MAKING
WASHINGTON
WORK

*An undertaking
of the
Innovations in
American Government
Awards Program
of the
Ford Foundation,
Harvard University's
John F. Kennedy School
of Government,
and the
Council
for Excellence
in Government*

MAKING WASHINGTON WORK

Tales of Innovation in the Federal Government

JOHN D. DONAHUE, EDITOR

With a foreword by
ALAN ALTSHULER AND PATRICIA MCGINNIS

Published for
COUNCIL FOR EXCELLENCE IN GOVERNMENT

BROOKINGS INSTITUTION PRESS
Washington, D.C. WITHDRAWN

Copyright © 1999
COUNCIL FOR EXCELLENCE IN GOVERNMENT
1301 K Street, N.W.
Suite 450
Washington, D.C. 20005

Making Washington Work: Tales of Innovation in the Federal Government
may be ordered from

BROOKINGS INSTITUTION PRESS
1775 Massachusetts Avenue, N.W., Washington, D.C. 20036
Tel: 1-800/275-1447
     202/797-6258
Fax: 202/797-6004
www.brookings.edu

Library of Congress Cataloging-in-Publication data

Making Washington work : tales of innovation in the federal government / John D. Donahue, editor ; with a foreword by Alan Altshuler and Patricia McGinnis.
    p.   cm.
"An undertaking of the Innovations in American Government awards program of the Ford Foundation, Harvard University's John F. Kennedy School of Government, and the Council for Excellence in Government."
Includes bibliographical references and index.
ISBN 0-8157-1895-0 (alk. paper)
1. Political planning—United States. 2. Administrative agencies—United States—Management. 3. Organizational change—United States. 4. Government productivity—United States. I. Donahue, John D. II. John F. Kennedy School of Government. III. Council for Excellence in Government.
JK468.P64 M33 1999   99-6552
352.3'0973—dc21   CIP

9 8 7 6 5 4 3 2 1
The paper used in this publication meets the minimum requirements of the American Standard for Informational Sciences—Permanence of Paper for Printed Library Materials, ANSI Z39.48-1984

Typeset in Sabon and Penumbra

Composition by Betsy Kulamer
Washington, D.C.

Printed by R. R. Donnelley and Sons
Harrisonburg, Virginia

Dedicated to the memory of
Marty Slate

CONTENTS

ACKNOWLEDGMENTS

THIS VOLUME IS the product of an uncommon collaboration among many individuals and organizations. The idea of a book profiling the federal winners of the Innovations in American Government award originated with Patricia McGinnis and Anne H. Lewis of the Council for Excellence in Government, who commissioned me to organize a recounting of the award-winners' stories. The project's other institutional anchor was the Innovations Program at Harvard's Kennedy School, whose longtime director, Alan Altshuler, urged me to add the introductory essay and engineered support for that part of the project.

Chapters 3 through 15 were complexly cooperative undertakings, with the bulk of the work carried out by a team of contributors. While I helped to frame the structure and reworked the drafts of each narrative, much of the writing and virtually all of the research for the individual cases was done by John Buntin of the Kennedy School's Case Program, John Trattner and Laura Ziff of the Council for Excellence in Government, and freelance writer Dalit Toledano. The fifth contributor, Kirsten Lundberg of the Kennedy School's Case Program, deserves special mention. She produced a substantial part of the material in this volume, and her professionalism and good judgment sustained the overall enterprise.

Sally Sachar and David Sheldon of the Council for Excellence in Government enlisted the cooperation of the innovating agencies and managed every aspect of the enterprise but the writing itself, with the able assistance of Andrea Mitchell, Ron Redmon, and Elizabeth Rogers. At Harvard, William Parent (the executive director of the Innovations Program) along with Elaine Kamarck (the program's faculty director) offered wise counsel at several key junctures, while Amy Christofer, Caroline Marple, Liz Rosenstock, and Patience Terry delivered logistical support.

Literally scores of people in the innovating agencies themselves provided data, endured interviews, or fact-checked intermediate drafts of the cases. The project would not have been possible without the cooperation of Patricia H. Adkins, Jane Axelrad, Dana Banks, Kathleen Begala, Jeff Bromme, Linda Brophy, Paul Bryant, Dick Burk, Ronald Chesemore, Frank Claunts, Cindy Coe, John Dougherty, Tina Downey, Lorraine Drolet, Crockett Dumas, William Freeman, Maria Garcia, Pamela Gilbert, Eileen Rae Glass, Ellen A. Hennessy, Karen Hinton, William Hubbard, Don Hunt, Neil Jacobs, David Kaminsk, Rob Kehlet, Susan King, Carveth Kramer, Robert Kulick, Audrey Kuykendall, Susan Linden, Jonathan Linton, Caryl Lummis, Murray Lumpkin, Adrian Linz, Terence H. Lutes, Eluid Martinez, Carmen Maymi, Maureen Morrill, Norman Oliver, Robert Pitulej, Ernie Renner, Terri Rogers, Janet L. Rose, Laura S. Rosenberg, Barbara Rosenfeld, Joel Sacks, Walt A. Sanders, Andrea E. Schneider, Alan H. Schoem, Marc J. Schoem, Suzanne B. Seiden, Janice Sheehy, Nancy Smith, Robert Stamer, Anne Marie T. SuPrise, Sue K. Turchan, Gilbert Vigil, Janet Woodcock, Randolph F. Wykoff, and Kathryn C. Zoon. An even longer list of Innovations in American Government evaluators, judges, and site visitors contributed to the information pool from which these profiles draw.

Nancy Davidson, Christopher Kelaher, and Susan Woollen at the Brookings Institution Press have been instrumental in shepherding the volume to publication, and Deborah M. Styles edited the manuscript.

Finally, special thanks are due to the Ford Foundation, and particularly senior program officer Michael Lipsky, for sponsoring the Innovations in American Government Program itself and for encouraging this effort to tell the tales of the fourteen federal award winners.

JOHN D. DONAHUE
Cambridge, Massachusetts
June 1999

FOREWORD

AMERICA'S STATE AND LOCAL governments, according to conventional wisdom, are the nation's principal laboratories of democracy. And indeed, significant policy initiatives at the national level almost invariably do have precursors at the state or local level. Naturally, then, the Innovations in American Government program first looked to the state and local level when it set out systematically to identify and celebrate exemplary innovations in the public sector.

Gradually, however, those responsible for the Innovations Program became aware that the federal government was in ferment as well. So the annual Innovations in American Government competition—financed by the Ford Foundation and administered by Harvard's John F. Kennedy School of Government in partnership with the Council for Excellence in Government—was opened to federal contenders in 1995. Since then, hundreds of impressive federal initiatives have been considered in the Innovations competition each year, and roughly one-third of all Innovations award winners have been federal agencies. The fourteen award-winning federal programs are profiled in the following pages.

The spirit of innovation's ability to remain vigorous in the federal system is in one sense rather surprising. Stability, consistency, and equal treatment for all are cardinal public values, most deeply ingrained at the national level since it is there that the most critical tax, regulatory, and social insurance rules are established for a highly diverse society. These values are often interpreted so as to dictate rigid, by-the-book administrative arrangements. Yet the public's ever-rising expectations are all but impossible to meet without continuous gains in efficiency and effectiveness—particularly in view of the companion public desire for tax stability or reductions. In brief, citizens want the federal government to be predictable yet creative, responsive yet focused, energetic yet parsimonious—and these desires, of course, are perfectly legitimate. The challenge for public-sector managers and employees is to engage these pressures in ways that yield mission-appropriate adaptation rather than stagnant defensiveness. The cases presented in this volume demonstrate that the challenge can be met, indeed *has* been met frequently, in a wide variety of federal circumstances.

This volume explores a diverse set of federal enterprises that, after several stages of winnowing, were judged (by an eminent panel) to be among each year's top ten public-sector innovations during the period 1995 through 1998. Like the 106 other winners recognized since 1986, these are held up as sources of inspiration and as starting points for future adaptation (often to meet challenges quite different from those that the original innovators faced), not as templates to be slavishly copied. Progress in improving American government depends on deep reflection on such experiences and broad diffusion of their lessons.

The designers and managers of these programs started with profound commitments to a mission. Anchored by clear conceptions of purpose, they were flexible and ingenious about the means of accomplishing their goals. Never forgetting their mission assignments or the need for approval from higher levels when they ventured very far from established routines, they stretched their minds and resources to use whatever tactics—interagency and public-private partnerships, new information technologies, performance measurement, market incentives, employee and citizen participation—appeared likely to yield better results. They displayed habits observed among innovators everywhere, in the private no less than in the public sector. They were committed. They were willing to accept risks in the service of mission. They were courageous. Their stories are likely to prove fascinating and instructive to others currently charged with public responsibilities or preparing for careers in public service. They illustrate the challenges public servants face, and they may reassure readers that many public servants are both passionately and creatively committed to—serving the public.

ALAN ALTSHULER
PATRICIA MCGINNIS

Alan Altshuler is the Ruth and Frank Stanton Professor at Harvard's John F. Kennedy School of Government and Graduate School of Design and director of the Kennedy School's A. Alfred Taubman Center for State and Local Government. From 1988 through 1998 he also served as director of the Innovations in American Government program.

Patricia McGinnis is president and chief executive officer of the Council for Excellence in Government, a nonprofit organization that works to raise public trust in government and improve its performance. She served previously in a number of senior budget and management posts in the federal executive branch and Congress.

MAKING
WASHINGTON
WORK

1

JAMMING
IN THE SYMPHONY

WHEN WE THINK of the federal government's working smoothly—for those of us who are not disabled, by ideology or experience, from harboring any such thought—one conventional metaphor might be a thoroughly rehearsed symphony orchestra. Each member acts in concert with the rest of the section. Each section, in turn (oboes or second violins, the FBI or the Federal Reserve), delivers—in the right sequence, in the right key, at the right tempo—its own contribution to the overall effort. The ensemble follows a score written out in advance, which each of the players understands but which none, by all odds, had any hand in composing. The leader sets the tone and the pace (within the narrow range of discretion the scripted score allows) and coordinates the components into a harmonious whole, scanning for missed beats and sour notes and herding errant players back into line. And the performance unfolds with a majestic predictability. The repertoire is essentially the same from one performance to the next, varying little even if some (or indeed all) of the players change. Novelty, almost by definition, constitutes error.

Imagine, then, that a handful of players stray from the program. They segue to a different key, shift the tempo to their own syncopated rhythm, synthesize riffs never written in any score. Even if the audience applauds, and even if the conductor encourages the improvisation, the performance poses a startling challenge to convention.

This chapter was written by John D. Donahue.

1

No federal agency operates in quite so robotic a fashion as this stereotype suggests—nor, for that matter, does even the starchiest symphony orchestra—but the metaphor sets the stage for the tales to be told in this volume: fourteen federal organizations, each in its own way compelled or inspired to suspend the score and improvise, each running risks and even courting chaos, each racking up achievements and raising questions (at once heartening and unnerving) about the meaning of "good government."

Why Is It Hard to Innovate in the Federal Government?

Let's not kid ourselves. Innovation may never be Washington's strong suit. The federal government *does* enjoy some obvious advantages when it comes to adaptation, to be sure, including a strong executive branch periodically infused with fresh leadership and more fiscal freedom than state or local governments. But its characteristic features of scale, complexity, monopoly, and indirect accountability (each taken up in more detail shortly) render the federal government less amenable to innovation than other kinds of organizations. Creativity, boldness, intuition, and initiative tend to rank lower in the bureaucracy's pantheon of virtues than do continuity, predictability, accountability, and impartiality. Compared with a solitary entrepreneur or a small private company—indeed, compared with a *large* private company, or a foundation, or even a major university—the federal government is not built for flexibility.

In an unchanging world, governmental rigidity might be tolerable, even admirable. But the federal government's challenges and constraints do change, and an atrophied capacity to innovate can result in the wasteful pursuit of yesterday's imperatives, delay in addressing citizens' priorities, and squandered opportunities to do things better. Citizens become disenchanted with Washington and hesitate to entrust it with important tasks or empower it with resources. Political pressures grow to write off our shared aspirations as unachievable or to reallocate responsibilities to state and local governments, which are presumed to be nimbler and more responsive to new goals and possibilities. For anyone who harbors some faith that the federal government retains a central role in the pursuit of Americans' common purposes, the stakes of federal innovation are immense.

Before reading the stories of the fourteen federal enterprises that were selected, from among many contenders, for special recognition by the Ford Foundation's "Innovations in American Government" award, consider the hurdles the innovators had to overcome. The federal government has four features that pose special impediments to an aspiring innovator.

Scale

Whatever else it may be, the federal government is *big*. Its spending in fiscal year 1998 approached $1.7 trillion. Even after rounds of downsizing over the previous several years, it employed around 2.8 million civilians, plus almost 1.5 million uniformed military personnel. The Department of Defense alone employs nearly 750,000 civilian workers. Three cabinet agencies employed more than 100,000 each in 1997 (Veterans Affairs, with 212,000; Treasury, with 146,000; and Justice, with 111,000), while five others (Agriculture, the Social Security Administration, Interior, Health and Human Services, and Transportation) employed more than 50,000 each.[1] It is a cliché but nonetheless (like most clichés) rooted in truth: the federal government is an ocean liner of an institution, its maneuverability hindered by far more inertia than that of the speedboats that typify the private economy. If Washington's *only* distinctive feature were a matter of scale, it would face special challenges in meeting new missions and adopting new approaches.

Yet size cannot be the whole story. Wal-Mart has more employees (825,000) than the Defense Department's civilian work force, and quite a few U.S.–based companies—including Boeing, Sears, General Motors, K-Mart, Motorola, J. C. Penney, General Electric, IBM, and Ford—employ more people than does any civilian department in the federal government.[2] So there must be something other than scale at work.

Complexity

It may be that no organization—even a taco stand or a day-care center—feels all that focused to the people on the inside, but even the largest private institutions tend to enjoy a blessed clarity of purpose compared with the federal government. International Business Machines makes and sells business machines internationally. United Parcel Service ships parcels. Tootsie Roll produces Tootsie Rolls. Many firms have subsidiaries and affiliates, to be sure, but they are usually integrated in some fairly simple way with the main line of business. General Motors has a financial affiliate that makes loans for car purchases, but not for movie production; U.S. Airways has alliances with hotels, car rental chains, and other airlines, but not with bakeries or brokerage houses. The corporate world's fling with conglomeration a generation or so ago ended badly, for the most part, and "stick to your knitting" has become a durable theme of business orthodoxy. Rare is the corporation that wanders too far from its core competency and avoids making a hash of it.

Simple missions have obvious advantages when it comes to innovation: it is easier to think up new ideas, and easier to tell whether they work, when you have some reasonably coherent conception of what it is you are trying to do. Corporate "mission statements" are soft targets for comic-strip satire, but the mission-statement fad does demonstrate the usefulness—and, for most private organizations, the feasibility—of encapsulating an institution's purpose in a sentence or two.

The federal government's closest analogue to a mission statement, the preamble to the Constitution, proclaims that the goal is to "establish Justice, insure domestic Tranquility, provide for the common defense, promote the general Welfare, and secure the Blessings of Liberty to ourselves and our Posterity." Words to stir the blood—but a bit imprecise as workaday guides to action. In practice, the federal government inspects meat, sends robots to Mars, reroutes rivers, delivers the mail, takes care of ailing veterans, guards against danger or discrimination in the workplace, negotiates trade deals, subsidizes dance troupes and ethanol producers and about one-fifth of everything that state and local governments do, mows the grass at military cemeteries all over the world, deals with natural disasters, looks for cancer cures, manipulates the price of milk and the supply of money, broadcasts propaganda to Cuba, rescues stranded hikers, counts everybody in the country every ten years, patrols the borders, breaks up monopolies, lends money to college students, reverses invasions in the Middle East, maps the human genetic code, chases drug dealers, makes hydrogen bombs, writes Social Security checks, listens to the stars in case somebody out there sends a message, and prevents airplanes from running into each other. Among other things.

No single department has quite so vast a mandate, to be sure, but even the most focused agency will usually have a mission sufficiently sprawling and tangled to chill the blood of the average corporate acquisitions manager. The Immigration and Naturalization Service, for example—just one element within the Justice Department's organizational portfolio—is responsible for keeping track of the whereabouts and circumstances of every foreigner inside U.S. borders, welcoming new citizens with suitable ceremony into the American family, and checking to be sure that nobody employs a person who may not legally work in this country. The Food and Drug Administration—a subagency of the Department of Health and Human Services—monitors the quality of most of the nation's food and drink and regulates the safety and efficacy of all drugs and medical products—goods and services that claim about 25 cents of every consumer dollar.

Moreover, the missions of different agencies tend to be interconnected, making the federal government's overall complexity an ever-present factor in how individual units operate. The State Department cannot put pressure on China by denouncing prison labor, for example, without stepping on the toes of the Bureau of Prisons, which believes in putting inmates to work and opposes international conventions forbidding it. When an interagency working group meets to coordinate policy, it is not in the least remarkable to have six or eight chairs around the table for the delegates of departments that can claim perfectly legitimate stakes in the outcome—even before the deputies and support staffers and representatives from the metropolitan White House complex (Office of Management and Budget, National Security Council, Domestic Policy Council, National Economic Council, and so on) crowd the room.

The impediments to innovation this complexity introduces are not particularly subtle. Interagency coordination, no matter how protracted and painstaking, is unlikely to yield more than a tiny number of approaches that are simultaneously acceptable to every agency, and the odds are very long against a consensus solution that breaks new ground. The coordination process itself absorbs prodigious amounts of time, ingenuity, and managerial attention. This deters creativity both directly (by gobbling up the resources that might otherwise be devoted to the development of new approaches) and indirectly (by making federal managers groan at the prospect of reopening any issue that has been tolerably laid to rest, even in the name of the most sparkling new idea).

The characteristic complexity of the federal government tends to make continuity and standardization more important than they are in most other settings. Except for problems of exceptional urgency, only issues with staying power can make it through the process by which a potential mission gains political endorsement and then incorporation as a federal institution. International travelers have long required a piece of paper affirming their identity and attesting to their citizenship, and the State Department has provided passports for two centuries, with a reasonable degree of efficiency and by a process that has not changed in any fundamental way. Even if the mission's continuity does not rule out incremental change—and while increments can surely aggregate over time to become major transformations—the procedural tracks established during an agency's early days tend to put boundaries around subsequent innovation.

More than other institutions (with some obvious exceptions, such as the Roman Catholic Church), the federal government is organized around the expectation that its core missions will change only slowly, pushing flexibility and creativity downward in the hierarchy of institutional priorities. Citizens, businesses, state and local governments, and even foreign governments come to depend, in ways large and small, on the stability of federal policies and processes. The worker looking toward retirement, the investor structuring a real-estate deal with an eye to tax liabilities, the auto maker designing the safety features for cars to be marketed five years hence, the mayor planning a waste-treatment plant, or the governor contemplating options for highway construction all anticipate and rely on continuity from the federal government. Change—even change that is a clear-cut improvement from Washington's perspective—tends to disrupt such plans. Constituencies' reliance on federal stability narrows the range of innovation an agency can contemplate without damaging (or undergoing intricate negotiations with) those who had accommodated themselves to the status quo. Even if we approve of creative adaptation, as a general matter, many of us may have qualms about the federal officials with whom we do business noodling around with new ways of doing things.

Monopoly

The federal government—unlike all but a few private organizations, and even unlike state and local governments—faces no rivals for most of what it does. The implications for innovation are profound. While there are some caveats and complications, it is a bedrock axiom of economic theory (and justly so) that competition fuels innovation. Private firms are bestirred to innovate by the recognition that stasis means extinction, as rivals race to deliver better results or lower prices. In the nonprofit world as well, innovation is often essential to finding a sustainable niche where unmet needs and willing donors coexist. The market metaphor is less applicable to government than some careless theorists suggest. Nevertheless, it is true that citizens' option to "vote with their feet," if their current jurisdiction fails to meet their priorities, does tend to discipline state and (to a greater extent) local governments in ways to which the federal government is all but immune. Without competitive pressures, obsolete missions can continue to absorb resources, approaches that are tolerable but very far from ideal can endure indefinitely, and the generation of new ideas can recede from a sine qua non to a dispensable frill or even a disruptive distraction.

Indirect Accountability

The single most important feature distinguishing government from business is the public sector's lack of a direct link between resources and results. This is a more nuanced matter, to be sure, than is commonly asserted. The conventional view, reprised routinely on the Sunday morning chat shows and around countless dinner tables, is that the federal government has become arrogantly indifferent to public opinion or to the judgments of the citizenry's representatives. Any federal veteran who has labored to improve some department's image, or who knows the alacrity with which an agency responds to congressional concerns, is aware of just how preposterous this notion is. The federal government is by no means insulated from accountability. But the mechanisms by which it is held to account are indirect, aggregated, uneven in their effectiveness, and notoriously error-prone.

In business, delivering better value to customers tends to generate higher revenues with a fair degree of reliability and without too many intervening steps. So there is both a bright star by which to steer efforts at innovation and a bottom-line measure by which to gauge whether a particular change actually constitutes improvement. Pleasing customers all but automatically means also pleasing stockholders, the other (or, perhaps more accurately, the ultimate) constituency to which private managers are accountable. Not-for-profit private institutions are not accountable in precisely the same way, but there is usually a reasonably sturdy link between performance and resources: donors are free to supply or to withhold funds based on their assessment of the organization's work.

Not so in the public sector. Resources originate with taxation or borrowing, which conveys next to no information about how individuals value particular governmental activities, and they are allocated in ways that have much more to do with the perceived importance of an agency's mandate than with how well that mandate is pursued. The agency's "customers," if they can even be identified, generally contribute no more to its budget than noncustomers. ("User fees," while growing more common, still account for a tiny fraction of most agencies' resources.) It is seldom sufficient, and sometimes flatly perverse, to define the mission as gratifying those with whom the agency most directly interacts (consider the agencies whose "customers" are industrial polluters, or federal prisoners, or illegal aliens, or the managers of sweatshops). Even when learning and serving customer priorities is a major part of the mission—as it is, in fact, for many federal agencies—it is almost never the *only* goal. If a mission claims public resources, it is (inevitably and appropriately) subject to diverse public demands.

But this diversity of legitimate goals makes *value* a radically ambiguous notion for the public sector. And since innovation less often results from Darwinian selection among random deviations than it does from informed speculation about how better to create value, indeterminate priorities can confuse or paralyze potential innovators. To blaze new trails, one must know which way is forward. Instead of the clear beacon of profit and loss guiding his or her private-sector counterpart, the public manager must recognize and reconcile many different kinds of signals about the relative value of alternative activities. These signals are dimmed, distorted, filtered, or refracted in complex ways by electoral politics, interest-group activity, or strategic behavior on the part of individuals. There is a temptation to favor the more visible or vocal interests (or those that accord with a manager's own priorities) at the expense of longer-term or more diffuse dimensions of value.

At the same time, federal institutions are riddled with channels through which interests can make themselves heard. The most vivid signals, however, may not be the most valid. For example, in the mid-1990s the Labor Department received two messages about the value of the programs that one community-based organization had been running, with federal support, for many years. One message was delivered by evaluation researchers in the form of statistically convincing, if arid, analyses showing that the programs were ineffective. The other message was delivered by demonstrators who stormed and occupied the department's headquarters to protest cuts in funding for the programs. A single prime-time exposé on food-stamp fraud or military waste, similarly, can obliterate the signals sent by a million well-nourished children or a thousand days of peace.

Indirect accountability greatly complicates the innovator's task. He or she must make a convincing case that an innovation will *work*—the far-from-trivial burden shared by a private-sector counterpart. Then it must be established that the values the innovation will advance are more important than the values that will be sacrificed, or reduced in priority, by departing from the status quo. Then the innovator must argue persuasively that the political system will affirm that judgment. The old way of doing things almost always represents an uneasy equilibrium of competing priorities—an equilibrium that an innovation is bound to disrupt. And since the ranking of priorities is seldom settled once and for all, the players in the federal arena are poised for perennial vigilance. Congressional patrons, constituency organizations, advocacy groups, and employee unions are always ready to push back against any perceived threat to their interests. Significant changes must pass through many settings in which a veto can be exercised, including the review process of the Office of Management and Budget, congressional authorization and appropriations, the federal courts, and a gauntlet of other perils.

Potential innovations must thus navigate a hazardous route from idea to action. And since government's attenuated link between resources and results means that even the most successful innovation may not pay off very directly or very tangibly for the proponent or the agency, a potential innovator may well balk at attempting the journey—even if duty bound to try.

This brings us to the most general, and most disheartening, implication of indirect accountability: the links between results and resources can become so twisted and attenuated that accountability simply ebbs, allowing federal agencies to stick with the status quo not because it works for the public, but because it works for agency insiders and for privileged constituencies. Garden-variety indolence, self-dealing, and indifference to the public interest are less common in Washington than folklore suggests, but they are by no means unknown.

A deliberate and defensible inclination toward established routine, driven by these four distinctive features, is only part of the reason why Washington can be so inhospitable to innovators. There is another layer of explanation—more primitive, less logical, less rooted in reasoned responses to the federal system's distinctive purposes and constraints, but no less potent for all that. This is the accretion of checks and double checks, rules and regulations, restrictions, guarantees, legally mandated administrative procedures, and so on. This superstructure of safeguards can be thought of as institutional scar tissue, the legacy of wounds left by scandals large and small since the 1780s. History offers ample excuse for the prejudice that unusual behavior indicates bungling or corruption rather than ingenuity or ambition, and this prejudice motivates a profusion of rules constraining discretion. Such scar tissue makes federal institutions stiff and awkward, even relative to the far-from-limber ideal that a counterfactual federal government, free from historical trauma, might attain.

So for some perfectly good reasons (as well as some bad reasons), reverence for standard operating procedure is woven into Washington's genetic code. Departures from the norm are conventionally presumed to signal pathology. And a daunting immune system—with administrative law judges, inspectors general, employee organizations, and congressional investigators serving as the institutional analogues of the macrophages and antibodies coursing through the bloodstream on the lookout for intruders—remains poised to identify and annihilate alien processes and unfamiliar structures.

Why Do Federal Workers Innovate Anyway?

Yet innovation *does* happen in Washington. New missions are taken up; old missions are pursued in novel ways; standard approaches are refined to the point of real reinvention. The stories summarized in this volume offer only a small, unsystematic sample of the adaptation that goes on within federal agencies and thus cannot support conclusive generalizations about the sources of innovation. But they do suggest a few of the forces that cause agencies to do things differently, a set of catalysts that might be summarized (straining only a little in the name of alliteration) as *pressure*, *promises*, and *pride*.

Pressure

No matter how intimidating the impediments arrayed against it, innovation becomes more probable once the status quo is rendered unbearable. World War II required a wrenching transformation of the federal government, made up of hundreds or thousands of separate innovations (including the successful campaign to harness then-mysterious atomic forces to the war effort) that became possible only because the alternative to entering and winning the war was indisputably hideous. Few examples are quite so dramatic. But pressure—the prospect of dire consequences as the price of rigidity—quite frequently inspires change.

Sometimes the pressure comes in the bluntest possible form, as a mortal threat to an institution's existence. If the death penalty for failing to deliver value is seldom as clear and present a danger for public organizations as it is for their private-sector counterparts, it is by no means unknown. The Bureau of Reclamation's traditional mission had become patently unsustainable by the early 1990s. Its founding raison d'être—building dams—had been eroded not only by a shift in public priorities but also, ironically, by its very success in completing most of the more valuable potential projects within its domain. The bureau's traditional constituencies, feeling betrayed by the diminished pace of dam building, withdrew their support. Its traditional adversaries, in turn, were disinclined to waste many tears over the abolition of a lightly altered bureau.

Thus deep reinvention became the only alternative to more traumatic change imposed from outside the agency. As this perception spread, it gave resonance to internal calls for change.

Similarly, the budgetary fallout from the end of the cold war tightened the resource constraints facing the Defense Personnel Support Center's customers in mess halls and quartermaster's offices throughout the armed services. As dwindling appropriations left supply officers progressively less slack, they became eager to ease their own budget pressures by seeking better deals on blankets, bug spray, bayonet scabbards, and the countless other items the center had traditionally delivered. When the center lost its monopoly on military supply in 1994, its future was suddenly put in jeopardy, triggering a campaign of root-and-branch restructuring. Similarly, the Consumer Product Safety Commission, after years of wasting away as an organizational invalid, had to make a case for its existence if it hoped to endure.

External pressures need not be quite so stark. Even as budgets and head-count ceilings have tightened in successive deficit-reduction campaigns, very few federal institutions have actually been abolished. If nothing but the prospect of organizational oblivion could concentrate the minds of potential innovators, the payoff would be meager. Dysfunctional or redundant bureaus can linger for decades as the institutional undead—drained of vitality, but still issuing paychecks. More commonly the pressure that inspires innovation comes in the form of new or intensified challenges, or a concatenation of separate stresses that together trigger change. The much-publicized prospect of a financial catastrophe echoing the savings-and-loan meltdown forced congress and the administration to deal with the problems at the Pension Benefit Guaranty Corporation and made possible a series of innovations that might otherwise have been blocked. Congress's flat refusal to allow the Internal Revenue Service to simply update and expand its established procedures, as aging computers and growing demands rendered retooling imperative, created an internal seller's market for new ideas that sped the transit of over-the-phone tax filing from the drawing board to implementation.

By the early 1990s tightening budgets, expanding missions, and endless choruses of reproach from management and labor—similar in intensity, pulling in almost exactly opposite directions—made business as usual an excruciating prospect for the Occupational Safety and Health Administration. Elsewhere in the Labor Department, the Wage and Hour Division of the Employment Standards Administration found its traditional inspection model an increasingly futile method for holding accountable a complex, institutionally fluid, and highly competitive garment industry. And the sudden imposition of a new imperative—limiting environmental damage—inspired the Air Force's Aerospace Guidance and Metrology Center to rethink its technological fundamentals. While it differs in degree and character, external pressure helped lay the foundation for change in every case profiled here—and in most of the less heralded innovations throughout the federal government.

Promises

On the day John F. Kennedy challenged the United States to send a man to the moon, neither the technology nor the institutions existed to make the mission happen. But the audacious dream galvanized action, and in less than a decade the goal was accomplished. High-profile promises can alter the calculus of possibility and catapult missions to the front of the queue. Particularly when the promise serves to augment the resources devoted to an enterprise, it can powerfully catalyze innovation. Yet even if budgeted resources stay the same, the priority that comes with visible commitments can make it easier to sacrifice other institutional goals in the name of the explicitly anointed priority.

Several of the innovations profiled here owe much of their momentum, and sometimes their origins, to the national performance review (NPR), which was unveiled with great fanfare at the start of the first Clinton administration. Clinton and (even more directly) Vice President Al Gore wagered their reputations on the promise to deliver "government that works better and costs less." Federal appointees, from the cabinet level down, had personal and political stakes in delivering on the promise, given Gore's prominence in the administration and his obvious positioning for a presidential race himself.

The NPR featured a certain amount of hoopla and hucksterism, no doubt, but few who passed through Washington after 1993 would deny that it provided a thematic focus and institutional anchors that made it easier to market potential innovations internally. The visible commitment of top officials sent powerful signals throughout the bureaucracy—reassuring the enthusiasts and warning the recalcitrant—that the campaign would not fade away once a few speeches had been made. Explicit reinvention promises made by senior Labor Department officials (including Secretary Robert Reich and Joe Dear, the political appointee responsible for occupational health and safety) empowered people like Bill Freeman, the front-line architect of the "Maine 200" experiment with a workplace safety policy based on results. Many career officials at the Department of

Housing and Urban Development (HUD) had long been frustrated by the clutter of separate programs that made their dealings with states and localities so awkward and process-ridden. But not until Assistant Secretary Andrew Cuomo decided to make his mark through administrative consolidation could the impediments be overcome.

Leadership matters, in short.[3] But these cases suggest that a particular type of leadership spurs innovation. It is not so much a matter of pep talks and uplifting slogans, but of senior officials who put their reputations on the line with concrete public promises. Only by burning their bridges can leaders credibly commit that they will not retreat to business as usual when the status quo bites back. Leaders' promises, moreover, must be anchored in the organization's underlying mission and consistent with career staffers' seasoned assessments of what that mission means in practice. With the possible exception of HUD's Consolidated Planning, none of these reforms can be characterized as top-down. Most were fueled by an interdependent blend of front-office and front-line initiative, and several—including the innovations at the Immigration and Naturalization Service, the Federal Emergency Management Administration, the Internal Revenue Service, the Labor Department's Wage and Hour Division, and the Forest Service—clearly started with career bureaucrats.

Professional Pride

Pressure and promises can help to overcome the federal government's special impediments to innovation, but they are not enough. Necessity may be the mother of invention, but the record attests that this mother's fecundity is remarkably uneven. There are *always* pressures to deliver more with less, since federal resources fall short of claims even in the flushest of times. But these pressures only sometimes lead to true innovation. Similarly, a great many promises—even high-profile presidential promises—go unfulfilled. Challenges from the head office can improve the climate for innovation, but they cannot on their own force growth from barren fields. Other factors must aid in incubating innovation, and the cases here suggest the importance of intrinsic commitment and professional pride on the part of front-line federal workers.

Not one of the innovations celebrated in this volume would have been possible without the purposeful engagement of bureaucrats in the trenches. Personal commitment to an agency's goals among its workers can do much to counter the federal government's special impediments to innovation. Such motives are not unique to public workers, to be sure. But intrinsic commitment to the organization's mission is more indispensable in the public than in the private sector. A for-profit business could still operate, albeit badly, if its workers were motivated by nothing more than eagerness for income and the fear of its loss. But the federal government would promptly collapse. The innovations described here, like the many that remain unheralded, may have been nurtured by political pressure and committed leaders, but their parentage is usually found among front-line workers who were determined to make a difference.

Failure, futility, and irrelevance are soul-destroying for anyone with the slightest self-regard. Few federal workers can live comfortably with the thought that their work is pointless. When an agency fails to deliver on its mandate, or when that mandate drifts out of alignment with the public's desires, some bureaucrats salvage their dignity through self-deception; others seek more satisfying work elsewhere. But for many federal workers, pride forces reflection about how to do things better. By no means all such reflection is fruitful. Some potential innovators are earnest but inept; others lack a wide enough perspective to make reasonable judgments about what can and should be done; a great many assume, often correctly, that their superiors are not interested in new ideas and solace themselves with daydreams of what they could accomplish were it not for the chowderheads in the front office. But on any given day, at any given agency, there are likely to be any number of latent innovations in the works.

Bureaucrats at the Internal Revenue Service's Research Division had long sought ways to simplify tax filing, and they dreamed up on their own the idea of filing by phone (along with other ideas for simplification that foundered short of implementation). External pressures for change helped them overcome the lawyers' objection that a tax return required a signature, and a signature required paper. Why couldn't a "signature" be a personal code, the improvisers asked? This time the stars were in the right alignment—congressional politics, administration slogans, and budget cycles were all favorable—and the internal promoters of procedural simplicity won the day.

The intense eighteen-month reform campaign that reworked the Bureau of Reclamation's mandate while trimming the agency's personnel by one-fifth was, for the most part, the aggregate result of innumerable improvements suggested by front-line workers that leaders picked up once they started listening. The dismay of Forest Service workers at the declining health of the Carson National Forest played at least as great a role as the grief they were getting from environmentalists, loggers, and local residents in inspiring a new way to balance claims on the land.

The Immigration and Naturalization Service's policy of helping employers find legal workers sprang directly from the wounded pride of street-level agents. "There was a sense of frustration that we were really not doing the job," recalled one of the initiative's pioneers. "We would arrest the aliens and they would come back the next day, but everybody still got their paycheck. So we decided we were going to do something different."[4] That "something different"—getting the jobs previously held by aliens filled by U.S. citizens, thus reducing the temptation for the employer to return to illegal labor—became national policy.

Bureaucrats at the Pension Benefit Guaranty Corporation (PBGC) were chagrined at being outmaneuvered by their corporate counterparts (to the detriment of retirees and of taxpayers); this eventually led to tougher PBGC policies and to new legislation that gave the rules teeth. A small group of career civil servants at the Labor Department, frustrated that the old strategy of raids and inspections was not curbing the growth of sweatshops, dusted off an obscure legal detail to amplify their leverage over companies that sold goods made in violation of the law.

Often the new ideas front-line workers develop require higher budgets. This is perfectly normal; it is always easier to think of ways to do more *with* more. Any healthy organization, whether in the public or private sector, chafes at resource constraints and can instantly summon a dozen plausible uses for a budget increase. Since cutbacks require more managerial effort than do expansions—especially in the federal government—innovation is almost always easier if new missions are accomplished with new resources, rather than with budget and personnel wrenched away from older missions. In recent years, as budget pressures reinforced the reigning imperative to do more with *less*, some workers dismissed the new dogma as self-evident nonsense. Others, however, like the compliance officers at the Consumer Product Safety Commission, chose to emphasize economy and in so doing found a particularly hospitable climate for their ideas.

The power of professional pride as a spur to bureaucratic innovation is mostly good news for sympathetic observers of government reform. (It is not news at all, to be sure, for those who have worked much with federal bureaucrats.) Yet the good news is alloyed with some cause for anxiety. One worry is that bureaucrats may anchor their self-regard so solidly in accustomed ways of pursuing their missions that they resist radical shifts in strategy. For example, Wage and Hour investigators had come to score their successes by the number of employers caught in the act of shortchanging workers and forced to make good on the wages they owed. The "no sweat" initiative put the emphasis not on catching scofflaws, but on creating new incentives within the garment industry to raise the rate of voluntary compliance. In the (admittedly unlikely) event this strategy succeeded completely, wage and hour enforcers would never nail an offending employer. Veteran investigators had a hard time stretching their sense of professional satisfaction to include deterring violations, not just catching violators, and this presented a significant challenge to expanding the initiative. Other innovations will surely experience similar complications.

More generally, the greater the weight we accord professional pride as a motive for good performance—including innovation—the greater Washington's vulnerability to degraded effectiveness from any threat to the quality and morale of its personnel. This raises the stakes of attracting bright, energetic Americans into federal service and retaining them long enough for experience to season their idealism. As a casual contempt for federal workers becomes the unremarkable norm, self-respecting young men and women can be expected to shun the civil service, with a growing risk of poisoning the well of federal innovation.

Why Innovation Matters

The innovations profiled here record the stories of the fourteen federal agencies included among the forty innovations winners recognized since 1995, when the federal government first became eligible for the annual competition sponsored by the Ford Foundation. Winners were sifted through a sequence of evaluations by progressively more demanding judges under the aegis of Harvard University's Kennedy School of Government. A panel of distinguished public and private leaders made the final selection. The process is painstakingly thorough. But it is not scientific, by the scrupulous standards of social-science research—this is not that kind of book—and there is no way to be sure that these stories are representative or that they are the fourteen most significant recent innovations in Washington.

Nor is there any easy way to measure the staying power of these innovations, or the capacity of the innovators to continue evolving to keep pace with changing conditions and needs. One of the organizations celebrated here (the Aerospace Guidance and Metrology Center) no longer exists. Marty Slate of the Pension Benefit Guaranty Corporation, the cornerstone of another innovation, died young in office before his reform campaign was completed. And some signs of backsliding can no doubt be found for each of the stories told here. But that is not really the point. Some of the private firms heralded in the 1982 book *In Search of Excellence*, by Thomas J. Peters and Robert H. Waterman Jr., have since stumbled, which neither negates their erstwhile accomplishment nor undermines the validity of the principles they embodied.[5]

Fixing problems, not infallibility, is what we expect of the private economy. For the public sector as well, the real challenge in an ever-changing world is not to find the one best way and stick to it, but ceaselessly to adapt, revise, and readjust. Readers are not asked to believe that the public organizations profiled here have attained some kind of ideal. Any citizen has a right to quibble with an agency's new agenda or even denounce the whole enterprise. We are all bosses, after all, entitled to weigh in on what the mission should be and render our judgment of how well it is pursued. Indeed, one need not even concur that the transformations described here constitute clear-cut progress to accept the central, unfashionable, profoundly consequential claim that innovation, after all, lies within Washington's repertoire. Creative improvisation, of the sort depicted in these stories, is the best hope for progressively improving the score that guides the whole federal symphony, in the never-ending search for a better fit between what the citizenry values and what the government delivers.

Hopeful anecdotes do not make the case that the federal government has a pervasive predilection to innovate (any more than selective stories of brain-dead torpor prove the opposite). But the tales told here do present a counterpoint to the conventional depiction of the federal government as an inert behemoth immune to adaptation. And they celebrate, appropriately, the tangible triumphs of federal workers who summoned the courage to change.

Notes

1. Agency-specific employment figures are from the Office of Management and Budget, *Budget of the United States Government, Fiscal Year 1999*, "Analytic Perspectives" volume, table 10-1, "Civilian Employment in the Executive Branch," p. 228. The figure for all federal civilian employment (which includes around 850,000 postal workers) is from data compiled by the Office of Personnel Management and published on the Census Bureau's online data source, "Federal Government Civilian Employment by Function, 1997," at http://www.census.gov/govs/apes/97fedfun, accessed in October, 1998.

2. Employment figures for the private corporations listed are from *Fortune* magazine, August 3, 1998, "Global 500" table, pages F-1 and F-2.

3. While I cannot claim to be an unbiased observer on this point, it is probably no coincidence that former Labor secretary Robert B. Reich was involved in three of these fourteen innovations.

4. Neil Jacobs, Federal Innovators Roundtable, Council for Excellence in Government, Washington D.C., January 16, 1998.

5. Thomas J. Peters and Robert H. Waterman Jr., *In Search of Excellence: Lessons from America's Best-Run Companies* (Harper and Row, 1982).

2

FAST TRACK
PRODUCT RECALL

L ATE ONE SATURDAY evening in the spring of 1998, at a suburban Washington restaurant, a man in his forties was having dinner with his wife and friends when his pager beeped. The man put down his fork, checked the number on the pager, and explained that he had to handle some business right away. He called, connected, got an update, and made some quick decisions. A quarter-hour later he rejoined his party to catch up on the dinner and the conversation.

On the surface there was nothing remarkable about this slice of 1990s life. But the man was not a surgeon fielding a nervous intern's questions about a post-operative patient, or a portfolio manager keeping tabs on off-hours currency trading, or a political consultant monitoring the polling data for some dicey campaign. He was a federal bureaucrat named Marc Schoem, who ran the Recalls and Compliance Division in the Office of Compliance at the Consumer Product Safety Commission (CPSC). The call was from a Honeywell Corporation team scrambling under deadline to film a video describing a subtle hazard in a new Honeywell humidifier. They needed Schoem's reactions to a script detail for the video, which was being readied for a Monday morning press conference at which CPSC and Honeywell would announce together that the humidifier was being recalled for repairs. As was his custom, especially when a recall plan reached the tricky final stages, Schoem had urged his

---

This chapter was written by John D. Donahue.

19

industry counterparts to get in touch with him any time to keep the process moving toward deadline.[1]

This is not quite the conventional image of bureaucratic work habits, or the style of interaction between federal regulators and the firms they oversee. But it has become business as usual for Schoem and his colleagues since 1995, when the Consumer Product Safety Commission adopted a new approach for working with business to find and fix dangerous products.

The Consumer Product Safety Commission (CPSC)

The CPSC never really had a golden age. It went straight from birth into decline, without the honeymoon of vitality and high hopes that even the most troubled agencies usually enjoy. Congress created the CPSC, through the Consumer Product Safety Act of 1972, to "protect the public against unreasonable risks of injury associated with consumer products."[2] This was a vast and vague mission, formulated during the last gasp of a federal activism that had faded before the ink was dry on the CPSC's authorizing legislation. It was unclear at the start precisely what the commission—headed by the president's appointed chairman, and backed by a staff of hundreds—was supposed to do.

The CPSC's jurisdiction included virtually any risk posed by virtually anything anyone in the United States brought home from a store (other than goods monitored by specialized regulators like the Food and Drug Administration or the National Highway Traffic Safety Commission). Its domain covered some 15,000 types of products, from toys to tools, cribs to Christmas ornaments, apparel to appliances. Carving out a workable agenda posed a daunting challenge to the new agency. How was the CPSC to define its own special product-safety mission, given the incentives of tort liability and market reputation that presumably made most firms prefer not to hurt their customers? How should it complement the efforts of consumer groups, trade associations, and other regulatory agencies at the state and federal levels? Congress provided few guidelines for balancing consumer risks and the costs of regulation, leaving it to the CPSC (and, inevitably, the courts) to figure it out.

It took years to translate the abstract mandate of the Consumer Product Safety Act into the practical operational instruments of offices, regulations, laboratories, and lawyers. And when the CPSC did gear up to do something specific to "protect the public against unreasonable risks," it had a calamitous debut. The first regulation to make its way through the commission's comment and review labyrinth entered the rulebooks in 1976 as 16 CFR Part 1207; it imposed safety standards on swimming-pool slides.

This was not, on its face, an ill-conceived goal—at least eleven people had been paralyzed in pool-slide incidents in the preceding six years. After years of CPSC staff analysis and consultation, the commission concluded that misuse (in particular, poor technique in head-first "belly sliding") and misplacement of the slides (delivering users into water that was too shallow) were the principal hazards. The agency issued a regulation requiring that henceforth any pool slide sold in the United States must feature signs, of a specified size and format, installed in a specified sequence on the slide's steps. One sign described the proper form to use for belly sliding; another explained the correct procedures for sliding in a sitting position; a third pointed out the wisdom of checking for people and objects in the way before zipping into the water. Still another sign, this one especially vivid, featured a large-type WARNING about the dangers of ignoring the guidelines on belly-sliding if the water was less than four feet deep. This sign included, as a visual aid, a tableau of a little stick figure breaking its neck. While the CPSC lacked the authority to *require* consumers to use products in a particular way, the regulation issued strong guidelines urging deep-water placement of pool slides. In response to observations that this might be expected to decrease the risk of paralysis but increase the risk of drowning, the regulation instructed manufacturers to bolt on another WARNING sign. This one depicted a little stick figure lying at the bottom of a pool, a thin trickle of bubbles grimly drifting to the surface.

Shortly after this debut regulation went into effect, a pool-slide manufacturer named Aqua Slide 'n' Dive filed suit against the CPSC to overturn the warning-sign rule.[3] The company pointed out that some 350,000 pool slides were in use and that most were used many times by many people over the course of a year. It offered the calculation—apparently not disputed—that the annual odds of a slide user's suffering a paralyzing accident worked out to less than one in 10 million, or something under the average person's annual risk of being killed by lightning. Moreover, Aqua Slide argued, there was little evidence that the barrage of warning signs the CPSC required it to install on its products would deter the kinds of gross foolishness—including at least one instance of drunken sliding—that had been behind most previous cases of paralyzing injuries. In short, the company claimed, the rule would not do much to reduce consumer risk. But the icons of stick-figure death and mayhem, attached to slide ladders by federal fiat and visible before every splash into the water, might well dampen that spirit of carefree joie de vivre with which a normal person should expect to approach a swimming-pool slide. And this kill-joy factor, Aqua Slide complained, would shrivel the market for swimming-pool slides, inflicting certain losses—far beyond the direct costs of the signs—in exchange for only the most speculative benefits.

Despite the efforts of CPSC lawyers to defend the rule, the U.S. Fifth Circuit Court of Appeals broadly agreed with Aqua Slide's objections. In an opinion studded with withering comments on the quality of the agency's data and logic, the court ruled that "the Commission has failed to provide substantial evidence to demonstrate the reasonable necessity of the warning signs" and struck down the requirement.[4]

After this inaugural misstep, the CPSC continued to stagger through much of the next fifteen years. The Reagan era began before the commission could recover from its Aqua Slide debacle. Advocates for aggressive federal action on consumer protection found themselves political outsiders. Free-market purists were in the ascendancy, and the CPSC was a soft target for scornful denunciations of government meddling. The new administration shrank the commission's budget sharply, cut its work force by nearly half, and exiled it from downtown Washington to a nondescript building overlooking a supermarket loading dock in suburban Bethesda. The *Washington Post* profiled the CPSC in a scathing 1989 piece entitled "The Little Agency That Can't," in which outside experts called it "emasculated," and "a regulatory speck." Even a conservative Reagan appointee lamented that "this whole place has been traumatized, tortured, and drop-kicked around since 1981."[5]

Yet the CPSC soldiered on. Political appointees came and went. Some of the new political appointees (who by statute constituted a majority of commissioners and included the powerful chairman) seemed skeptical about the basic mission; others were apparently sold on the act's goals but displayed an honest caution about burdening business. (At least one Reagan-appointed commissioner, Anne Graham, was seen as seriously committed to consumer protection.) Amid the turnover at the top and the general absence of zeal in the front office, the professional staff demonstrated a remarkable resilience. While many were banished through mandated staff cuts and a few left voluntarily, a surprising number stayed. Where else, after all, was a lawyer or scientist passionate about enforcing product safety laws supposed to go?

As budget reductions thinned the ranks of field inspectors, office staffers scanned for hazards by calling coroners or reviewing obituaries to see if some product seemed to be linked with suspicious frequency to fatal accidents. When there was no money to rent a studio, a product-safety video was filmed in a staff member's house. Another staffer habitually scouted out dangerous products on her own time, even returning from her honeymoon with a cache of toys that she suspected could choke a child.[6] There were some undeniable successes during the 1970s and 1980s for the CPSC, including standards for cribs to prevent babies from strangling between slats and standards for the size and construction of rattles and toys that by all accounts reduced the number of choking hazards American children encounter. In 1986 the CPSC launched an effective partnership with the Customs Service to block at the border products that violated U.S. safety rules. But even after Graham moved up to chair the commission in 1989, few would have called the CPSC a vigorous agency. By the early 1990s, charged Ralph Nader (the consumer movement's stern godfather), the agency had "been dormant for fifteen years."[7]

Ann Brown, the chair of a leading consumer advocacy group and a former vice president of the Consumer Federation of America, was the Clinton administration's pick to head the CPSC. A dynamic, charismatic, and media-savvy woman, Brown took charge in early 1994 amid widespread speculation about her plans for the troubled agency. "She has her own agenda," worried the National Association of Manufacturers' general counsel, "and we want to know what it is."[8] Industry's fears mirrored the hopes of consumer groups that Brown would usher in a renaissance of hard-charging safety regulation.

But Chairman Brown had something subtler in mind. Neither her marching orders from the Clinton administration nor her own instincts—Brown was a veteran consumer advocate, but also a shopkeeper's daughter—pointed her toward a product-safety jihad against American business. Even had she been so inclined, her resources rendered impossible any command-and-control offensive against thousands of consumer-goods companies; the CPSC's staff had dwindled to fewer than 500, and administration higher-ups had warned Brown not to expect major budget increases.

Brown set the stage with a series of partly symbolic measures. She encouraged staff to drop by her office; hosted award ceremonies and pep rallies and pizza parties; enlisted the actor James Earl Jones to lend his resonant voice to a reinvigorated "consumer safety hotline"; and worked the talk-show circuit preaching product safety, with a special focus on children. She orchestrated voluntary industry standards on high-profile but relatively uncontroversial hazards like dangling drawstrings on children's jackets and window-blind cords that could entangle a playful toddler, and she created a "chairman's commendation" award for firms displaying exemplary initiative on product safety. These tactics proved highly effective in boosting the agency's morale and visibility, but Brown knew they only bought time while the CPSC framed its new regulatory strategy.

The problem, simply put, was that the CPSC had never mastered the balancing act Congress bequeathed it in 1972—to intervene in consumer-product markets when intervention is "reasonably necessary to eliminate or reduce an unreasonable risk." After all, only extremists (whether on the right or the left) could object to the underlying principle: enforce requirements that cut a lot of risk for a little cost (in terms of procedural hassle or market disruptions) and forswear interventions that impose heavy burdens but have limited effect. But for most of its history, the CPSC had been preoccupied with internal and external disputes over which side of the scale mattered more and the proper calibration of risk and cost. In its earliest days it declared risk reduction paramount and discounted business costs; under different management, in a different political context, it stressed the damage done by shrunken markets and procedural burdens. Brown and her team knew this cycle of competing priorities reflected an honest political conflict. But instead of simply presiding over another spin of the ideological wheel, she opted to stress better bargains—cheaper, more effective ideas for making people safe.

One challenge for Brown, as she sought to transcend the CPSC's legacy of conflicting imperatives and as business and consumer advocates flexed their political muscles, was that she could not be sure the commission would get the running room to pursue such an agenda. Another challenge, even more fundamental, was that she came in with no detailed blueprint of just how to advance this goal of efficient, nonadversarial risk reduction for a vast and complicated economy. But she became convinced, as she settled into her job, that the CPSC staff was a latent reservoir of expertise on how to get more safety bang for the regulatory buck. So in meeting after meeting, Brown delivered the message to the commission's lawyers, economists, scientists, press experts, and engineers: We're serious about making consumers safer. There aren't very many of us. We can't pick fights with business. *You* figure out how we're going to pull this off. Get me your ideas, and I'll do everything I can to make them happen.[9]

Beyond authorizing regulations and standards to head off hazards in advance, the Consumer Product Safety Act authorizes the commission to demand a recall, at the manufacturer's expense, of any product found to pose a serious risk. A potential product defect can reach the CPSC's attention through complaints from consumers, tips from insurance companies or liability lawyers, investigations by field staff, or a suspicious pattern of deaths or injuries associated with some product. One common way, however, is a report by the manufacturer itself. Firms are legally obliged to report suspected defects to the CPSC, and they are usually the first to know when there may be a problem with a product. Once a potential defect is reported, the CPSC's job is to determine what sort of corrective action is required and to ensure that the firm follows through—notifying retailers to stop selling the item, attempting to reach consumers who are already using the product, and repairing the defect if possible or, failing that, offering replacements or refunds. A recall happens, on average, about once each working day.

During the CPSC's long years in the political wilderness, internal frustration about accomplishments led to an obsession with the recall process. While it is not prescribed by statute, an intricate process for responding to a suspected product defect became standard operating procedure. One key step in this procedural ballet was the drafting of the preliminary determination that a product was defective, the piece of paperwork that advanced a problem to the front burner. The preliminary determination—usually abbreviated as PD—was the watershed of the process. An intensifying flood of staff work—field inspectors exploring incidents associated with a suspect product, engineers doing lab tests to pinpoint flaws and test potential remedies, specialists in "human factors" studying how consumers are likely to use or abuse a product—flowed toward the PD; a formal decision to seek a recall flowed from it. The process was administratively tidy and produced an orderly record documenting why the CPSC believed there was a problem and what it wanted done about it. While the CPSC rarely had to go to court to trigger a recall, if it did need to file suit the PD process ensured that the evidence was there to convince a judge. But the process was expensive, adversarial, and slow. By the time all the compliance officers and technicians and lawyers had come to closure on the preliminary determination months might have passed. During those months, however, people were buying and using the defective space heaters and swing sets and playpens.

Soon after Ann Brown rallied the staff to find better ways to keep consumers safe, the forty or so workers at the Office of Compliance—which took the lead in product recalls—started a series of informal brainstorming sessions. (Alan Schoem, a career employee who would later head the office, is seen within the CPSC as the midwife of the compliance initiative.) How could the small team get more leverage over its ultimate mission? If only they could spend less time wrestling with manufacturers when a product hazard surfaced, they could catch more defects and get products off the shelves faster once a recall was needed. They could also economize on political capital if they could crank down the adversarial tone of their dealings with business. But how?

A Two-Track Approach

The insight that eventually emerged from these sessions was that the CPSC did business with at least two quite different categories of companies. Some were ready and willing to recall a defective product right away. Others disputed (for sound or unsound reasons) the need for corrective action.[10] Under the standard PD process, any potential defect required the same internal investigation, which often but not always led to a PD and a legal mandate for action. But the compliance staff was well aware that many manufacturers of defective products had no desire to wrangle with the government before initiating a recall. Often corporate officials were horrified to discover a product defect and anxious to put things right as fast as possible. If a company knows what is wrong and wants to fix it, compliance staffers mused, what is the point of the process? Would it not be better for all concerned—the company, the CPSC, and especially the consumer about to buy something dangerous and bring it home—to just agree on a plan and get moving? The compliance staff sketched the logic of a two-track recall system. If a company wanted to play tough, or honestly doubted the need for a recall, the standard process still made sense. Otherwise, why should the CPSC not simply take "yes" for an answer?

The conversation broadened within CPSC. Quite a few people, in the Compliance Office and elsewhere, were initially reluctant to surrender the formal paper record the PD process produced. What if a company changed its mind, or bungled the recall? What if the company (by accident or by design) misconstrued the hazard and fixed the wrong defect? But these and similar objections were countered by advocates' assurance that the standard track would still be there if the new approach failed. Internal skepticism gradually gave way.

Other staffers pointed out some subtle advantages to the two-track idea. The relative size of those two groups of companies—those who were ready to initiate a recall as soon as a problem surfaced and those who resisted the idea—was not set in stone. The decision by a particular company to fight or to cooperate was the result of internal debates. Some within the firm—especially the engineers and marketers, anguished by the idea of dangerous products on the market with the company's name on them—tended to favor immediate recall. Others—especially lawyers who were wary of inviting liability lawsuits—wanted to wait for rock-solid proof of a problem before going through the recall ordeal. Thinking through the bureaucratic dynamics within regulated firms, CPSC staffers reasoned that a less traumatic recall option could tilt the corporate debate toward rapid compliance. It could be "a way for the doves within the company to win the internal argument," explained a commission lawyer.[11] "Do the recall," the doves could argue, "and we can get the problem behind us without all the paperwork and red tape." Even the corporate lawyers might be induced to agree to a recall by the prospect of avoiding the potentially damning documentation assembled in the course of the PD process. The CPSC, for its part, would give up something of secondary value (a detailed, documented process) in exchange for something absolutely central to its mission—rapid corrective action.

Once she was briefed on the emerging idea, Chairman Brown was an instant supporter and gave the go-ahead for a formal initiative. In mid-1995 the Office of Compliance formally proposed an alternative to the standard recall process. If a company and the CPSC could agree on a remedy and get it under way within twenty working days after a hazard reached the commission's attention, the PD process could be bypassed. Companies had to be willing to share data on the nature and extent of the problem, and CPSC experts had to be convinced that the proposed remedy—whether repair, replacement, or refund—was a reasonable response to the hazard. But most of the procedural hurdles could be skipped, and the interaction between government and business would be dominated by technicians and public-affairs staffers cooperating to get the recall done instead of lawyers debating the need for one. The commissioners—Bush appointee Mary Sheila Gall, Clinton appointee Thomas Moore, and Chairman Ann Brown—blessed the plan unanimously. In August a pilot of the "no preliminary determination corrective-action program" was announced in the *Federal Register*.[12] Soon thereafter, Barbara Rosenfeld, a one-time career staffer at CPSC who had returned as senior advisor to the chairman, suggested the less cryptic label "Fast Track."

Within less than a week, Fast Track had its first test. Support cables holding up some playground structures made by B.C.I. Burke turned out to be too flimsy to take the pounding they would likely get. The problem surfaced August 22. By early September, CPSC staff and the company agreed on a remedy and started the recall. Before the end of October, 93 percent of the faulty products had been fixed—an astonishingly high fraction of hazards caught, by historical standards, in an astonishingly short time. No kids got hurt. Thirty-three additional recalls went forward under Fast Track during 1995, and early the next year the pilot was extended. In mid-1997, after hundreds of successful recalls under the pilot program, Fast Track was made a permanent alternative to the traditional process.

The mechanics of a Fast Track recall can seem like simple common sense. For example, Sunbeam one day discovered some sloppy design in a new line of crockpots. An electrical wire had a little too much room to rattle around inside the heating unit. Over time, with the shaking and banging the crockpot could endure, the wire might work its way into contact with the metal shell and deliver a dangerous shock. The company notified the CPSC, and soon a Sunbeam technician was on the phone comparing notes with Julie Ayers, an electrical engineer at the commission. The company technician thought the problem could be fixed by simply crimping a plastic insulator onto the end of the errant wire. Ayers got one of the crockpots, took it apart in her lab, tried out the plastic-insulator trick, and judged that the fix would work just fine. With no disagreements on the technical front, a recall plan was quickly written up. Nearly 5,000 of the crockpots were on the market; within a few weeks, all but a few had been found and fixed, and nobody got hurt.

Unremarkable as this sequence might appear, consider what would have happened under the traditional process: The CPSC would have kept its distance from Sunbeam, collecting its own samples of the suspect crockpot. Ayers would have started her own technical diagnosis from scratch. Had she determined independently that the loose wire was indeed long enough to reach the metal shell, she would have passed the case over to CPSC experts in consumer behavior. These experts would apply models of product use and abuse to calculate the odds that somebody would knock the crockpot around enough to bring the wire and the shell into contact. Then the health scientists would calibrate how bad an electrical shock an unlucky consumer might suffer. Then the results of all these analyses would be drafted into the precise and detailed language of a preliminary determination. The CPSC would then send a letter to Sunbeam informing it of the preliminary determination. Sunbeam and the compliance office would settle down to negotiate a technical fix and recall procedure, and once the lawyers had worked out the language of the recall notice, consumers would finally start to get the word. In the meantime, some guy in Fargo might have caught 110 volts while stirring the chili.

Sometimes the stakes are higher. The Tonka division of Hasbro Toys launched its new "Soft Walkin' Wheels" line in early 1994. The toys were stylized trucks, cars, and other vehicles with cheerful faces and a soft fabric surface that appealed to toddlers and battery-powered wheels to provide the kind of action that could keep older preschoolers interested. Three years later, after Hasbro had sold well over a million of the toys, reports began to filter in that wheel hubs were separating from the axles on some of the Soft Walkin' Wheels. A Hasbro subcontractor, it turned out, had botched the assembly work on a batch of the toys. Two children were known to have started choking on the loose hubs. Both had been rescued. But with a million small children doing what came naturally—trying to take toys apart and popping into their mouths any small pieces that broke off—the odds were high that some child would be hurt or killed.

This was the toughest kind of product-safety challenge. The dangerous units were scattered throughout the country. Most of the toys had left store shelves years ago, and rarely was there any traceable purchase record. Even if parents who had bought a Soft Walkin' Wheels happened to see a recall announcement, after so much time the dangerous toy was likely to have become an unnoticed part of the playroom clutter. Once products are in the home, traditionally, it is extraordinarily difficult to get them out again. The longer the time since purchase, and the smaller and cheaper the product, the lower the odds of capturing consumers' attention and catching the hazard in time.

But this also turned out to be where the CPSC's accelerated and cooperative recall option, coupled with broader changes engineered on Brown's watch, could make the biggest difference. Hasbro reported the problem in the second week of January. Far from disputing the need for a recall, Hasbro's fondest hope was to get the toys out of kids' hands. With $3 billion in annual sales of its Tonka, Kenner, Playskool, Parker Brothers, Milton-Bradley, and other lines of toys and games, the public-relations and legal repercussions of a Soft Walkin' Wheels debacle could be devastating. The company immediately opted for Fast Track, and in less than two weeks the company and the CPSC had come up with a strategy to boost the odds of a successful recall.

One part of the strategy was simply an intensified version of classic recall tactics. It was standard practice for CPSC to send out press releases announcing a recall. But when Brown took over, the public affairs office had only one fax machine, and it could take three days to issue a press release. Under Kathleen Begala, the top-flight public affairs chief Brown had recruited, the CPSC had built a bank of sixteen fax lines with automated "send" lists of media outlets, pediatricians' offices, and day-care centers. The press release in which Hasbro and the commission called for Soft Walkin' Wheels to be returned for a refund was issued nationwide on January 29, mere hours after it was written. Begala also made heavy use of the video news release. As broadcast media had grown in importance and print receded, short videos explaining the hazard and announcing the recall had obvious advantages over traditional paper announcements. Video news releases about the Soft Walkin' Wheels, prepared by CPSC and Hasbro staffers working together, were fed by satellite free of charge to TV stations across the country. Another tactic involved concentrated attention to key distributors. Upon learning that Toys "R" Us sold over a quarter of all the toys in America, for example, the Brown team had cultivated relationships with the massive retailer. When the Soft Walkin' Wheels crisis broke, the CPSC was able to get recall posters prominently placed in Toys "R" Us outlets.

Ann Brown also decided to cash in some chits with the top-drawer media. Since taking charge at the commission she had appeared regularly on news and talk shows. She had proven herself lively, articulate, and telegenic—quite the opposite of the hazard to ratings a TV producer might anticipate from a federal regulator. Brown and her staff worked their rolodexes and persuaded the popular program "Good Morning America" to devote a segment to the Soft Walkin' Wheels problem. On the morning the recall was announced, Chairman Brown appeared before millions of viewers with a Soft Walkin' Wheels toy in her lap to demonstrate the choking hazard. On the air, as in all her public statements, she took pains to depict Hasbro as a responsible firm trying hard to do the right thing. And in tones of calm concern, she urged viewers to help get the toys out of children's hands. Between "Good Morning America" and the video news release satellite feeds, nearly 25 million television viewers got the word on the recall.

The campaign worked beyond anyone's expectations. Over a million toys were returned for replacement or refund. Hasbro emerged with its reputation intact—even, perhaps, enhanced—and the Soft Walkin' Wheels incident made not a dent in its 1997 earnings or list of legal worries.[13] Alan Hassenfeld, the head of Hasbro, became an enthusiastic cheerleader for the CPSC in general and Fast Track in particular. Most important, no child was killed or badly hurt by a loose hub from a Soft Walkin' Wheels toy.

Since the option was first offered, nearly half of all recalls have proceeded under the Fast Track alternative—a total of close to 400 by the end of 1998. Almost by definition, this accelerates recalls: if the company cannot get the recall underway within twenty business days, it cannot use Fast Track. In practice, however, the average Fast Track recall is launched nine days after the CPSC learns of a hazard.[14] Related to the speedier recalls, but ultimately more important, is the superior return rate under Fast Track. It is much easier to pull a product from a warehouse or retail store than from a consumer's home—the information channels are more reliable, the logistical challenges simpler. The fraction of recalled products that are actually returned for repair or replacement has averaged well above fifty percent under Fast Track; for the traditional process, it is around 17 percent.[15]

Firms benefit, too. "It used to be like the stereotype of dealing with the feds," according to an attorney who represents consumer-product firms. "My client would have a factory shut down awaiting the OK from the government [on a corrective-action plan] and it would be 4:30 in Washington and everybody's gone home. It's real different now."[16] When a Fast Track recall is under way, key CPSC staffers routinely work late, wear pagers, and share home phone numbers with their corporate counterparts. As the program's merits become better known, some firms facing a recall have begun instructing their attorneys to "make sure this gets done through Fast Track."[17] The CPSC knows a lot about how to run a successful recall, and the collegial approach Fast Track makes possible allows firms to tap that expertise. Much less legal work is involved when the preliminary determination process can be bypassed. This saves firms money (Honeywell, for example, has found it can do without outside counsel in its Fast Track recalls[18]) and, more subtly, improves product safety by letting company engineers deal directly with CPSC engineers without the attorneys as go-betweens.

Fast Track complements—partly relies on and partly enables—the Brown team's broader strategy to leverage the commission's limited resources by using public visibility, moral suasion, and reputation-based enforcement tactics. As the CPSC establishes its bona fides as a reasonable regulator, it can more credibly put public pressure on companies that resist recalling dangerous products. For a consumer-product company, leverage over its reputation can be a more powerful motivator than the other arrows in CPSC's quiver, and Fast Track gives firms the option of visibly cooperating in a rapid recall, with some influence over how the problem and the solution are presented to the public. The CPSC gives regulated firms much more powerful incentives to be one of the product-safety good guys.

Fast Track does not cover all product recalls, and it probably never will. Some issues are simply too complex to process so quickly. Some managers fight to the bitter end the possibility that something is wrong with their company's product. But one reason for the durability of the old process is that most companies have little experience with its downside. Serious product defects, fortunately, are rare events. Except for the largest consumer-product companies, corporate managers involved in a safety-hazard case know little about what it involves. They understandably start out with the hope that a recall can somehow be avoided. Many firms find it difficult to come to terms with the need for a recall within the twenty days Fast Track requires, since there is always a possibility that the traditional process will lead to a determination that no recall is needed after all. So the original, slower track remains in use—though Fast Track's stepped-up efficiency allows more staff resources to be concentrated on conventional recalls, accelerating them as well.

Despite Fast Track and the CPSC's broader reforms, perfect harmony does not reign—if it ever could—between regulators and regulated. There was a bruising fight with industry over the commission's 1995 standard that packaging for medicines, household cleaning products, and other potential poisons had to be resistant to curious children but also usable by senior citizens—though the CPSC and industry did eventually reach agreement. And a late-1990s initiative to require furniture upholstery to be flame-resistant sparked furious opposition from politically well-connected furniture manufacturers.

Yet Fast Track, as a concrete example and an emblem of the CPSC's wider reforms, clearly improves the tone and boosts the productivity of relations between business and government. There are fewer sterile standoffs and more displays of teamwork. Less time and money are spent on process and more on results. There is less ideological sniping and more practical cooperation on product safety. Consumer advocates and corporate managers, as little inclined toward agreement as their habits or experience render them, broadly concur that Fast Track makes things better.

Notes

1. Interview with Honeywell attorney Jean Flynn, July 8, 1998.

2. The CPSC gained additional responsibilities under the Federal Hazardous Substances Act, the Flammable Fabrics Act, the Poison Prevention Packaging Act, and the Refrigerator Safety Act.

3. *Aqua Slide 'N' Dive Corp* v. *Consumer Product Safety Commission*, 569 F.2d 831 (5th Cir. 1978). Many of the details in this section are drawn from this appellate-court decision. There is some reason to believe that the commissioners went beyond their staff's recommendations in drafting the pool-slide regulation.

4. Ibid., at 843. While the warning-sign requirements were struck down, other parts of the slide safety regulation were retained. During his career as a law professor, Supreme Court Justice Stephen Breyer often used the Aqua Slide case as a textbook example of misguided regulation.

5. Dale Russakoff, "The Little Agency That Can't," *Washington Post*, February 2, 1989.

6. Ibid.

7. Brian Steinberg, "Ann Brown Has Revived an Agency That Nearly Suffocated in the Reagan Days," *New York Times*, September 11, 1994.

8. Ibid.

9. This section draws on an interview with Ann Brown, July 8, 1998, and an interview with Alan Schoem, July 9, 1998.

10. A third category of companies simply dodged their legal obligation to report product hazards and hoped for the best.

11. Interview with Jeff Bromme, CPSC general counsel, July 8, 1998.

12. "Announcement of Amnesty and Conditions under Which the Staff Will Refrain from Making Preliminary Hazard Determinations," *Federal Register,* Vol. 60, No. 159, August 17, 1995, p. 42848.

13. Soft Walkin' Wheels was not among the legal issues warranting mention in Hasbro Inc.'s 1997 annual report or 10-K submission to the Securities and Exchange Commission.

14. Internal CPSC performance data as of December 15, 1998.

15. N. J. Scheers, "Evaluation of Fast-Track Product Recall Program," CPSC Office of Planning and Evaluation, July 1998.

16. Interview with Peter Winik, attorney with Latham and Watkins, July 8, 1998.

17. Ibid.

18. Interview with Honeywell attorney Jean Flynn, July 8, 1998.

3

TRANSFORMING MILITARY SUPPLY

AMONG THE MOST MEMORABLE characters in *Catch-22* (Joseph Heller's dark satire about military life in World War II) is Milo Minderbinder, the bomber-squadron mess supply officer who manipulates a web of commerce stretching throughout a war-wracked continent to keep his kitchen stocked and his "syndicate" thriving. Milo smuggles frozen eclairs out of Paris, traffics with Italian endive exporters, commandeers planeloads of figs, and engages in byzantine cycles of egg arbitrage. Little of Europe's economy remains unaffected by the manipulations of this shrewd American lieutenant, who achieves nearly mythic (but hardly heroic) status by the end of the book.[1]

Milo is not alone. The street-smart and resourceful—if slightly shady—supply officer is an American cultural convention.[2] The same theme runs through every incarnation of the archetype: Whether dealing in artichokes or auto parts, playing by the book is a sucker's game. Guile and drive are the only ways to sidestep a pettifogging bureaucracy, entangling red tape, and regulations that seem untouched by common sense.

Art does imitate life, as many veterans can attest. The same U.S. military that has earned so proud a tradition on the battlefield has at times displayed breathtaking inefficiency in provisioning the troops. But the next generation of novelists and screenwriters may be forced to pick

---

This chapter was researched and drafted by Dalit Toledano.

another aspect of military life to lampoon, because the organization in charge of supplying the armed forces has done a sharp about-face.

The Challenge

The enterprise in question is the Defense Logistics Agency's Defense Supply Center Philadelphia (DSCP).[3] Headquartered on a military base in South Philadelphia, the DSCP delivers logistical support services for U.S. soldiers, sailors, airmen, and marines (and their dependents) around the world. The DSCP procures and transports everything from fresh fruit to combat boots to aspirin. It is responsible for the food served up in military dining halls (formerly known as messes), for the medical equipment and pharmaceuticals in military hospitals, and for the clothes on every warrior's back. Napoleon is said to have observed that an army marches on its stomach, and an old verse tells us how a kingdom was lost for want of a nail. The little things—things like socks, flu shots, and field rations—still shape the fate of grand forces.

Just such mundane items figure prominently in the mental image of military preparedness held by many Americans. When an isolationist United States was dragged into World War II, it was ill-equipped to fight a multifront war. That changed quickly, when the country mobilized the seemingly limitless resources and ingenuity of U.S. industry—the "arsenal of democracy." Star-spangled newsreels featured assembly lines churning out everything from blankets to bayonets for our boys abroad, and faith in eventual victory was fortified by the wide-angle vistas of overflowing warehouses.

Postwar defense policies were driven, at least in part, by the determination never again to be caught short-handed. Procurement policy quickly grew to encompass a vast array of statutes and regulations designed to guarantee that American armed forces would always be well equipped and well prepared. In order to ensure top quality and the requisite standardization, the Pentagon drafted elaborate guidelines for virtually anything the forces might need; military specifications—or milspecs, as they are known—stipulated the color, shape, size, strength, and life expectancy of everything from shoelaces to smoke grenades. The procedures for soliciting and choosing bids from manufacturers were painstakingly regulated, and the production methods and balance sheets of the chosen manufacturer were subject to scrutiny by Defense Department auditors and quality-assurance specialists.

The DSCP is responsible for food, clothing, medical supplies, and what are termed general and industrial goods, letting other agencies handle the assault helicopters and nuclear submarines. Its role as a middleman between the factory and the fighting force has nonetheless been regulated by many of the same restrictive federal rules that govern the acquisition of weapons systems. The DSCP would solicit offers from contractors willing to produce items in accordance with the milspecs, accept the lowest bid, monitor contractors to ensure correct procedures were being followed, and oversee the storage of the completed items in its own cavernous depots and in smaller depots on local bases.

By the 1980s, after decades of following this pattern, the system had produced what it had seemingly been intended to produce: warehouses brimming with inventory. Two billion dollars' worth of supplies sat in depots, ready to be shipped to any corner of the world at a moment's notice.[4] But this stockpile turned out to be not such a triumph for the DSCP. Instead, the agency was approaching a crisis, centered on soaring costs, that would culminate in a fight for its life. Nearly every aspect of the way the DSCP did business had proven expensive in an era when cost was coming to matter more.

The milspec system was at the root of the trouble. Standard commercial products rarely met stringent military specifications, so the DSCP dealt mostly with niche manufacturers who specialized in complying with Pentagon guidelines. When faced with detailed instructions about how to make underwear or chocolate chip cookies, many major manufacturers decided the business from the Defense Department simply was not worth altering their regular products or setting up parallel assembly lines. Those who did agree to follow Pentagon specs faced extra costs, but little competition, and therefore military supplies were consistently higher priced than their commercial counterparts.

Many of the small businesses that the DSCP relied on, in turn, depended almost completely on military contracts for survival. This was especially the case for the manufacturers of those items with little or no commercial application and thus a small or nonexistent market during times of peace. Meals-Ready-to-Eat (MREs)—the rations used by troops in field operations—are one example: the requirements for MREs depart somewhat from the supermarket norm. The foil-wrapped meals must be able to withstand the rigors of combat-zone transportation and storage and must hold up without refrigeration for the duration of a conflict. This durability comes at a cost. It will not surprise former servicemen to learn that there never has been a big civilian market for the military rations.

Similarly, a firm in Bethesda, Maryland, produced atropine injectors to treat people exposed to chemical-weapons attack—another item in limited demand at the corner convenience store. Because this one small supplier was the only company that made such a product, its survival was critical to the DSCP, which felt compelled to tide the company over even when injector supplies seemed adequate.[5] Such mutually dependent relationships tended to become quite costly for the DSCP.

In the meantime, the DSCP's customers—the personnel in charge of feeding troops, or keeping commissaries well stocked, or equipping pharmacies and hospitals—were growing dissatisfied with this very system that the DSCP was hemorrhaging money to maintain. In the first place, customers' choices were limited to the narrow list of items that met Pentagon specifications. As one DSCP official conceded, "More than 40 percent of everything we bought was not what our customers wanted."[6] Delivery timing seemed to be a guessing game, with some customers waiting months for shipments—and some customers receiving the wrong supplies altogether. Nervous that they might run out of supplies and confronted with an inconsistent system, each base's supply personnel had ample incentive to over-order and stockpile goods.

So the DSCP was doling out huge sums of money to produce items that conformed to milspecs, shouldering the expense of storing these supplies, insulating some of their manufacturers from the ups and downs of military demand, and facing increasingly unhappy customers.

The milspec system was based on good intentions informed by bad experiences. Horror stories about shoddy goods punctuate U.S. military history. (Indeed, the word "shoddy" originally referred to a type of fabric sold to the Union Army during the Civil War.) The risk of inflicting low-quality or inappropriate supplies on U.S. fighting forces was by no means imaginary, nor was the taxpayer's risk of being gouged by suppliers. But the system put in place to manage these risks was backfiring. Defense contractors were spending forty cents of each dollar on administrative costs, and industry executives estimated that they were charging the Pentagon nearly 50 percent more than commercial firms for the same work.[7] A senior procurement official for the Pentagon described the problem this way: "We have become so risk averse that we end up spending billions to make sure we do not lose millions."[8]

The cost overruns in the Defense Department had not gone unnoticed by Congress, and procurement reform was a perennial topic. Since the mid-1980s, bipartisan groups had worked to revise laws governing contract audits, to consolidate contract payment and financing laws, and to allow procurers to include factors other than price—such as the supplier's delivery history—in purchasing decisions. But despite these and other important efforts to simplify and streamline regulations, the acquisition process remained stubbornly resistant to large-scale reforms.

Congressional efforts to reform defense procurement remained—as did the trials and tribulations of the DSCP—largely outside the glare of the public spotlight until Saddam Hussein strained the system by invading Kuwait in August of 1990. The sudden U.S. involvement in the Gulf conflict—first in Operation Desert Shield and then in Operation Desert Storm—left the DSCP scrambling to supply the largest deployment of troops since the Vietnam War. The task of feeding, clothing, and otherwise equipping hundreds of thousands of troops was an enormous one—and one in which the DSCP ultimately succeeded—but its initial troubles revealed deep faults running through the military's supply system.

The manufacturing base that the DSCP relied on was neither large enough nor flexible enough to meet the sudden expansion in military demand. Many suppliers had begun downsizing to brace for defense budget cutbacks and were ill-prepared to handle the huge new orders from the DSCP. The owner of a small Texas company that makes bread and other rations for the armed services complained, "Companies like mine contracted capital spending; now the government calls and asks how fast can you make it."[9] When it was clear that its regular, smaller suppliers could not handle all the government orders, the DSCP had no choice but to turn to alternative suppliers. Emergency waivers let it bend the rules and quickly sign contracts with the kinds of commercial firms that had been out of the loop on defense supply. The jeans maker Wrangler was first contacted on October 2, 1990; two weeks later, it had begun production of 1 million pairs of battle fatigues, part of a contract totaling more than $17 million.[10] Many manufacturers, however, were unwilling to take on new government contracts because they were afraid their commercial customers—who would still be buying when the shooting stopped—might react badly to having Uncle Sam cut in line.

It was not only the sheer number of orders and the tight time frame that overwhelmed the DSCP. The military simply had not been ready to supply an engagement in the Middle East. The notion that stockpiling in depots equaled defense readiness was shattered when searches through the vast DSCP warehouses turned up boots for the Korean War, millions of bottles of nasal spray, and World War II–era hospital gowns, among other items that had limited usefulness in the sands of Saudi Arabia. There were uniforms—400,000 of them, in fact—but they were brown and green woolen uniforms that would make combatants about as inconspicuous as a Christmas tree on a beach. "We were prepared for a war in eastern Europe, not a war in the desert," confessed Dennis Dudek, the chief of apparel production for the DSCP.[11] Desert camouflage uniforms were needed, as were boots that contained a thermal barrier against the hot sand. Food contracts had to be revised, too, to take into account the special dietary laws of the troops' Islamic hosts. Spam, that mainstay of military cuisine, was thrown off the menu, along with other items containing pork.[12] And food manufacturers struggled to provide edibles that could withstand the extreme desert heat.

In the end, the DSCP came through. Supplies to U.S. troops in the Middle East included hundreds of thousands of water purification tablets, sunscreen lotions, cans of foot powder, and chemical-protective suits.[13] But as one DSCP official acknowledged, the Gulf crisis had "exposed all the blemishes."[14] It was not good enough that the DSCP had managed to pull it all off. More permanent reforms would be needed for the military—and the nation—to be confident about defense readiness in the future.

Shrinking defense budgets and a new national deficit consciousness also forced the Pentagon to make a priority of fixing procurement practices. The nation's defense budget had peaked in the mid-1980s and then declined rapidly as the Soviet Union crumbled. Cold war budgets had been so large that the high costs associated with even the most wasteful of practices had been absorbed, but fewer resources meant closer scrutiny of all expenditures. And it was clear that the old way of doing things—stuffing military depots with items that past experience suggested might turn out to be handy—was no longer affordable.

It was also no longer desirable. Stockpiling had proven grossly insufficient and had actually harmed readiness by hogging resources. If the prospect of a large-scale war was receding, the likelihood that U.S. troops might be drawn into regional conflicts anywhere in the world was increasing. Defense experts warned that the future held rapid mobilizations and deployments of short duration, requiring that the DSCP be more flexible and more effective than stockpiling had permitted.

Had the internal pressures of trying to maintain enough fighting power to win two major regional conflicts—simultaneously, and without help from other nations—while adapting to significant budget cuts not been enough to force the Pentagon to make major changes in its acquisition procedures, there was plenty of external pressure as well. The media had begun to pick up on the military's troubles—fairly or not, $600 toilet seats make a great story—and their reports made the calls for reform even harder to ignore. In 1991 the Pentagon adopted new rules that, among other things, gave all branches of the military new discretion over their purchasing decisions. Supply officers were no longer required to buy through the DSCP or any other government provider.[15]

The DSCP's clients could now take their business elsewhere—a disquieting prospect, considering the level of customer dissatisfaction and their intensifying concern for bargain prices. Further cranking up the pressure was the announcement that supply centers would no longer receive appropriations from Congress to cover overhead; instead, thanks to another new Pentagon rule, they would have to sell enough to their clients to support their own costs.

The DSCP's troubles would get worse before they got better. Auditors from the General Accounting Office published a scathing report on procurement practices. In early 1992 the television news magazine "60 Minutes" ran a piece that ridiculed the DSCP, showing warehouses full of tennis shoes from the 1960s and Army medical paraphernalia that dated back to the 1950s.[16] And the DSCP was targeted for a traumatic relocation by the Federal Base Realignment and Closure Commission.[17]

The DSCP seemed to be facing a grim future in the early 1990s. But it survived, and indeed came to flourish, in the wake of a series of fundamental reforms. There is no solitary hero in the transformation of a $3.4 billion agency into an agile contract broker. Nor is there any one bold breakthrough that locked up the reinvention. Instead, in the years following the Gulf War, a multifront campaign of reform was waged by a force that included the 3,500 employees of DSCP, who discovered which local-level changes were making a difference; their managers, who encouraged their employees to experiment, raided the business world for the latest technologies, and merged several separate initiatives into one comprehensive whole; members of Congress, like Senator Jeff Bingaman of New Mexico, who would support the reforms with new legislation in 1994;[18] and an administration that was willing to make acquisition reform a priority. As Deputy Defense Secretary William Perry put it, "This is the window of opportunity for doing it. We're going to see if we can slither through that window."[19]

The most immediate priority for the DSCP was to reclaim its relevance for military supply. It would have to solidify its standing with its previously captive customers, who themselves were under pressure to get the most from their dwindling defense dollars. Winning their confidence would require offering a broader range of better products at lower prices with quicker delivery. What the DSCP needed was an open corridor to the commercial economy—and a frontal assault on the rigid milspec system.

This meant bringing antiquated procedures, long preserved in isolation from the economic mainstream, into sync with modern commercial practices. The DSCP had been experimenting with computerized ordering since 1987, but the experiments had not become standard practice. Now the DSCP purchased computers for its headquarters and developed new software so that its systems would be compatible with those already in place within the Army, Navy, and Air Force. As it trained its own employees, the DSCP also provided training for its customers in the separate services.[20] Supply officers can now "window shop" with on-line catalogues, order goods electronically, and receive confirmation of their orders within minutes. Inventories are immediately updated to reflect new orders, deliveries are invoiced instantly, and funds are promptly transferred over wires. Customers used to waiting months to receive orders now receive them within several days, and usually within forty-eight hours. Medical supplies can be delivered within six hours.

The DSCP has mobilized its vast buying power on the service's behalf to negotiate volume discounts. And when manufacturers post the prices for their wares on the electronic menus, they know computer graphics will display competitors' prices right alongside. The DSCP has set up a cost-saving distribution system that allows customers to choose among goods made by hundreds of different manufacturers, without sacrificing the convenience of dealing with a single prime vendor responsible for taking orders from and delivering supplies to military dining facilities or hospitals or clothing depots throughout a geographical region.

As customers have learned to trust the speeded-up delivery system, the value of supplies sitting in warehouses has dropped by 40 percent, and storage costs have plummeted.[21] Why hoard supplies once you are confident you can get what you need when you need it? Fort Lee in Virginia reduced the value of its food inventory from more than $500,000 to $40,000. Another customer decided it no longer needed the multi–million dollar cold storage warehouse it had planned to build. And some costly supply depots have been eliminated altogether; when pharmaceutical inventories at the Walter Reed Medical Center fell by 89 percent, the hospital stopped using six warehouses—at an annual savings of $7 million.[22]

The servicemen and servicewomen in military dining halls are not complaining about the new system, either. Under the old regime, supply officers would order food in bulk; the crates and barrels were stored in warehouses; items were eventually delivered to the kitchens in DSCP trucks. Most foods failed to benefit from aging. Now supply personnel can call the vendor less than twenty-four hours before a meal and order food based on the expectation of how many people will show up for that particular breakfast, lunch, or dinner. This new system means fresher food *and* lower costs. The success of the DSCP in this area has been so remarkable that the Department of Agriculture has asked it to take over the job of delivering fresh produce to school lunch programs in thirty-nine states.[23]

Just as electronic data interchange has made such significant contributions to the food, clothing, and medical operations of the DSCP, so has the same technology brought dramatic changes to the business practices of military suppliers. Copying methods used by retail giants such as Wal-Mart, J.C. Penney, and Sears, the DSCP uses electronic bar coding to keep track of actual demand, allowing suppliers to adjust their production schedules based on real-time information instead of blue-sky forecasts. Again, stockpiling could be reduced.

But if reducing its reliance on warehouses was becoming a new measure of success for the DSCP, defense readiness still depended in some part on being able to supply the armed services with huge quantities of custom-made items on short notice. The DSCP needed to build that which had eluded it in the past: a network of raw material suppliers, manufacturers, and distributors with the demonstrated capacity to churn out huge orders and the flexibility to respond to rapid changes in demand. And now, with large military contracts likely to come along unpredictably, the DSCP could not restrict itself to dependent suppliers who relied on government contracts to ward off bankruptcy.

The eventual solution was an organizational and economic innovation, not a simple technical fix, and it was inspired by the insight of front-line DSCP employees. They saw that the manufacturers they had always done business with were having difficulty finding commercial customers to pick up the slack left by shrinking military orders. Many of these were small firms that did not know how to operate in the commercial world. The DSCP determined that helping these firms make the transition to commercial markets made good business sense: the suppliers would be strengthened and disciplined by exposure to the commercial world, enabling the DSCP to rely on them without having to support them during times of peace with make work or subsidies.

So the DSCP began to help firms formerly dependent on the government modernize their plants and install dual-use technology that allows them to make civilian as well as military goods. And to make sure its investment pays off, the DSCP orchestrates triangular partnerships. The DSCP and a commercial customer contract to share the manufacturer's production capacity, each agreeing to adjust its own requirements to accommodate the other's emergency needs. Both customers are assured of having their urgent orders filled, and both can feel confident about investing in long-term relationships with a firm that has the volume of business it needs to survive.

The DSCP has set up one such three-way production agreement with Terry Manufacturing, a small, minority-owned business in eastern Alabama, and the fast-food giant McDonald's. Terry produces clothing for the military and also makes civilian uniforms; McDonald's is its biggest commercial customer. In the event of a military emergency, Terry's production of uniforms for the fast food chain's restaurant employees is delayed or sent elsewhere. In the fall of 1994, just four weeks after U.S. forces were mobilized in response to Iraqi troop movements, the DSCP was able to send 100,000 new uniforms to Kuwait— thanks to the shared production agreement.[24]

Each shared production agreement is different, tailored to meet the specific needs of the businesses involved. Take, for instance, the Phoenix-based company Atlas Headwear. After more than a decade of manufacturing military caps for the DSCP, the company began to train its employees in commercial production methods as well. It now has a contract to produce a certain percentage of all the golf hats, tennis visors, and baseball caps sold by Nike, the athletic-wear company. If the DSCP should need Atlas to scramble on an emergency order, Atlas will use overtime and second (and even third) shifts to fulfill its contracts with Nike. And Nike will have access, should it need it, to Atlas's full productive capacity during times when military needs ebb. Nike's director of corporate development, Michael Lewellen, commented: "Our product cycles vary, and there are times when demand for certain products exceeds our original production allocation. We never want to be in the position of not being able to provide a Nike product at retail, and this relationship allows us—at times of peak need—to access additional production time with Atlas."[25] DSCP employees have taken what were shaky, specialized companies and nudged them into commercial viability.

Just as our nation was able to rely on U.S. auto makers and steel companies to build the planes and bombs and tanks it needed to fight World War II, the Pentagon today hopes to be able to call on the country's commercial, as well as defense, industries. The DSCP's innovations are a part of the larger Defense Department strategy of creating a single industrial base whose defense and commercial sectors are all but indistinguishable.

The DSCP encountered many obstacles along the road to building a competitive and self-sustaining operation. It has fought for the waivers and exemptions that it needed to circumvent statutory barriers; its continued success will be predicated on relentless efforts to keep its customers happy and on vigilance against the regrowth of red tape. Working to maintain the capacity to equip its customers (not just for military emergencies—but also for nonwar defense assignments such as disaster relief missions, humanitarian aid efforts, and drug enforcement programs), the DSCP is committed to using the latest software programs to solve thorny logistical problems, reduce paperwork, and lower costs. It will face competition from other agencies clutching for every available federal dollar, and its private sector competition will always be aggressive—and answerable to fewer regulatory requirements.

In 1999 the nation's defense budget is projected to account for a smaller percentage of Gross Domestic Product than any time since 1940.[26] But the DSCP's mission has shrunk far less than its budget. The DSCP buys fresh and frozen food for 360 commissaries worldwide, for the Veterans Administration, for federal prisons, for Job Corps centers, and for school lunch programs. Its apparel division outfits the armed forces with everything from flags to dress uniforms to specialized flight clothing—and also supplies apparel to the Department of Immigration, federal prisons, and the Federal Aviation Administration. Millions of active and retired military members and their families are treated at hospitals and dental clinics that use medical equipment and pharmaceuticals supplied by the DSCP.

We Americans have our own version of Napoleon's adage about the importance of supply. Texas journalist William Cowper Brann once wrote: "No man can be a patriot on an empty stomach."[27] In the past several years, none of our fighting men—or women—have had to put this proposition to the test, because every time the United States dispatched military forces to Somalia, Haiti, Bosnia, or Rwanda, the DSCP was there, right along with them.

Notes

1. Joseph Heller, *Catch-22* (Dell, 1955).
2. Another example of the icon is Master Sgt. Ernie Bilko, whose inept superiors are dimly aware that all is not well in the motor pool but are no match for

the scheming sergeant. In "Kelly's Heroes," Don Rickles plays the hustling supply officer who bypasses the brass to scrounge up some tanks for Clint Eastwood's freelance offensive.

3. The operation's former name, in use until early 1998, was the Defense Personnel Support Center.

4. Lisa Corbin, "Retooling the Supply Chain," *Government Executive,* November 1995.

5. Michael Totty, "Gulf War Crisis Catches Suppliers Unprepared," *Dallas Times Herald*, August 30, 1990.

6. Corbin, "Retooling the Supply Chain."

7. John Mintz, "In Pentagonese, 'Milspec' Spells Trouble," *Washington Post*, June 27, 1993.

8. Greg Schneider, "Armed Forces Are Becoming Smart Shoppers," *Baltimore Sun*, December 15, 1996.

9. Totty, "Gulf War Crisis Catches Suppliers Unprepared."

10. Benjamin Weiser, "Firms Rush to Keep U.S. Troops Supplied," *Washington Post*, December 18, 1990.

11. Anne D'Innocenzio, "DSCP Goes to War," *Daily News Record*, January 25, 1991.

12. Douglas Frantz, "Armies of Workers Gear Up to Supply Troops in the Gulf," *Los Angeles Times*, January 22, 1991.

13. Sally Solo, "Supplying an Army," *Fortune*, December 31, 1990; and Frantz, "Armies of Workers."

14. Anne D'Innocenzio, "DSCP Marches into State-of-the-Art Manufacturing," *Daily News Record*, April 7, 1993.

15. Corbin, "Retooling the Supply Chain."

16. "60 Minutes," CBS, January 19, 1992.

17. "Aspin Lists 31 Bases for Closure," *St. Louis Post-Dispatch*, March 13, 1993.

18. Federal Acquisition Streamlining Act of 1994.

19. Mintz, "In Pentagonese, 'Milspec' Spells Trouble."

20. Innovations in American Government, 1995 Awards Program, Site Visit Report.

21. "Pentagon Reforms Its Purchasing," *Philadelphia Inquirer*, October 28, 1995.

22. David Warren, director of Defense Management Issues, General Accounting Office, Testimony, Government Reform and Oversight Committee, National Security, International Affairs and Criminal Justice Subcommittee, July 24, 1997.

23. Anne Lindberg, "Fresh, Healthy Innovation Goes to School," *St. Petersburg Times*, October 17, 1994; updated by John Dougherty of DSCP, February 1999.

24. Corbin, "Retooling the Supply Chain."

25. Monica Greco, "A Flexible Alternative," *Apparel Industry Magazine*, May 1995.

26. Ted Shelsby, "Defense Companies Struggle to Survive," *Baltimore Sun*, April 2, 1994.

27. William Cowper Brann, *Old Glory*, July 4, 1893.

4

SHUTTING DOWN SWEATSHOPS

IT IS MARCH 1911. Smoke erupts from a ten-story building in New York City. Horse-drawn fire engines clatter to the scene. But their ladders reach barely half the building's height. Young women lean screaming from windows on the top three floors. As the fire engulfs them, some of the women jump. They plummet to the pavement, their burning skirts trailing flames. When it is over, 146 women lie charred in the ruins or crushed on the street. The dead, mostly Jewish immigrants, had been working at the Triangle Shirtwaist Factory—a "sweatshop," in the day's slang. The women had been locked into the workrooms, stitching clothes for the fashion trade, when the building began to burn.

It is August 1995. Women are discovered living and working behind a barbed-wire barricade in El Monte, California. There are dozens of them, Thai immigrants, most of them very young. They are compelled to sew sixteen hours a day, sometimes much more. Most speak no English; all are forbidden any uncensored communication by phone or mail. If they try to leave, or refuse to work, or complain about the conditions or the pay (sometimes 70 cents an hour), the women face threats of beating, or rape, or death. Some of them have been held for years, stitching clothes for the fashion trade.

Few Americans in the early 1990s gave much thought to sweatshops, or indeed even encountered the word except as a faint echo from the

This chapter was researched and drafted by Laura Ziff and John Trattner.

days of bustles and whalebone corsets. Blurred black-and-white images of young immigrant girls, thin and unsmiling, crowded shoulder to shoulder in front of piles of garments, seemed like relics of an older, harsher America left behind long ago. Surely such antique abuses had no place in the glamorous, crisply corporate fashion industry of today. Surely the government could prevent such blatant breaches of the laws that long-dead crusaders had shamed the nation into adopting early in the century.

But the sweatshop was once again tarnishing America's garment trades. The El Monte raid, and others like it, unveiled for the public the troubling truth that sweatshops exploiting a new generation of immigrants had emerged and spread within the $45-billion apparel industry. Another truth, not so well publicized but at least as troubling to some, was that the modern-day sweatshop was no news at all to the Labor Department investigators who were supposed to make sure that nothing of the sort could exist in this country.

How had it happened? Had the labor laws been repealed or fatally weakened? Had federal regulators somehow lost their will to act even in the face of gross abuses? Nothing so simple explained the recrudescence of sweatshops in the fashion industry, and nothing as conventional as revised regulations or stepped-up inspection would turn out to be the most promising modern weapons against an age-old shame.

There is no question that what happened in El Monte was flatly illegal. An imposing edifice of labor laws, mostly erected in the first half of the twentieth century, is meant to protect workers from exploitation on the job. The most prominent such law is the Fair Labor Standards Act of 1938, but a long list of legislation at the federal and state levels bars work hours that are too long, wages that are too low, or working conditions that are too grim. Regulations render these laws explicit, often with painstaking precision. Investigators are empowered to detect breaches of the law; courts are authorized to punish them. The U.S. Department of Labor was established in 1913 "to foster, promote, and develop the welfare of the wage earners of the United States" and was assigned responsibility for enforcing federal labor laws as each was enacted—laws setting minimum wage levels, for example, or forbidding child labor, or requiring overtime pay for long work weeks. Enforcement officers at Labor Department field offices and other compliance officials in state government are charged with guarding against precisely the kind of working conditions that were discovered in El Monte.

Enforcement

The key office within the Labor Department was the Wage and Hour Division of the Employment Standards Administration. "Wage-Hour," as the division was generally referred to, had a deep-rooted organizational culture built around a tough enforcement ethos. By the early 1990s, however, Wage-Hour was troubled by a growing disparity between its capacity and the scale of the economy it was meant to regulate. While the number of workers and workplaces had climbed, the ranks of Wage and Hour investigators had been held down by budgetary concerns and, some charged, by political pressures to go easy on enforcement.

But however serious the shortage of investigators may have been, something more subtle was also behind the new wave of garment-trade sweatshops. The industry was developing a structure that thwarted conventional enforcement strategies.

The apparel industry had evolved into a "food chain" of interdependent but separate private companies. At the top of the chain are the large retailers—many of them household names, with carefully nurtured images in the international fashion world. One level below the high-profile retailers are roughly a thousand major clothing suppliers. While these companies are sometimes termed manufacturers, the designation is imprecise. These suppliers plan, design, ship, and broker lines of apparel, but for most of their product they do not do the actual stitching. Most of the production is farmed out to the bottom of the chain, where small sewing shops assemble garments under contract. While nobody knows exactly how many such contractors there are, something over 20,000 are probably in operation at any given time.

The bottom of the fashion food chain features an uncommonly harsh business environment. Order volumes ebb and flow seasonally and in response to unpredictable market changes. Product designs change continuously. Business links between the manufacturers and the contractors are shifting and short-term. An impending large order from a major manufacturer triggers a competitive frenzy among sewing shops. Each scrambles to submit a bid that will win it a piece of the action; each of the winners then scrambles to deliver the goods as cheaply and as quickly as possible. As orders are completed, a sewing shop usually gears up for the next one—but it may downsize, or go out of business, or merge with another, or change its name or location.

This environment proved ideal for incubating sweatshops. Tight deadlines and razor-thin profit margins tempt sewing contractors to cut corners. Labor constitutes most of their production cost, and disregarding minimum-wage and maximum-hour rules can drive costs down dramatically. The workers are generally transient, almost always lacking in political or economic clout, and as vulnerable to exploitation as their counterparts in the early 1900s. Many of the contractors—most of them, perhaps—have scruples against exploiting their workers. But the unscrupulous minority enjoys a built-in edge when it comes to winning bids. If scofflaws are able to evade regulators' radar, they can undercut the contractors who play by the rules and claim a larger share of the market. If a shady sewing shop attracts unwanted attention from the government, it is often able to pack up and move—literally overnight— to shake off enforcers, leaving behind workers with unpaid wages.

Such behavior is rare among the manufacturers in the middle of the food chain, and all but unheard-of among the high-profile marketers at the top. Even if their managers were utterly lacking in ethics, it simply would not be good business to court fines or (even worse) bad publicity for the sake of shaving payroll costs. But the retailers and manufacturers can nonetheless benefit, invisibly and even unknowingly, from sweatshop conditions. A penny less paid for cutting and sewing contracts can mean a penny more profit for manufacturers and retailers to divide, after all. That gratifyingly low bid may be due to efficient organization, cutting-edge technology, and top-flight management on the part of a contractor. Or it may signal a sweatshop. It is not always easy for a manufacturer to know which it is; harder still for a retailer, an extra step removed from the actual production. And traditionally, it has been much better *not* to know. In such an industrial climate, natural selection works against the good guys in the sewing business as the bottom-feeders prosper.

Wage-Hour enforcers had long been aware of this grim dynamic, and they had struggled to curb the growth of sweatshops. Investigators stepped up their efforts to visit sewing contractors, spot abuses, and sanction the bad actors. But in the early 1990s Wage-Hour had fewer than a thousand investigators to police 6.5 million workplaces. Even if it ignored the rest of the economy—concentrating on protecting America's million garment workers and leaving the 109 million other workers to fend for themselves—constant monitoring of cut-and-sew operations would have been beyond the resources of the Wage and Hour Division. And when investigators did succeed in spotting a sweatshop, all too often the operation would simply melt away to evade sanctions, only to reopen the next day under some other name in some other dingy building and reclaim its place in the food chain. Even if Wage-Hour nailed a sweatshop owner, levied fines and made them stick legally, the assets of the operation—a few sewing machines, typically, and the lease on some low-end space—were trivial, and bankruptcy could make the fines irrelevant. And if a determined campaign by investigators succeeded in shutting down one sweatshop, new operations were always forming, and existing contractors were under intensifying competitive pressures to turn to the low road. Using traditional enforcement with a limited corps of investigators to police the bottom tier of the fashion food chain was like moving a sand dune with a dessert fork.

Labor-law enforcement in the sewing industry was made even more frustrating by the industry's invisibility. Some trades that are equally prone to exploitative practices are at least exposed to public view, with the opportunity for somebody—a supplier, a customer, a cop on the street, a worker herself—to spot abuse and tip off an inspector. But sewing shops were typically tucked away in lofts, warehouses, or low-rent industrial parks, seldom visited by anyone outside the industry, populated by powerless workers who were often immigrants, sometimes illegal, unaware of their rights, and reluctant to turn to authority even if they knew where to turn. A huge boost in the number of Wage-Hour investigators might help some. But given continuing budget pressures, no major increase was in the cards, Wage-Hour officials knew, even under a new administration that was avowedly concerned about workplace law enforcement. And some officials had their doubts that more manpower could do the trick on its own. The Labor Department needed to come up with something different.

The invisibility of sweatshops was maddeningly ironic to the enforcers. The cut-and-sew trade among which sweatshops lurked, after all, formed the underpinnings of perhaps the most glitteringly visible industry in the country. The fashion business lived or died by image. The industry's distinctive features—celebrity designers, supermodels, ferociously promoted and frenziedly reported runway shows to announce each season's new styles—were all devices to attract the public's eye and burnish a label's image. So there was an irony that beneath the hype and glamour, hidden from public view, festered a supplier industry marred by spreading exploitation. An irony—and also, Wage-Hour enforcers began to think, perhaps an opportunity.

A strategy began to take shape at the start of the 1990s, emerging first from long and painful discussions among Labor Department field staffers in California, including assistant district director Rolene Otero and associate regional solicitor John Nangle. *Why is it so hard to root out the sweatshops?* they asked. Because we cannot get at the bottom of the food chain where the abuse happens. *Who* does *deal, every day, with the cut-and-sew operations?* The manufacturers and, through them, the retailers. *Why don't these top-end players care about sweatshops?* Because they have little incentive to care. And gradually from these conversations the central question emerged: *How can we* get *them to care?*

One possible answer to this question crystallized from a close reading of the Fair Labor Standards Act. A dusty provision of that act bars "shipment in interstate commerce" of goods made in violation of the labor laws. *So did that mean that shipping sweatshop-made goods across state lines is illegal?* The lawyers read the law and the precedents and issued their judgment: It means precisely that. If a dress is produced in violation of the labor laws, anyone who knowingly puts that dress into interstate commerce is in violation of the Fair Labor Standards Act. It does not matter if you are the supplier, who contracted out the actual production. It does not matter if you are the retailer, two steps removed from the stifling loft where the dress was sewn. If it is produced in a sweatshop and you put it on the national market, you are breaking the law.[1] This provision, termed the hot goods clause, was to become a powerful lever to pry open sweatshop doors.

Armed with the hot goods clause, Wage-Hour staffers realized they could enlist the manufacturers—who had expertise and clout within the fashion industry—as allies in enforcement. The regulators drafted the Compliance Monitoring Agreement, which codified manufacturers' obligations to ensure that their contractors obeyed the labor laws. By late 1998 nearly fifty manufacturers had formally signed the agreement. More important, perhaps, was emerging evidence that the middle-tier manufacturers, whether signatories or not, were taking their obligations seriously. A 1998 compliance survey of the Los Angeles garment industry showed dramatic improvement since a similar survey four years earlier. Nearly half of the area's sewing contractors were being monitored by manufacturers, either through direct agreement between the manufacturer and the Wage and Hour Division or in voluntary programs undertaken by manufacturers. Of the shops subject to effective monitoring, only around one-fourth were cited for minimum wage violations. Nearly two-thirds of the sewing contractors that were not being monitored by the next tier in the food chain were found to be in violation of the law.[2]

A Winning Strategy

In early 1993, the strategy went national. When investigators discovered a garment-industry contractor breaking labor laws, they still cited the sewing shop. They no longer stopped there, however, but moved up the food chain to the organizations with more durable stakes in a clean fashion industry. The manufacturer for whom the contractor was working would be reminded of the wage and hour laws and informed of the hot goods provision. And the retailers who did business with the manufacturers learned that a tainted shipment could be embargoed from interstate trade. The message spread quickly through the industry: Get your sewing done by the good guys, and keep an eye on labor-law compliance by the operations you deal with lower in the food chain, or face the consequences of moving hot goods. "It was a credible threat," Labor's Suzanne Seiden recalled. "We didn't have to go to court very often."[3] This became the foundation of a four-part strategy termed enforcement, education, recognition, and partnership.

One part of the new strategy focused on the middle of the food chain, using the leverage of the hot goods law. Another part focused on the top of the chain—the brand names that are recognized by millions of Americans—and added the subtler but potentially even more powerful lever of public opinion. This was uncharted terrain for the Department of Labor, but it soon developed into an intense team effort, uniting by-the-book civil-service enforcers and media-savvy political appointees brought in by Labor Secretary Robert Reich.

For most of its history, the Labor Department had not been a particularly high-profile operation. Most of its work—issuing regulations, distributing training funds to states and localities, drafting codes, mediating labor disputes, and enforcing labor-law compliance—struck the general public as technical, complex, and perhaps a little dull. Several specialized publications covered Labor, but were read only by insiders, whether lawyers, lobbyists, or regulated companies. On those few days each month when the Bureau of Labor Statistics released numbers on employment trends or consumer prices—data that could, and did, move the financial markets—reporters from big-time papers or news shows would drop by. But otherwise Labor was not much of a player in the media world. Susan King, a Washington news anchor who later headed Labor's public-affairs office, described Labor's historical status with the press as a backwater. The appointment of Robert Reich as labor secretary in 1993 marked a break with this convention. An academic and author wise in the ways of the media, Reich constantly invoked the triad of "policy, politics, and message" as interconnected arenas for advancing an agenda. Reich was a poised and practiced television presence who relished taking his case to the airwaves (whether on the Sunday morning TV debates or the "Tonight Show"), and he became one of the administration's most visible members. He enlisted top-flight talent—first Anne Lewis, then Susan King—to handle press and public affairs for Labor. The next stage of the antisweatshop campaign proved tailor-made for Labor's fortified outreach operation.

By 1995, Wage-Hour officials were already working closely with the public affairs staff at headquarters to boost the visibility of the sweatshop problem. And then the El Monte story broke. Conditions at El Monte were horrific enough to penetrate the media's traditional indifference to labor-law issues, and stories about "slavery in California" filled the news. The Labor team seized the moment to trigger a public awareness campaign, coordinated with Wage-Hour's enforcement offensive, that came to be called No Sweat. The El Monte contractor, it turned out, was producing garments for some of the most recognizable names in retail apparel. Wage and Hour let reporters in on the story as it developed, supplying background information and access to senior officials for on-the-record interviews. Some enforcers were uncomfortable with the high-profile approach. A public-relations push was an unconventional adjunct to law enforcement, and it struck some as undignified. But boosting the visibility of garment-industry abuses, they realized, could catalyze compliance. The enforcement veterans believed that if consumers knew about sweatshops, many might shun the tainted labels, providing a bottom-line incentive for the fashion industry to root out labor abuses. "But if you can't tell it," said Wage and Hour's Seiden, "you can't do much about it."[4] The No Sweat effort, enforcers came to realize, offered an opportunity to arouse public opinion and leverage their traditional compliance efforts. "The press office made Reich available, which struck me as an effective means of telling the government's side of the story," one reporter recalled; another reported, "I've never had such access at an agency."[5]

The modern American sweatshop, long a fact, suddenly became a story. Weeks of headlines, television discussion, business page analysis, and editorial page comment ensued. Reich and Wage-Hour administrator Maria Echaveste became news-show fixtures, retelling grim tales of conditions in the garment trades. Labor staffers strategized to keep the momentum going. Shortly after El Monte, Labor announced it was organizing a retail summit meeting and (very publicly) invited the retailers who had received goods from the El Monte contractor and other major players in the fashion industry to join the conversation about cleaning up the industry. With every subsequent development in the El Monte case—a suit filed to recover back wages owed to the workers; the indictments of the sweatshop owners; the request that retailers who had sold the tainted goods help compensate the El Monte workers—a media effort accompanied the enforcement action. Enforcement data were assembled into a quarterly report that was not only used for internal management, but was published in coordination with the antisweatshop campaign. When the seven Thais who had run the sweatshop were convicted in 1996, the story was still being covered.

The historically anomalous level of media interest in labor-law enforcement was about to intensify. In May of 1996 investigators raided a particularly nasty sweatshop in New York City. The conditions the Wage-Hour enforcers uncovered, while abusive and glaringly illegal, may not have been the worst to be found. But a glance at the shop's paperwork revealed that abused workers were stitching clothes destined for Wal-Mart's Kathie Lee apparel line. Wal-Mart was the biggest retailer in America; by some measures the biggest retailer ever, anywhere. Kathie Lee Gifford, the cohost of the morning television show "LIVE with Regis and Kathie Lee," was an A-list American celebrity with a perky mom-next-door image. Suddenly the sweatshop scourge became front-page fodder from the tabloids to the *New York Times*. What had begun with Wage-Hour investigators in California struggling to energize their obscure enforcement mission had evolved into a cause célèbre. "I'm not sure you'd get that without the celebrity," recalls Susan King.[6] Public awareness, however, was not the purpose of the campaign, King stressed, but a means to the end of antisweatshop vigilance at the top of the food chain. "We then had to sustain the effort" by showing the brand-name players that "we could help them deal with their problem."[7]

And here, Kathie Lee Gifford became an unexpectedly avid ally of the Wage-Hour enforcers. Ms. Gifford was embarrassed, of course, by the tabloids' gleeful revelations that America's sweetheart was profiting, if indirectly, from sweatshops. But beyond concern about bad public relations, she was by all evidence honestly anguished to learn of her links to an abusive workplace. A week after the New York strike, Gifford joined Reich on a podium in New York's Fashion Cafe to announce a fashion industry forum to combat garment-trade sweatshops. As the cascade of press reports fueled consumers' concerns about how their clothes were produced, and as companies fretted about stains on their images, other major figures in the fashion industry signed on. A well-publicized Washington conclave drew celebrities like former model Cheryl Tiegs, representatives of major companies such as Nicole Miller and Nordstrom, and sweatshop workers themselves.

No Sweat

Later that summer, Congress held hearings on the sweatshop problem, at which Gifford and others testified, spurring a fresh round of coverage in news and entertainment media. On the first anniversary of the El Monte raid, President Clinton called for enlisting consumer choice as an instrument of labor law enforcement when he challenged the apparel industry to label its wares to reflect production practices. A No Sweat label would indicate that a garment was made under legal conditions. The basic approach had been used in other areas—recycled packaging, for example, or "dolphin-safe" tuna. The expected consumer appeal of goods certifiably produced by well-treated workers was meant to offset the temptation to trim costs by skirting the law. Meanwhile, the Labor Department created and publicized a Trendsetters List to celebrate fashion industry retailers and manufacturers who took the lead in industry-wide reform. (In 1998, the list was superseded by the Apparel Industry Partnership, a voluntary industry-driven effort involving manufacturers, nongovernmental organizations, and consumer groups.) Labor continued to reinforce street-level enforcement with a series of forums, seminars, public service announcements, and on-line data to apprise workers of their rights; contractors, of their obligations; manufacturers, of effective monitoring practices; retailers, of techniques for avoiding hot goods; and consumers, of how to use their market muscle to help combat sweatshops.

U.S. News and World Report devoted a cover story to the sweatshop issue late in 1996, and the next spring President Clinton announced the first stages of an international campaign against sweatshops. "In our system of enterprise, we support the proposition that businesses are in business to make a profit," he said at an Apparel Industry Partnership event in the White House. "But in our society, we know that human rights and labor rights must be a part of the basic framework within which all businesses honorably compete."[8] He unveiled a voluntary workplace code of conduct protecting worker rights, along with new industry-developed standards for internal and external monitoring to ensure the code's enforcement.

Common action did not imply complete consensus, to be sure, nor was the No Sweat formula of direct enforcement, bolstered by hot goods and public opinion pressure, uncontroversial. Some critics in labor, consumer groups, and even industry charged that the public-awareness campaign was a shallow substitute for old-fashioned enforcement. Established trade groups resented being bypassed by new organizations going directly to the retailers and manufacturers. And some observers were troubled by what could be cast as government complicity in besmirching the reputations of private firms.

Yet Labor was convinced that the No Sweat campaign was a legitimate and sustainable lever to amplify the force of what would inevitably remain inadequate resources for traditional inspection. Conventional enforcement, moreover, retained a central role; by 1998, labor enforcement officials and lawyers had recovered nearly $18 million in back wages for 54,000 garment workers since the start of the initiative. Even if the novel legal and public-relations strategy "was what really shook up the industry," Labor's Seiden emphasized that "it had to have substance behind it." Former Labor Department official Anne Lewis thinks that "it took someone at the top who understood that media alone and enforcement alone weren't going to work. You have to put them together." "Some people think the work of an agency is its product, but its message is the product that reaches most people," Susan King observes. "We've got to show the public what they're getting for their tax dollars—and how government works for them."[9]

Industry sensitivities, meanwhile, were soothed somewhat by the department's willingness to define sweatshops as a shared failing and to concede candidly the public sector's limits. "Reich openly admitted that many of the sewing shops in the country resembled sweatshops," says NBC producer Kelly Sutherland. "He wasn't hiding from the fact there were problems on his watch. Instead, he explained what the constraints were. You build credibility by being up-front." "The Labor Department succeeded in making progress on an issue that is tremendously complex and ripe for many conflicts," according to Roberta Karp, general counsel to the Liz Claiborne fashion house. "That is no easy task."[10]

And it was undeniable that labor practices in the garment industry, however improbable this may have seemed a few years earlier, had gained a place on the public agenda. Companies continued to sign on to the No Sweat campaign. In 1998 Reich's successor, Labor Secretary Alexis Herman, launched a new skirmish in the struggle against sweatshops by focusing on apparel bearing the names or insignia of American universities. School and team apparel alone accounts for $2.5 billion in annual sales, and colleges tend to be particularly eager to avoid even indirect links to exploitative cut-and-sew operations. Duke University gave the initiative momentum when it established a code of conduct for its 700 apparel licensees, which make everything from sweaters to sweatpants bearing the Duke seal. Secretary Herman gathered college officials and students to a forum labeled "No Sweat University" to enlist new recruits to the university code of conduct campaign. That same year the Smithsonian Institution set up an exhibit on the history of sweatshops in its Museum of American History, sponsored by major companies including Calvin Klein, K-Mart, and Levi Strauss along with the National Retail Foundation and labor and consumer groups. "There is a tremendous amount of momentum right now," said Secretary Herman at the exhibit's opening. "We need to keep building on it."[11]

Notes

1. There is an exception for "good faith purchasers" who can demonstrate they were deceived, or could not have known, about the origins of the goods they sell.

2. U.S. Department of Labor, Compliance Surveys in Garment Manufacturing, May 1998.

3. Interview with Suzanne Seiden, October 26, 1998, at the Labor Department.

4. Ibid.

5. "No Sweat" case prepared for Leadership Conference for Presidential Appointees and Nominees, May 31, 1997 (hereafter Leadership Conference case).

6. Ibid.

7. Ibid.

8. Remarks made by President Clinton on April 14, 1997, at an Apparel Industry Partnership event at the White House.

9. Leadership Conference case.

10. Ibid.

11. Remarks of U.S. Secretary of Labor Alexis M. Herman, Smithsonian Sweatshop Exhibit, Washington, D.C., April 21, 1998.

5

COLLECTING TAXES BY TELEPHONE

I N EARLY 1996, the Internal Revenue Service (IRS) had a lot riding on a technology project that it hoped would greatly ease annual tax filing for many taxpayers. The tax collection agency—historically, and almost inevitably, unloved among the citizenry—was in the midst of an especially difficult period. Congress and the media had spotlighted rude treatment of taxpayers, unproductive expenditures, errors in processing tax returns, and lost records. But special scorn was reserved for repeated IRS failure to modernize its 1960s–era computers and processing equipment despite an investment of billions of taxpayer dollars.

So it was with somewhat greater than usual apprehension that the IRS awaited the results of a pioneering tax-filing program that promised to allow millions of taxpayers to send in tax returns using a tool as universal and simple as a touch-tone telephone. TeleFile, as it was called, had passed its pilot testing with flying colors. But the IRS had seen too many other promising technological innovations founder to count on an untroubled national roll-out. The first nationwide use of TeleFile was scheduled for the 1996 tax filing season. Not until April 15 had come and gone would the hard-pressed IRS know whether it had racked up a customer-service win.

This chapter was researched and drafted by Kirsten Lundberg.

The Background

The history of taxation, and tax collectors, is not tranquil. In Biblical times, tax collectors were on occasion stoned to death. Americans have a long-standing (if less physical) tradition of hostility to taxation: the United States, some might argue, originated with a colonial tax revolt. The "revenooers" of a later era were suspect characters in at least part of the popular image. When our nation was young, however, fewer citizens had much direct contact with Uncle Sam's collection agents, as most federal revenue came from customs duties and excise taxes. The first official income tax was not levied until 1862, when Abraham Lincoln imposed an emergency tax of 3 percent on income of more than $600—meaning it affected only the wealthy—to pay for the Civil War.[1] To collect it, he established the Bureau of Internal Revenue, precursor to the IRS. But Lincoln's tax lapsed within a decade. For more than twenty years, U.S. citizens paid no tax on income until Congress instituted a modest 2 percent federal income tax in 1894. Even that did not last long, as the U.S. Supreme Court ruled the tax unconstitutional in 1895.

By 1909, however, government recognized that it needed a reliable source of revenue, and the sixteenth amendment, which would permit Congress to collect taxes on income, was proposed. The amendment became law in 1913 when Wyoming became the thirty-seventh state to ratify it. Even then, only one in 271 people paid income taxes. Over the next forty years, however, the tax system became ever more inclusive, although tax rates were still low by contemporary standards. World War II accelerated considerably the process of broadening the tax base: in 1939 one in thirty-two citizens paid the 4-percent income tax; by 1943 one in three people paid, and the system of withholding taxes from wages was introduced.[2] In 1952, in response to charges of corruption and political patronage, Congress passed a massive overhaul of the Bureau of Internal Revenue. To reduce political influence, all jobs in the bureau became part of the civil service; only the commissioner remained a political appointee. In 1955 the bureau was renamed the Internal Revenue Service.

To accommodate the vastly larger number of taxpayers, the IRS implemented new technology that would allow it to process returns accurately and quickly. In the 1960s, the agency put in place mammoth mainframe computers that were state of the art. The computers enabled the IRS to remove the processing function from local offices and concentrate it, instead, in regional centers around the country. The computers went into nationwide operation in 1967.

From the time that the new system was put in place, the IRS prudently looked to the future and the need for continuing renovation and upgrades of its computer capabilities. Unfortunately for IRS funding requests, however, the Watergate scandal of the early 1970s—which revealed that the IRS had conducted politically motivated audits—left Congress indisposed to support the agency. Protection of the privacy of individuals became a congressional rallying cry. Enhanced IRS computer capability seemed to summon an Orwellian vision of government intrusion into individual affairs, and the agency's plans to upgrade its aging technology were blocked by Congress.

By the 1980s, however, it had become clear to congressional oversight committees as well as to staff members within the IRS that the 1960s' equipment still handling the nation's tax returns was obsolescent and in danger of breaking down. The computers were so old that whenever Congress passed new tax legislation, the IRS had a hard time finding programmers familiar with the antique computer language needed to translate the new law into computer code.

In the era of automatic teller machines and on-line investment trades, with customers accustomed to prompt and informed service from businesses such as banks, retailers, and credit card companies, tax return processing remained mired in a bygone technological era. Some 700 clerical workers still hand stamped paper returns with serial numbers. Other employees removed staples, held envelopes up to the light to check for overlooked sheets of paper, and entered millions of pieces of information into a central computer data base known as the general master file. Returns were sorted on devices called tingle tables, purchased in the 1960s and better suited to museums than front-line agencies. The labor costs for this antiquated system were high. The processing center in Cincinnati alone hired 2,600 seasonal workers to handle more than 10 million paper returns.[3]

IRS service to taxpayers was frequently denounced—and part of the problem was inadequate computerization. The master file could handle only 40 percent of the information in a typical 1040 (the centerpiece of an individual U.S. tax return). It took from eighteen to twenty-four months for the IRS to check a filed return against the wage (W-2) and interest (1099) reports submitted in conjunction with that return.[4] The result was that when taxpayers called to ask about puzzling notices from the IRS or with other questions, the employee on the other end of the line was usually unable to access the file and answer the question.

Even the toll-free 800 number that the IRS created to help taxpayers with their tax-filing questions suffered from inadequate technology. A 1989 report charged that taxpayers had only a 63 percent chance of getting a correct answer from the tax information line.[5] If the IRS phone operators had had access to computerized records, their performance might well have improved. Early and tentative IRS attempts to modernize were plagued by inefficiency and lack of funds. As a former IRS commissioner, Larry Gibbs, put it "We are administering the largest tax system in the world with computers and an information system that is one of the most antiquated in the world."[6]

The IRS was the largest agency within the Department of Treasury (which held ultimate responsibility for its performance). It employed, in the early 1990s, more than 105,000 people across the country. The IRS collected $1.4 trillion in taxes—making it arguably the largest financial institution in the country, charged with administering the almost impossibly complex 3,000-page tax code written by Congress. The agency processed more than 200 million returns annually (some 114 million from individuals), which had to be received, sorted, distributed, processed, verified, corrected, debited or credited to individual accounts, and, on occasion, audited.

The IRS prided itself on an 83 percent compliance rate—meaning that 83 percent of taxpayers voluntarily paid taxes owed, strikingly high by international standards.[7] But the agency's technological backwardness threatened, many feared, its ability to maintain that rate of tax collection. The burdens on the IRS were increasing. IRS figures showed that the number of tax returns rose 46 percent between 1979 and the mid-1990s, while the number of documents submitted nearly doubled.[8] The overburdened computer system increasingly imperiled the agency's ability to uphold any clause of its mission statement, which read: "The purpose of the Internal Revenue Service is to collect the proper amount of tax revenue at the least cost; to serve the public by continually improving the quality of our products and services; and to perform in a manner warranting the highest degree of public confidence in our integrity, efficiency, and fairness."[9]

Early Reforms

In 1988 Congress had approved what the IRS promised would be a comprehensive, integrated overhaul of the agency's computer system. It was called Tax Systems Modernization (TSM). The IRS projected that TSM would cost $8 billion and be completed by the year 2000. All TSM programs, said IRS commissioner Margaret Milner Richardson in March 1995, "are designed to ease the burden and increase the fairness of our federal tax procedures."[10] Larry G. Westfall, who led the IRS modernization effort, added his voice. "There is an enormous cost associated with processing paper, storing paper and accessing paper. The IRS is the largest information organization on the face of the Earth. It is critical to us and to the public that we become electronic [given] the commercial environment in the country."[11]

But TSM did not go as hoped. By early 1996, it had become clear that there was no integrated approach and no end in sight. The IRS itself conceded that the eventual projected cost of TSM had spiraled to $20 billion with no firm completion date. Instead of a comprehensive, well-synthesized modernization program, the IRS had funded upward of fifty discrete projects that could not necessarily even speak to one another electronically. Congress responded with anger.

"To date this has been a $4 billion fiasco," fumed Representative Jim Ross Lightfoot (Republican of Iowa), chair of the House Appropriations subcommittee with oversight for the IRS budget. Lightfoot, a former IBM engineer, declared at a hearing March 14, 1996, that Congress had had enough. He said: "This committee is, as of today, out of the business of providing the department with billions of taxpayer dollars for what is in essence the construction of a house that lacks a blueprint."[12]

A House Appropriations Committee report of 1996 took a similar view, more moderately voiced. It noted: "Unfortunately, there is only modest evidence that concrete actions for improvement have been taken. . . . It appears while there is much movement at the IRS, there is no discernible forward progress."

The *Los Angeles Times* quoted a senior executive at an information technology firm working for the IRS, in whose view "the IRS underestimated the complexity of the challenge. The IRS decided that a large IRS work force was the way to do this job. They hired more of the same kind of people they already had without investing in new skills."[13] Senator Robert Dole (Republican of Kansas), at that time running for U.S. president against incumbent Bill Clinton, adopted in his campaign platform a pledge to "end the IRS as we know it."

The IRS protested that it had incorporated hundreds of improvements into the original approach, that there had been some noteworthy accomplishments, that TSM had cost $2.7 billion—not $4 billion. The protests availed little. True to Lightfoot's word, Congress slashed funding for the modernization program from $859 million to $274 million for the budget year beginning October 1, 1996. Overall, it cut $1 billion from the IRS budget request of $8.2 billion. It mandated that the IRS eliminate all but 150 of its 2,016 modernization jobs and turn the effort over to private contractors. Added Lightfoot: "It's clear after eight years and almost $4 billion spent that the IRS cannot handle the job."[14]

TeleFile

It was in this atmosphere that the IRS received its first solid indications that TeleFile—an electronic filing system in the pilot stage since 1992—looked as if it just might work.

TeleFile was conceived sometime in 1990, according to IRS internal legend, when a group of senior managers convened for a postmortem on a pilot tax project that had had disappointing results.[15] As the executives debated the program's weaknesses, one man leaned back in a chair and knocked a telephone off a desk. As he retrieved the phone, he reportedly blurted out: "Why can't we use *this* for filing taxes?" Why not, indeed, the group concurred. And the notion of TeleFile took root.

Its birthplace was the Technology Department, under the control of the IRS director of technology. The Technology Department had a reputation as a skunk works, a place where ideas could be tested and developed without fear that failure would wreck reputations. The Technology Department decided to use staff from the IRS Development Center in Cincinnati to develop the actual product. From its inception, the project benefited from support at both the national and the field level. National management worked to obtain broad institutional approval for the concept, while the field staff were responsible for making sure that it was useful and practical. At the same time, TeleFile promoters—well aware of the difficulties besetting TSM—took pains to keep TeleFile both operationally and fiscally separate from the broader modernization program.

Electronic filing was already a reality at the IRS, though a circumscribed one. Since 1986, professional tax preparers such as H&R Block had sent clients' returns to the IRS directly from their computers. The IRS licensed such firms to file electronically, and by the mid-1990s such filings accounted for some 12 million returns a year. Providing privacy and security for ordinary citizens to file electronically proved daunting, however. A program known as CyberFile, intended to roll out in 1995 or 1996, was supposed to permit taxpayers to file over the Internet from home computers. In fact, the program was canceled in September 1996 after the General Accounting Office (GAO) determined that it was "hastily initiated," that "development and acquisition were undisciplined, and Cyberfile was poorly managed and overseen."[16] Among other shortcomings, it allowed IRS employees to share computer passwords so that it became impossible to know who had accessed a particular file for what reason.[17]

TeleFile, by contrast—and despite some pressures for a quick rollout—went through careful pilot stages before expanding nationwide. It had, moreover, the advantage of using an ordinary telephone rather than a computer, which was still nowhere near a standard fixture in American homes. The IRS executive board gave TeleFile conceptual approval in 1991. The TeleFile project managers developed a prototype filing program, which they demonstrated both inside and outside the IRS in an attempt to gauge understanding and support. A two-year pilot of TeleFile was inaugurated in Ohio in 1992.

The primary goal of return-free filing was to reduce the amount of time and effort taxpayers needed to invest in filing tax returns. The TeleFile creators wanted to design a system that would allow taxpayers to use a toll-free 800 telephone number to report the income information the IRS required to calculate taxes due. One of the first issues the designers of TeleFile had to settle was: Who would use it? For reasons of simplicity and security (a concern never far from the minds of IRS innovators), the creators decided to design TeleFile for those taxpayers with the most straightforward tax situation. Filers who used form 1040EZ usually needed no supporting documents beyond a W-2 wage report. They claimed no deductions or exemptions. They were single, or married with no children. They generally earned less than $50,000 a year.

The progression from research to implementation was handled with particular care. Often new projects, say IRS officials, were "tossed over the wall" into implementation. But for TeleFile, development staff worked closely with the field implementation staff—all in Cincinnati. The work group was interdisciplinary from the start, which greatly enhanced both the speed of the project's development and its institutional support among technical staff.

The management for TeleFile was also, in a sense, interdisciplinary. To handle TeleFile, the IRS implemented for the first time so-called matrix management, which cut across traditional hierarchies and brought together necessary experts from various sections of the agency to work on the project. While popular in corporate America, such an approach was new to the IRS. Typically, IRS projects must navigate numerous committees and processes as they work their way through the hierarchical organization of the agency. The matrix system allowed speedy approval at various stages of development and reduced the number of points at which the project could be delayed or halted. Indeed, the Tele-File project manager, Robert Hare, had explicit authority from IRS executive leadership to seek necessary endorsements at senior levels, without going through channels. As a result, TeleFile received all required internal approvals within a single two-year budget calendar.

In addition, while primary responsibility for TeleFile development remained with the Technology Department, the IRS did go outside the organization as needed for expertise in voice-processing technology. The agency brought in cognitive specialists, behavioral experts, research scientists, and telecommunications engineers, as well as engineers with expertise in voice and data system integration. These experts were instrumental in conducting target market analysis, testing the practicality of the system, and designing it to be user-friendly. TeleFile managers were determined not to let the "not-invented-here" syndrome get in the way of top-flight advice. Institutions that assisted with the development of Tele-File included the University of Michigan Survey Research Center, the American Institute for Research, the Klemm Analysis Group, and the Bureau of Labor Statistics.

While the specifics of how taxpayers would use TeleFile evolved over time as a result of the pilot tests, the profile of a typical TeleFile user was established from the start. Eligible taxpayers were those who had already used a 1040EZ (no first-time filers). They claimed no special exemptions or exclusions, lived at the same address as the previous year, and spoke English (an initial effort to include a Spanish version did not generate enough response to justify its continuation). Even with these constraints, the eligible clientele included some 23 million American taxpayers. Overwhelmingly, given these criteria, the target population was young adults. To enhance security, no one could *apply* for a TeleFile packet. Rather, the IRS identified eligible taxpayers from the master file and sent these prospective TeleFile users a package of explanatory materials. The packet included instructions as well as a unique customer ID number of five digits. This assigned number, in conjunction with the taxpayer's Social Security number, allowed the IRS to verify an individual caller's identity.

After dialing the 800 number, the taxpayer entered data from his W-2 wage statement along with other information. The TeleFile system was able to calculate automatically the amount of tax owed or the refund due, and it validated the transaction with a confirmation number. The taxpayer then finalized the transaction by "signing" the return—entering the ID number. If the taxpayer did not accept the IRS calculation, he or she could simply hang up. The entire process took an average of ten minutes. If tax was owed, the taxpayer would send in a payment; if a refund was due, the IRS could authorize a check, and it would arrive in the taxpayer's mailbox within a maximum of three weeks.

Despite significant staff turnover on the TeleFile project—a common occurrence in the technology field, where private firms can easily outbid the government's salary offers—the IRS was able to expand the pilot in 1994 to seven states. First results from this expanded pilot indicated that the concept would be popular. TeleFile packets were mailed to 4.7 million eligible taxpayers. Some 11 percent, or 518,000 taxpayers, used TeleFile. In 1995, when the program expanded to three additional states, the eligible population grew to 5.9 million. The user rate went up slightly to 11.5 percent, or 680,000 returns filed via TeleFile. The 1995 filing season marked the first time that TeleFilers could claim the Earned Income Tax Credit.

In 1996 the program went nationwide. TeleFile was offered as an option to 23.5 million taxpayers. Some 2.9 million, or 12.5 percent, elected to use it. To handle the extra volume, two processing sites were brought into service in addition to Cincinnati: Memphis, Tennessee, and Ogden, Utah. As Commissioner Richardson put it: "TeleFile is a hit."[18]

TeleFile had a variety of benefits. For one thing, it did away with the need for 1040EZ filers to use paid tax preparers (surveys showed 25 percent had used such services, at considerable expense). It virtually eliminated the errors (roughly half due to taxpayer mistakes and the other half to incorrect entries by IRS data entry personnel) that plagued paper returns. With TeleFile, the error rate was .0002 percent, compared with 6.6 percent for 1040EZ returns on paper.[19] Taxpayers also benefited from faster refunds—between one and three weeks, compared with the standard six weeks—made possible by the automatic confirmation that the return was correct. The IRS also conducted surveys that demonstrated that taxpayers saved an average of 125 minutes using TeleFile compared with the old way of filing their taxes.

Customer satisfaction appeared high. Fully 99 percent of those TeleFile users the IRS polled said they would use the new system again. Eighty-eight percent said TeleFile was faster than a paper return, and 87 percent said it was easier than filing a paper form 1040EZ. The IRS benefited, too. Although TeleFile designers had focused on the advantages it could offer taxpayers, it also saved the IRS money; the agency estimated a roughly two-to-one return on its investment in TeleFile.[20] The savings came mostly in the form of reduced labor costs to receive, open, and sort returns and to enter data. At the Cincinnati center, for example, thirty to forty individuals could process 4 million electronic returns.[21]

An additional boost to IRS morale was that other IRS technology efforts were also proving successful. The number of correct answers the IRS provided callers to its toll-free information line had jumped to 91 percent in 1996 (from the embarrassing 63 percent of 1989). In a separate effort, the IRS set up another 800 number dedicated to helping taxpayers already in communication with the agency over a specific problem. Employees answering this number had data retrieval capabilities and could review the caller's records on-screen during the call. The world wide web page that the IRS posted in January 1996 to assist taxpayers with questions also proved hugely popular. In its first four months, it registered 41 million hits. Taxpayers used it not only for information, but also to download 29,000 tax forms and publications a day, saving numerous trips to the Post Office or local library.[22] *Money* magazine, in an otherwise unflattering article about the IRS, noted appreciatively: "Your home page on the world wide web (www.irs.ustreas.gov), where taxpayers can retrieve forms and get answers to frequently asked questions, is first rate."[23]

In 1997 TeleFile was further refined. For the first time, the IRS offered the added option of direct deposit of refunds to a taxpayer's bank account. The 1997 form also allowed married taxpayers filing a joint return—not just unmarried individuals—to use TeleFile. In anticipation of higher numbers, the IRS doubled the number of TeleFile phone lines to 6,048 nationwide. In 1997, 27 million eligible taxpayers received the TeleFile packet in the mail.[24] Of those, 4.7 million (17 percent) chose TeleFile. In what could only strengthen TeleFile's appeal and promote its use, by 1997 at least eleven states, like Massachusetts, piggy-backed on the TeleFile example and implemented a telephone-filing system for simple state income tax returns.

In making TeleFile succeed, the IRS uncovered hitherto unsuspected in-house skills, such as marketing. The IRS discovered that it had to market TeleFile to persuade taxpayers to give up the familiar paper forms, though most people became avid converts once they tried it. Moreover, because 1040EZ filers are not a stable population—couples have children or individuals move into a more complex tax situation—the IRS faced a task of constant reeducation to maintain TeleFile participation rates. So the IRS devised a $5 million public service announcement campaign telling taxpayers to look for the TeleFile packet in their mailboxes. TeleFile managers also had to design novel packaging for their product. At first, the cover they devised was so creative that some recipients thought it was junk mail and threw it away; in a second round, the packaging identified the mailing as clearly from the IRS, but with its own logo and other markings.

There were some kinks in the system that remained to be worked out. Some taxpayers complained about the lack of tax tables, meaning that an individual taxpayer had no means of verifying the tax figure computed by the IRS. In addition, some 90 percent of TeleFilers used the system within a two-week period. To meet these peak use times, the IRS had to maintain and pay for access to its 800 number on an annual basis. Moreover, unanticipated growth could mean busy signals or a system overload.

But the IRS could point to a welcome success in a sensitive area: technology. TeleFile was never envisaged as being able to serve all taxpayers—for one thing, surveys showed that the time a taxpayer with a complex return would have to spend on the phone would be unacceptably long. But for a significant portion of the taxpaying population, it offered a new and simplified way of doing business with the IRS. TeleFile had demonstrated that the IRS could preserve taxpayer privacy and security while offering stepped-up convenience. It was a practical display of the service mentality that IRS overseers had long urged the agency to cultivate. Paying taxes will never become something a citizen fondly anticipates. But TeleFile has taken some of the sting out of America's April ritual.

Notes

1. After $10,000, the rate went to 5 percent.

2. Helen Huntley, "Electronic Alternatives," *St. Petersburg Times*, February 13, 1995, p. 12. The preceding chronology is from this article.

3. Ralph Vartabedian, "To an IRS Mired in the '60s, '90s Answers Prove Elusive," *Los Angeles Times*, December 9, 1996, p. 1.

4. Don L. Boroughs and others, "Can the IRS Clean Up Its Act and Pacify the Nation's Angry Taxpayers?" *U.S. News and World Report*, April 8, 1996, p. 38.

5. Ibid.

6. Ibid.

7. The remaining 15 or so percent nonetheless constituted a whopping $150 billion "compliance gap," which could have easily paid off the federal budget deficit. The IRS aspired to a 90 percent compliance rate.

8. Robert D. Hershey Jr., "A Technological Overhaul of IRS Is Called a Fiasco," *New York Times*, April 15, 1995, p. B8.

9. Shelley L. Davis, *Unbridled Power: Inside the Secret Culture of the IRS* (HarperCollins, 1997), p. 202.

10. Margaret Milner Richardson, "The Role of the Internal Revenue Service," *Vital Speeches*, March 15, 1995, p. 330.

11. Huntley, "Electronic Alternatives."

12. Hershey, "A Technological Overhaul of IRS."

13. Vartabedian, "To an IRS Mired in the '60s."

14. Hershey, "A Technological Overhaul of IRS."

15. Under the pilot, taxpayers could elect to have the IRS prepare taxes for them. It proved cumbersome for both sides.

16. General Accounting Office Letter Report, "Tax Systems Modernization: Cyberfile Project Was Poorly Planned and Managed." GAO/AIMD-96-140. August 26, 1996.

17. Ann Reilly Dowd, "*Money* Audits the IRS," *Money*, January 1997, p. 78.

18. Hershey, "A Technological Overhaul of IRS."

19. The error rate on 1040s in general was considerably higher. The IRS estimated that 9 percent of the 91 million 1040s (excluding 1040 EZs) processed in 1995 contained data input mistakes. The IRS issued, by one estimate, 8 million incorrect bills or refunds every year. Dowd, "*Money* Audits the IRS."

20. The 1997 TeleFile budget was some $10 million. Of that, 48.7 percent composed telecommunications costs, 19.9 percent went for data processing, 22.7 percent to salaries, and 8.7 percent for maintenance, travel, and training. This represented 0.0014 percent of the total IRS budget and 0.0076 percent of the Information Systems budget. Innovations Award application, Robert Hare, Tele-File Project Manager.

21. Compared to the 2,600 personnel needed to handle 10 million paper returns, as noted above. Vartabedian, "To an IRS Mired in the '60s."

22. Hershey, "A Technological Overhaul of IRS."

23. Dowd, "*Money* Audits the IRS."

24. Those 27 million represented 22 percent of all filers using forms 1040, 1040A, or 1040EZ.

6

BANISHING CHLOROFLUOROCARBONS

MANY BABY BOOMERS harbor vivid grammar-school memories of the Cuban missile crisis. Scrambling to the floor during a nuclear drill, children reflected on what their teachers had intended to be a reassuring thought: the Cubans brandished Soviet missiles, but the United States had its own arsenal at the ready. If the president "pushed the button," America's missiles would surge from their silos, thunder through the skies, and rain wrathful fire on distant enemies. The comforting part was that this prospect should, in principle, deter anyone from venturing an attack on *us*. A generation grew up with earnest hopes that this principle would turn out to be sound. But one detail doubtless failed to preoccupy the second-graders huddling under their desks (or, for that matter, their teachers). The U.S. missiles may have been marvels of science and engineering. They may have been tipped with awe-inspiring weapons that turned the universe's fundamental forces to the service of destruction. But if they were to work as advertised, the missiles had to be very, very *clean*.

Clean Weaponry

It was the job of the Aerospace Guidance and Metrology Center (AGMC), located in Ohio, to maintain and repair inertial guidance and navigation systems for the nation's ballistic missiles and advanced mili-

This chapter was researched and drafted by Kirsten Lundberg.

tary aircraft. In the course of repair or refurbishing, the delicate components were meticulously cleaned with powerful chemical solvents. A speck of foreign material hiding within the precision-engineered machinery could result in a misguided missile.

The chemicals used to clean these components were mostly chlorofluorocarbons (CFCs). By the late 1980s, these chemicals were known to damage the vulnerable layer of ozone in the upper atmosphere. Unlike the fiery violence of the missiles that populated Americans' nightmares, CFCs float skyward silently and invisibly. But the damage they caused, if subtler than the effects of an ICBM, was also less hypothetical. Ozone blocks ultraviolet rays from penetrating to Earth's surface. Unbuffered ultraviolet radiation can ravage the genetic structure of organisms. The loss of ozone threatened increased cancer for humans, as well as unpredictable risks to plants and animals. The search was on, within private industry as well as within the government, for alternatives to CFCs.

The AGMC, one of the largest single users of ozone-depleting chemicals (ODCs) in the world, became one of the pioneers in finding competitive alternatives to the newfound hazards. But the challenge was daunting. Time was short, given the complexity of the task at hand. And AGMC customers—the armed forces—could tolerate no sacrifice in the reliability of the weapons they deployed.

The AGMC was a U.S. Air Force organization embedded in the network of agencies that together compose the U.S. Department of Defense (DOD). It was located on the Newark Air Force Base in Heath, Ohio, some thirty miles west of Columbus. Its chief customer was the U.S. Air Force, but it also serviced equipment for other branches of the U.S. armed services and several foreign countries. For thirty years, the AGMC's Maintenance Directorate had been the sole repair facility in the nation for the inertial guidance systems on the Minuteman and Peacekeeper ballistic missiles—the systems that tell a missile how to get to its target. (The AGMC also repaired navigation systems for military aircraft, such as the B-1 bomber.[1]) These systems were so delicate that a misalignment of five microns (millionths of a meter) or even less could send a missile astray. A smear of cleaning residue, a film of oil, a fleck of dust—all could spell misalignment.[2]

To attain these exacting standards, AGMC employed some 1,500 workers in a sixteen-acre facility, Building 4, at the Air Force base. The workers had the tedious but crucial task of ensuring that the components of the systems the AGMC had repaired were thoroughly cleaned before being reassembled in their original configuration. The cleaning agent of choice, from the 1960s onward, had been CFC-113, a chlorofluoro-carbon-based solvent.

Not long ago CFCs themselves had been hailed as a high-technology innovation, replacing less effective or more obviously dangerous compounds such as methylene chloride, trichloroethylene, methyl alcohol, isopropyl alcohol, toluene, and benzene. They served a variety of industrial purposes. As refrigerants, they cooled air conditioners and freezers. As propellants, they forced out sprays and foams from cans at the touch of a button, powering fire extinguishers as well as hair sprays. As cleaning agents, CFCs were widely used in manufacturing. According to one enthusiastic technical writer, CFCs worked beautifully for such wide-ranging tasks as "removing flux from electronics assemblies, de-oiling stamped metal parts, removing particles from motion picture film, removing pitch, wax, and polishing compounds from optics as well as in the precision cleaning of gyroscopes, medical implants, and semi-conductors."[3]

CFC-113 was one of the stars of the chlorofluorocarbon family. Among its desirable properties were low surface tension, limited viscosity, and high density, which allowed it to get into the tiny spaces within complex machinery. In its gaseous form—used in the final cleaning phase—it left no residue. CFC-113 dried rapidly, accelerating repair operations and reducing the risk of corrosion. Its penetrating vapors were unhealthful, to be sure, but workers were accustomed to wearing protective clothing to defend against the fumes. And it was cheap compared with other high-performance solvents. CFC-113 did the job for the AGMC.

By the mid-1980s, however, its downside was becoming clear. Research started in the 1970s (and initially dismissed as overblown) had now shown persuasively that CFCs were damaging the Earth's protective screen. CFC-113 and its fellow compounds were found to form long-lived gaseous chemicals that floated up to the stratospheric ozone, where they triggered chemical reactions that tore apart the ozone molecules. If the ozone layer thinned or developed gaps, higher levels of destructive ultraviolet rays could reach the Earth's surface.

In the late 1980s and early 1990s, a global consensus against CFCs took root and grew. The first international treaty governing the use and production of ODCs was the Montreal Protocol on Substances That Deplete the Ozone Layer, signed in 1987. The signatories pledged to eliminate the production of ODCs by 1996. The U.S. Senate ratified the treaty in December 1988. The Montreal agreement called for production phase-outs to motivate companies to find alternatives to ODC–dependent manufacturing and cleaning processes. The phase-out schedule was accelerated by amendments to the Montreal Protocol agreed to in 1990 (London) and 1992 (Copenhagen).

In 1990 Congress amended the Clean Air Act to set limits on the release of ODCs into the atmosphere. As a result, the U.S. Environmental Protection Agency (EPA) developed domestic regulations to reduce and eventually eliminate ODCs. Among other efforts, the EPA began exploring methods of using water, instead of the harmful chemicals, for industrial cleaning. The Department of Defense, for its part, issued Directive 6050.9 as well as Air Force Regulation (AFR) 19-15 calling for compliance with the Clean Air Act and EPA regulations on CFCs, halons, and other ODCs.

Government agencies and private manufacturers alike were at first daunted by the prospect of doing without CFCs. They had to consider the cost and performance of alternative chemicals, potential redesign of equipment, retraining of workers, and anticipation of other environmental hazards. For the AGMC, abandoning ODCs would mean a massive redesign of the entire precision cleaning process on which it had relied for decades. The AGMC had actually taken the first steps down this path as early as 1985, though the search for alternative cleaning methods took on new urgency in the early 1990s. Yet it turned out that developing the technology would be the lesser of the two major challenges the AGMC faced. Far more difficult would be persuading its chief customers—the Air Force Missile Command in Ogden, Utah, and the Oklahoma City Air Logistics Center—that alternative approaches could produce acceptable results. "When the instrument you are washing has to guide a nuclear missile around the world and pinpoint a specific target, you can't exactly throw it in a dishwasher," observed Robert Campbell, the head engineer for the ODC project.[4]

In the early 1980s, the AGMC's top management had grown worried about the accumulation of spent CFC-113. Hundreds of barrels of the used chlorofluorocarbon were stacked at the Newark base. How to contain and dispose of these chemicals became a pressing concern, which inspired consideration of both recycling possibilities and alternatives to the ODCs. The AGMC had bought an average of 2 million pounds of ODCs every year during the 1970s. With the installation of a solvent recycling system in the early 1980s, the center was able to reduce purchases significantly. But it still bought 840,000 pounds of ODCs in

1985—mostly CFC-113, but also a few thousand pounds of methyl chloroform (MCF).

The AGMC's director of maintenance—on the lookout for alternatives to CFC–based cleaning processes—was impressed by a vendor's presentation of water-based cleaning equipment during 1985. As an experiment, the AGMC bought an ultrasonic cleaner using water. It seemed to work well, and an engineering team began inquiry into expanded use of this alternative. But there was limited follow-up to the purchase of the ultrasonic cleaner, and efforts to reduce reliance on CFCs, while under way in many parts of the organization, remained scattered and only partly coordinated.

In 1991 a new base commander arrived—Colonel Joseph Renaud— who stepped up the urgency, visibility, and organization of the CFC reduction campaign. Both Congress and the Defense Department had called for accelerated elimination of the chemicals. On October 28, 1991, the AGMC Directorate of Maintenance issued a new plan to formalize and coordinate the anti–ODC enterprise. That order was reinforced on March 11, 1992, with the "Aerospace Guidance and Metrology Center Policy for the Elimination of Ozone Depleting Solvents and Requirements for Its Implementation." It was one of the first such elimination policies enacted in any U.S. government agency.

The policy called for an overhaul of the way the center did business. It set ambitious goals:

—a minimum 90 percent reduction by December 31, 1993, from 1990 levels of purchases of ozone-depleting solvents through changes or substitutions to existing processes;[5]

—elimination of the remaining 10 percent of purchases by December 31, 1994;

—minimization of the release into the atmosphere of all ODCs.

Annual purchases of ODCs had fallen to 213,000 pounds by 1992, thanks to recycling and progress toward alternative cleaning techniques, but the AGMC was still far from weaning itself away from the chemicals. In 1992, the AGMC calculated that it used ODCs in 1,107 procedures. Many of these procedures involved highly advanced components, made from esoteric metals and epoxies, with bulging notebooks devoted to instructions for their care and maintenance. Repair jobs could take as long as six months.

Retooling the entire department would not be cheap; the leadership anticipated costs of more than $1 million. But the department knew it could draw on Air Force funds to support the conversion effort. A greater challenge would be to implement changes without disrupting the agency's work schedule. There was also the problem of how to define "clean enough." As the AGMC project engineer, Capt. Vernon Milholen, put it, "Quantifying the degree of cleanliness of a 'precision cleaned' component is an extremely difficult task. Techniques such as electron microscopy are effective in qualifying the cleanliness of parts with small flat surfaces; however, this technique is not very useful in determining the level of cleanliness of parts and assemblies which have complex geometries."[6]

Yet with solid institutional support for reform, both inside and outside the base, testing and implementation moved ahead. Meanwhile, the reformers at the AGMC set out to engineer concurrent innovations in the structure and culture of management to complement the technical efforts.

Management Innovations

Hierarchy is not traditionally a bad word in military settings. Obedience to one's commanding officer is, for excellent reasons, a cardinal martial virtue. Individual initiative is rewarded, to be sure, but in the service of the duly authorized objectives. Projects requiring creative contributions from individuals at all levels put a special stress on standard operating procedures. In order for the AGMC to redesign its cleaning processes, it first had to create a climate for experiment. This meant raising the institution's tolerance for failure; rare is the success that comes without the benefit of lessons from previous flops.

To create a haven for useful failures, the AGMC set up a "safe" site for ODC–elimination efforts in its engineering lab. Technological dead ends were quietly abandoned; successes were phased in to the AGMC production processes. As one article put it: "Early failures were shielded from outside eyes by a supportive and encouraging manager. As the technologies were developed, participation in technical conferences offered peer recognition of accomplishments. Once the technologies were ready to be used in production, seeing them used in regular production was further encouragement for the innovators."[7]

The AGMC's search for non–CFC based cleaning methods enjoyed the strong support of Colonel Renaud, the base commander since 1991, who made it clear that he wanted to be personally involved in finding a fix. As he told his staff, "If there is a problem at any time that cannot be resolved at a lower level, interrupt me." He regularly attended meetings that tracked the progress of the ODC project. As Renaud later elaborated, "It is not enough to have a goal. . . . I was demonstrating that I was *interested*."[8]

Renaud put in place a senior-level steering group spanning all the functional areas within the command—maintenance, civil engineering, logistics, financial management, environmental management, and engineering. The steering group had a simple mission statement: eliminate the use of ODCs. How they did so was up to them. The AGMC's chief scientist, Don Hunt, has been credited with shepherding the ODC–elimination effort through its most difficult stages. Anthony Skufca, AGMC director of maintenance, chaired the steering committee.

Renaud and other senior managers worked to maintain the project's momentum. If any ODC–related task stalled in an in-basket, Colonel Renaud demanded a personal explanation. To accelerate approval at any stage of the job, the steering group members used special red "ozone" stamps. It became understood that any ozone-stamped document had precedence over other paperwork. During phase-in of the ODC alternatives, all employees retained their regular supervisors. But the reporting chain of command changed to assist the project. Project engineers had the authority to initiate individual tasks. For example, standard reporting channels were modified so that, instead of working through his supervisor, a project engineer could deal directly with a pipe fitter. The job of supervisor, reports Dr. Jonathan Linton, "was transformed from controller and manager to coach."[9]

Responsibility—from concept to implementation—was deliberately driven downward toward the employees. Said maintenance director Skufca:

> From the very beginning, we used total quality management principles and integrated process-action teams to give decision-making authority to our employees, and that trust in our workers was key to our success. They were the ones who had the intricate knowledge of how to clean these instruments, and we were able to draw on that knowledge and technological know-how and transfer it to the new cleaning processes.[10]

The climate within the AGMC was so altered that technicians in different branches of the department competed among themselves to see who could reduce use of ODCs the furthest. Ozone posters appeared on office walls. One project leader was dubbed "Captain Ozone." Plans announced in March 1993—two years into the project—to close the Newark base and privatize the AGMC led employees to redouble their efforts to demonstrate the AGMC's value and competitiveness. To save money, staff members found ways to reuse equipment already available on the base in the new cleaning processes.

The new management methods introduced during the ODC–elimination project, in short, reshaped the organizational culture of the center. Employees, formerly focused exclusively on maintaining guidance systems, gradually developed a parallel commitment to environmental quality. Yet the management changes and the evolution of the AGMC's culture at once enabled and depended for their momentum on the remarkable success the center's scientists and engineers were having in the search for new technical solutions.

Technological Innovations

The AGMC set out to determine whether water-based cleaning would work and whether it had any unacceptable long-term consequences. Scientists used trial-and-error methods to determine whether it was possible to clean sensitive components using special baths with their cleansing power boosted with ultrasonics or advanced detergents. Many of the 1,107 cleaning processes required different combinations of water and detergent or other special technical fine-tuning. For each process, scientists had to evaluate the impact of a range of parameters—the temperature of the solutions, the duration of the bath, the amount and kind of detergent, the potential for ultrasonics, and so on. New drying techniques, including spray-air and vacuum-baked drying, were also evaluated. The potential pitfalls were numerous. Explained the chief project engineer: "What you find is that different solvents and cleaning agents react differently with the various types of epoxies, plastics, and metals used in these systems, and in some cases the chemical reaction can have a radically degrading effect. It was a nightmare."[11]

To make several of the new processes work, the AGMC found it had to construct entirely new equipment. The new apparatus included ultrasonic devices, fixtures to hold parts securely in the baths, specialized spray tools, and water recovery systems. AGMC technicians also developed new types of gloves. For all the new equipment, the AGMC set up seventeen "cleaning centers," outfitting them with new piping, heating, and deionized water systems. Technicians were individually retrained in the use and care of the new devices.

With funding from three Small Business Innovation grants, the AGMC also benefited from (and helped to orchestrate) the development of advanced equipment by private firms. At Membrane Technology and Research, Inc., scientists developed two vapor emission recovery systems that blocked almost all cleaning vapors from escaping into the atmosphere. Phasex Corp. developed a supercritical fluid system to remove silicon-based fluid from complex components. Entropic Systems, Inc., created two perfluorocarbon-surfactant based cleaning systems. They used laser light blockage particle counters, sensitive to the level of a single micron, to detect fluid contamination. The systems were completely enclosed to minimize vapor emissions.

The AGMC tested the new systems relentlessly; it was under no illusions that its clients would be satisfied unless they could be assured that the water-based cleaning matched the old system's effectiveness. But to meet its own deadlines, it had to make the case for soap and water not just convincingly, but *quickly*.

Convincing the Skeptics

The AGMC decided to bolster its case in part through meticulous record keeping. It set up and maintained a painstakingly detailed database on the reactions of various parts to solvents used in the cleaning process. Finding that it was unable to run all the necessary tests in-house as originally planned, the AGMC developed an unusually cooperative relationship with another Defense Department agency, the Directorate of Technical Operations at the Defense Construction Supply Center (DCSC) in Columbus, Ohio.

DCSC had standing contracts with a long list of vendors. Alliance with DCSC helped the AGMC sidestep what might otherwise have been a drawn-out process of forging new procurement contracts with thirty chemical and metallurgical laboratories in the area. The commercial labs were able to run tests, such as electron spectroscopy chemical analysis and auger electron spectroscopy, unavailable at the AGMC. "Because there was a preexisting contract and a pool of available money," recalled project engineer Captain George Letourneau, "we didn't have to go through a long procurement process every time we needed a lab to test the compatibility of different metals and detergents."[12] By using the DCSC channel, AGMC personnel could submit handwritten notes requesting specific lab tests and get the work under way quickly—often within the day. Said Letourneau: "Those quick turnaround times, which were extremely unusual in government contracts, allowed us to gather data in days or weeks rather than months." To get its customers to buy into the testing process, the AGMC took the further unusual step of inviting clients to participate in the assessment of test results.

The AGMC scientists knew that the most dangerous potential objection from missile operators was that non–CFC cleansers would degrade the components over time. To counter this worry, the team located a Minuteman missile that had been cleaned, three years earlier, using aqueous methods, and tore it apart for testing. The testing of this sample missile's components was contracted out to Draper Lab and TRW because of the high-quality work done by both independent laboratories and because the arm's-length assessment would lend some extra credibility. The report on the Minuteman missile teardown pronounced that the water-cleaned parts performed "at least as well as nonaqueously cleaned instruments." There was not a trace of corrosion that could be blamed on the water-based cleaning.

Finally, the project sponsors had to ensure that the new methods did not somehow introduce unanticipated environmental threats equal to or even worse than the peril of CFCs. The greatest worry was that the water used for cleaning would contribute to overload or contamination at a nearby wastewater treatment plant. A study by Battelle Lab, however, concluded that the discharge from the new cleaning processes would have "no significant impact" on the wastewater treatment plant.

By the end of 1994, the AGMC had developed alternative processes, free of ozone-depleting chemicals, for more than 95 percent of its 1,107 repair and cleaning processes, cutting its use of ODCs by 99.9 percent. The remaining procedures using ODCs were phased out by the end of 1995. By December 31, 1994—a year ahead of schedule—the AGMC had completely stopped buying ODCs. The center had fulfilled all of the four goals it set itself in 1992—without a single work stoppage and with no sacrifice in quality.

The conversion to aqueous cleaning processes generated some side benefits. One was financial. Had the center continued purchasing ODCs at the levels of the 1980s, the cost by 1996 could have reached $9.5 million. By comparison, installing the new machinery for water-based cleaning had cost $1.4 million, and annual operating costs ran about $200,000. Working conditions at the center had also improved. The stench of heavy solvents no longer permeated the cleaning rooms, and work areas were safer. Productivity was higher; before-and-after comparisons showed that parts got cleaner and were cleaned more quickly.

Chief Scientist Don Hunt felt the center successfully changed "long term, successful and accepted industrial processes . . . by overcoming the hurdles imposed by such things as technology barriers, mind sets, risk concerns, established requirements or specifications requiring the old process, lack of knowledge, shortage of funds, procurement and construction restraints."[13] Hunt himself had been named a member of the United Nations Environmental Programme Solvents, Coatings and Adhesives Technical Options Committee. Through this and other missionary efforts, AGMC personnel hoped to contribute to broader efforts to eliminate CFCs without sacrificing industrial imperatives of precision and reliability.

The odds have shrunk that America's nuclear missiles will ever be launched in anger. The end of the cold war has eased decades of hair-trigger confrontation, and the sharp sense of relief from the 1980s has become a comfortable status quo. Yet until we can do without the missiles entirely, they still have to be kept clean. The AGMC figured out a better way to keep them clean, in a small, happy footnote to late-century strategic transformations. Today's children, unlike their parents, can lie on the grass and look at the skies, their reveries uninterrupted by any plausible prospect of nuclear Armageddon. But the children also have a little less cause now to fear the silent, subtle threat of ozone damage miles above them. The history books might turn out to miss this detail, but the AGMC's quiet contribution to Americans' security nonetheless merits a moment of national congratulation.

Notes

1. The AGMC also managed the Air Force Metrology and Calibration Program, which provided measurement engineering services for the Pentagon.

2. Donald E. Hunt, chief scientist for the AGMC, clarified: "The systems for missiles and aircraft require that parts, because of their extreme precision, be very clean when they are assembled and repaired." David Jacobs, "French Get Defense Cleanup Tips," *Columbus Dispatch*, May 6, 1994, p. 2B.

3. Barbara Kanegsberg, "Precision Cleaning without Ozone Depleting Chemicals; Solvents and Cleaning Agents," *Chemistry and Industry*, October 21, 1996, p. 787.

4. James Kitfield, "Cleaner Cleanup Methods; Ozone-Depleting Chemical Elimination, Aerospace Guidance and Metrology Center, Air Force," *Government Executive*, November 1995, p. 27.

5. In 1990, the AGMC purchased 400,000 pounds of ODCs.

6. AGMC, Innovations in American Government application.

7. Jonathan Linton, "Harnessing and Managing Innovation: Lessons from the Aerospace Guidance and Metrology Center," *Engineering Management Jour-*

nal, December 1997, pp. 13–18. Many of the details on management changes at the AGMC come from this article.

8. Ibid.

9. Ibid.

10. Kitfield, "Cleaner Cleanup Methods."

11. Ibid.

12. Ibid.

13. Letter from Donald Hunt to Dr. Elaine C. Kamarck, senior policy advisor, Office of the Vice President, July 19, 1995.

7

BOOSTING
LEGAL HIRING

"THEY CAME IN like Jesse James, covering this door, covering that door," said Anthony Spinale, the owner of a produce packing company in New York City. "I thought it was a holdup." The armed men swarming over Mr. Spinale's fruits and vegetables turned out to be federal agents, not criminals: Mr. Spinale's business was one of hundreds raided by the Immigration and Naturalization Service (INS) during the spring of 1982.[1] With the country mired in an economic slump, the week-long nationwide sweep for illegal aliens was intended to open up jobs for out-of-work U.S. citizens.

The high-profile raids generated an avalanche of criticism: business leaders fumed about the disruptions and the sudden depletion of their work force. Civil rights advocates objected to the heavy-handed tactics used by some INS agents. Newspaper accounts of families torn apart and communities thrown into confusion by the raids prompted California senator Alan Cranston to warn that the agency was "sowing dangerous seeds of racial and ethnic conflict."[2]

The enforcement crusade had cost taxpayers a bundle and strained the INS's already tenuous relationships with employers and minority groups. True, the idea of replacing illegal workers with legal U.S. job-seekers had broad political support, and the INS sweeps had in fact resulted in more

---

This chapter was researched and drafted by Dalit Toledano.

than 5,000 deportations.[3] But the dust kicked up by the raids had barely settled before it was apparent that most of the jobs left vacant by the deported workers were being filled by more illegal aliens—not by unemployed U.S. citizens. In the end, the crackdown had yielded little more than a big public relations headache.

The Background

"All of our people, all over the country," said Franklin Delano Roosevelt, while campaigning in Boston one early November day in 1944, "are immigrants, or descendants of immigrants, including even those who came over on the *Mayflower*."[4] The president was tiptoeing through a minefield. The question of how the United States should respond to a steadily worsening European refugee crisis had inspired deep divisions in the electorate. Modern-day debates over immigration policy feature similar attempts to reconcile deep nativist instincts with the sorts of sentiments (etched equally deeply on the American psyche) inscribed on the Statue of Liberty ("Give me your tired, your poor. . ."). The tension makes for acrimonious politics and complicated policymaking. In the 1996 presidential primaries, even as a booming economy softened the edges of the issue, New Englanders were wooed by candidates eager to prove their tough-on-immigration credentials: Pat Buchanan promised to build a 2,000-mile-long wall along our border with Mexico, and Lamar Alexander pledged to create a new branch of the military devoted exclusively to controlling illegal immigration.

More than half a century after President Roosevelt struggled with the issue, a national consensus on immigration remains elusive. Emotions run high, factual issues are murky and complex, and a host of business, labor, ethnic, minority, and civil rights groups strain to influence legislative outcomes. In order to achieve a majority of votes in such an environment, lawmakers cobble together something-for-everyone propositions. Thus national immigration initiatives, faithfully reflecting the public's ambivalence, often include both harsh restrictions and generous gestures.

The Immigration Reform and Control Act of 1986 (IRCA) was one such set of compromises. The legislation, which was the first major revision of national immigration policy in more than two decades, offered amnesty to illegal aliens who had been living in the country since 1982. In addition, the law allowed for migrant workers to enter the country during harvest season. Both provisions had been heavily promoted by civil rights and agribusiness interests.

But the more controversial provisions of the legislation put in place a new regulatory scheme that made it illegal for U.S. employers to hire undocumented workers. The IRCA remedied a major inconsistency in immigration policy. It had been against the law for unauthorized aliens to work in the United States, but perfectly legal for employers to hire them. The new law required employers to maintain paperwork establishing that all of their employees were U.S. citizens or otherwise eligible to work. Employers could accept a variety of identification documents, including birth certificates, passports, driver's licenses, Social Security cards, and green cards, and they were not required to verify the legitimacy of the documents. But accepting obviously fraudulent documents or failing to meet the record-keeping requirements could result in fines— from $250 to $2,000 for each illegal worker. And employers who established a "pattern or practice" of knowingly hiring illegal aliens could face steeper fines and even jail. This was seen as strong medicine for an increasingly grave problem.

At the time the IRCA was enacted, the illegal alien population, by some estimates, had risen to nearly 12 million people.[5] In the 1930s and the 1950s, waves of illegal immigration had been followed by mass deportations. But between the 1960s and the 1980s, illegal entries into the country soared, amid heated discussion about their effect on the economy: Were illegal aliens taking jobs away from U.S. citizens, or were they mostly doing work eschewed by natives? To what extent were they responsible for declining wages among unskilled legal workers? Did their contributions to the economy outweigh their drain on public resources? Would removing unauthorized workers from the pool of labor available to U.S. businesses seriously damage competitiveness in certain industries?

But if the years of debate that preceded the IRCA had produced few definitive answers to these questions, they solidified one commonly held conviction: the integrity of the nation's immigration scheme was being seriously threatened. Relying exclusively on border enforcement had proven inadequate. The border was too porous and resources too few, and border agents could not monitor aliens who were entering the country on valid short-term visas but overstaying illegally. The IRCA did fund additional border patrols. More important, it recognized that since an overwhelming majority of immigrants entered the country in search of work, a coherent immigration strategy demanded workplace enforcement as well.[6] Employer sanctions were intended to discourage illegal immigration by walling off the job opportunities that drew people to the United States in the first place.

Critics of the new sanctions questioned how effectively they would deter immigrants fleeing the acute political crises or deep poverty of their native lands. Instead, they argued, illegal immigrants would just be driven deeper into the underground economy. Industries dependent on the ready supply of cheap, compliant labor provided by illegal aliens would continue to hire them—gambling that they would escape detection because of limited enforcement resources. Even if they were so unlucky as to have their violations uncovered, the financial penalties would not outweigh the extra costs associated with hiring legal workers—who were more likely to demand higher wages and better conditions than illegal workers nervous about being turned over to immigration authorities. Employers would just absorb the fines as a cost of doing business, the skeptics warned.

Despite these and other concerns, employer sanctions were approved by Congress, and the Immigration and Naturalization Service was charged with enforcing them. Although the IRCA's provisions took effect in May 1987, the INS focused on educating employers during the first year of the law's enactment. The following summer, after a brief period of issuing warnings, the INS began to enforce the law more vigorously. If police or agency investigative work had turned up evidence of wide-spread violations by a particular employer, the INS joined with local law enforcement to raid the work site. More commonly, if less dramatically, employers were targeted for compliance inspections (on the basis of previous history or unsolicited complaints) or were chosen for random checks and asked to present to the INS the documentation the IRCA requires for each employee. The agency issued subpoenas to those who did not comply voluntarily.

In their first three years of existence, employer sanctions were credited with sharply reducing the number of illegal entries into the United States.[7] But starting with the fourth year of enforcement, there was a dramatic drop-off in the law's impact. Paradoxically, the IRCA's ebbing effectiveness was accompanied by a high rate of technical compliance among employers. When it became apparent that most employers would not take on new workers unless they had the proper papers, the black market for fake documents expanded to handle the new demand. High-quality counterfeits became cheaper and easier to obtain through what had quickly grown into a nationwide network of vendors who could customize blank forms for customers. "Employer sanctions may have seemed a real barrier at first, but now they are just one more hurdle to overcome," said Wayne

Cornelius, the director of the Center for U.S–Mexican Studies at the University of California in San Diego.[8] Michael Fix, an immigration specialist at the Urban Institute, agreed: "Document fraud is the rock on which employer sanctions could founder."[9]

Because Congress had decided not to ask employers to become document experts—they incurred penalties only for accepting blatant forgeries—the increased availability and improved quality of counterfeit documents meant that employers who wanted to hire illegal workers could now do so with a diminishing risk of any sanction. "Compliance with the law has come to mean compliance with the paperwork requirements," noted Kitty Calavita, a professor at the University of California at Irvine. "Employers can comply and still employ the same people they always have."[10] A representative of a local carpenters union in El Monte, California explained: "It's become a standard joke. They say 'Just give me something so I can say I complied with the law.'"[11]

But the increase in document fraud put employers who were scrupulous about hiring only legal workers in a tough position. The fact that forgeries had become so sophisticated made it increasingly difficult to determine a job applicant's legal status. Employers knew that if they hired illegal workers unwittingly, conscientious record-keeping could help them avoid penalties. But they had more at stake than the possible imposition of regulatory fines—they wanted to make sure that the people they hired and trained would not later be led off in handcuffs. INS raids and inspections could disrupt operations and demoralize the rest of the work force. In some cases—because of the number and qualifications of the deported workers—they put employers out of business altogether. To avoid these misfortunes, many employers resorted to simply turning away anyone with a foreign appearance or accent, including U.S. citizens or legal aliens authorized to work. A 1990 study by the General Accounting Office found that hundreds of thousands of employers had adopted discriminatory hiring practices.[12] Efforts to comply with one law could put employers in violation of another; some were sued under antidiscrimination statutes. "The government gets you for trying too hard or not trying hard enough," complained Kay P. Norton, general counsel for Monfort, Inc., a Colorado beef-packing company.[13] In September of 1992, law enforcement officials—including INS agents, state troopers, and assistant U.S. marshals—removed more than 300 workers from Monfort's slaughterhouse in Grand Island, Nebraska. Monfort's angry president referred to the raid as a "media event" and a "waste of taxpayer money."[14] But when, as a result of that experience, Monfort adopted stricter hiring and document-screening procedures at its other plants, it was fined more than $45,000 for asking job applicants intrusive questions.[15]

If employers were increasingly resentful of the burdens imposed by the law (the IRCA, Norton grumbled, has turned employers into "involuntary deputies of the INS"[16]), INS officials were also struggling with their end of the enforcement relationship. During follow-up visits to work sites they had previously raided or inspected, they all too often found that employers had once again hired illegal workers equipped with bogus documents. The emerging pattern was dishearteningly reminiscent of the INS sweeps of the early 1980s, which were thought to have failed because employers had not faced penalties for rehiring illegal workers. Now the penalties were in place, but their effectiveness had been eroded by the widespread use of counterfeit documents. And the collateral costs of employer sanctions—increased employment discrimination and souring INS relationships with both business and minority communities—were continuing to pile up. But if the law had begun to produce diminishing returns, it was still, in the absence of a congressional directive to the contrary, the INS's job to enforce that law.

Closing the Revolving Door

One place where INS officials had grown particularly fed up with seeing their enforcement efforts come undone was Dallas, Texas. In a city where cheap labor was fueling the economic recoveries of many small businesses, INS agents were routinely coming across illegal workers they had shipped out of the United States just weeks earlier. Frustrated that all the time and money spent on enforcement was producing only temporary compliance, officials at the Dallas district office decided to add an extra step to their efforts. Late in the fall of 1992, they resolved to do what employers had been unable to do themselves—ensure that the jobs vacated by illegal workers were quickly filled with legal workers. That way, they reasoned, the IRCA's fundamental goals would be advanced more directly, and employers would be less sorely tempted to wink at counterfeit documents.

The Dallas INS officials began by establishing relationships with outside organizations that could supply local businesses with legally employable replacement workers. It made sense, they figured, to recruit workers from public and private agencies attempting to place people in the same kind of jobs—largely entry-level—that the INS was turning illegal immigrants out of. They reached out to the Texas Employment Commission, which could refer unemployed individuals looking for work; the Dallas, Denton, and Tarrant County departments of Human Resources, which were in touch with the area's welfare recipients; the Dallas Police Department, whose officers could suggest "at-risk" youth who could benefit from part- or full-time jobs; the Salvation Army, in touch with homeless and needy people able to work; and organizations like the North Dallas Refugee and Resettlement Services and the International Rescue Committee, which worked to find employment opportunities for refugees and aliens who were legal residents. INS officials developed contacts within each organization in a position to help employers tap legal labor pools.

It was clear, however, that success would depend heavily on cooperation from employers—who were not, after all, required by law to buy into this new scheme. Arthur Strapp and Neil Jacobs, two Dallas INS officials, recognized that many employers might need extra incentives to overcome their misgivings about cooperating with the agency. All too familiar with employers' distaste for traditional enforcement methods, Strapp and Jacobs decided their efforts to connect employers with legal sources of labor should be accompanied by some bold changes in INS procedures. In the past, when illegal workers had been found at a work site, they were carted off immediately—without regard for how their abrupt removal might affect a business. The law was the law, after all. But Strapp and Jacobs thought that if they offered employers advance notice of the arrests, along with adequate time to hire and train replacements—both startling departures from enforcement orthodoxy—employers might find it worth their while to participate in the new program.

It worked. When INS agents offered to delay arresting illegal workers so that an employer would not be left shorthanded, many employers responded first with shock, then with gratitude. "The employers stopped looking at us like we are Gestapo," said a relieved Mr. Jacobs.[17] His colleague Mr. Strapp agreed: "(We've) replaced an adversarial environment with one of cooperation and mutual respect."[18] But the idea, to be clear, was enforcement delayed, not enforcement denied. Employers were informed that the INS would be back to reinspect the premises after sixty days. They were accordingly enthusiastic about being put in touch with job placement agencies and volunteer organizations that could offer legal workers looking for opportunities.

Unorthodox, no doubt. But the model achieved the IRCA's purposes of dissuading illegal hires and boosting legal employment. The Dallas experience was so positive that the new model was expanded to include

123 counties in northern Texas. Within a few years, more than 3,500 positions formerly held by undocumented workers had been filled by legal employees.[19] By 1994 the program—which had been dubbed Operation Jobs—had caught the attention of national INS officials in Washington, who did not see why what had worked in Dallas could not be made to work in El Paso or Chicago or Salt Lake City. They began to implement the program in an additional eighteen states. In the first two months alone, 1,400 jobs were made available to legal workers.[20]

By cushioning the costs of compliance for employers, Operation Jobs proved a potent counter to the proliferation of bogus documents. In addition to providing INS officials with a more effective way to enforce employer sanctions, Operation Jobs is also responsible for enhancing employment opportunities for welfare recipients and "at risk" youth, reconnecting immigration policy to the broader jobs agenda. And the program's success at steering jobs to *legal* refugees has defused much of the hostility traditionally directed at the agency by immigrant advocacy groups.

Not everyone thinks that Operation Jobs is a good idea. Some critics find it objectionable that the INS allows illegal workers to remain in their jobs until new employees are recruited. The government, they charge, is aiding and abetting employers who break the law. One reader of the *Washington Post* was horrified to learn (from an article about the program) that surprise raids had largely given way to more cooperative measures: "Let me see if I got the facts right: Employers who have violated the law by hiring undocumented workers are given advance notice that the INS is aware of their unlawful conduct because the INS doesn't want to affect the offending employer's profitability? This gross failure of the INS to fulfill its law-enforcement responsibilities, should be condemned," he wrote to the newspaper, "not rewarded."[21]

Others are skeptical about the workability of substituting legal for illegal employees. Dr. Demetrious Papademetrieu of the Carnegie Endowment described what he called the "lump of labor fallacy": "That is if we replace a person from job X and we remove that person, the person who is unemployed or on welfare can somehow come in and do this job. This does not address the issue that even the lowest-skilled jobs require a bit of specialization, a little bit of training, and certainly some understanding of how one behaves in the labor market in any job."[22] Forging connections with legal workers, the argument goes, will not greatly lower the costs of compliance for employers, short-circuiting the basic logic of Operation Jobs. Some employers *have* been reluctant to rely on the candidates offered by public agencies as substitutes for illegal labor. But most, as the numbers attest, have proven willing to try the new arrangements, and INS officials point proudly to a job retention rate significantly higher than the national average. In addition, in 1995 the pool of labor available to employers participating in Operation Jobs was considerably enlarged when the program established links with agencies administering the Job Training Partnership Act, then the nation's main federal job training program.

Another criticism suggests that even if the legal workers prove acceptable to employers, ultimately the program will fail because so many of the jobs held by illegal aliens will not be considered desirable or even acceptable by most legal workers. "There's a perception that (illegal aliens) are taking jobs away from native-born Americans," contended Richard Vedder, a professor of economics at Ohio University. "But if you look at the overall big picture, immigrants do not raise unemployment rates in an area (because) they often take jobs no one else wants."[23] Yet such arguments miss the basic goal of limiting employers' access to the global labor market: If firms must attract legal workers, and know that none can gain a cost advantage through exploiting illegal labor, they will be more willing to offer prospective employees appealing wages and job conditions. When a 1994 INS audit found that one-third of the General Aluminum Corporation's workers were undocumented, the Carrollton, Texas, company (which makes windows and doors) raised its wages by more than ten percent—and then (through Operation Jobs) hired inner-city youth and refugees to fill the 200 jobs.[24]

The political salience of immigration control has raised the stakes for Operation Jobs and the overall mission of the Immigration and Naturalization Service. Congress has added to the agency's resources in the past several years, authorizing hundreds of additional agents for border and workplace enforcement. The INS has expanded its capacity to dismantle document-counterfeiting operations, reduced the number of random compliance inspections in favor of a focus on lead-driven cases, and stepped up criminal investigation and prosecution of egregious offenders. The INS is refining a new computer database program that will provide employers with electronic verification of worker documents. And legislation passed in 1996 made it harder to sue employers for discrimination as they try in good faith to comply with the IRCA, tilting the balance of incentives to favor legal hires. But the bottom line for any effort to limit illegal hiring is that employers need to see a legitimate way to keep their businesses staffed. Operation Jobs eases employers' access to the high road of compliance with the law.

Notes

1. Janice Castro, "Dragnet for Illegal Workers," *Time*, May 10, 1982.

2. Mary Thornton, "Raids Nab High-Pay Aliens, Make Jobs, Outrage Clergy," *Washington Post*, May 2, 1982.

3. Castro, "Dragnet for Illegal Workers."

4. Campaign speech, Boston, Massachusetts, November 4, 1944.

5. Roberto Suro, "1986 Amnesty Law Is Seen as Failing to Slow Alien Tide," *New York Times*, June 18, 1989.

6. Workplace raids had, of course, taken place before 1986, but the INS had prosecuted workers on charges stemming from their violation of the nation's borders. The IRCA was the first immigration law to regulate the employment relationship.

7. Roberto Suro, "Traffic in Fake Documents Is Blamed for Rise in Illegal Immigration," *New York Times*, November 26, 1990.

8. Ibid.

9. Roberto Suro, "Boom in Fake Identity Cards for Aliens," *New York Times*, February 19, 1992.

10. Richard W. Stevenson, "Jobs Being Filled by Illegal Aliens Despite Sanctions," *New York Times*, October 9, 1989.

11. Stuart Silverstein, "Seven Years Later, Many Scoff at Immigration Act," *Los Angeles Times*, August 28, 1993.

12. U.S. General Accounting Office, *Immigration Reform: Employer Sanctions and the Question of Discrimination*, GAO/GGD-90-62 (Washington, D.C.: GPO, 1990).

13. Catherine Yang, "Cheese It—The Boss," *Business Week*, November 27, 1995.

14. Jon Jefferson, "Is There a Legal Solution to the Immigration Mess?" *American Bar Association Journal*, September 1993.

15. Yang, "Cheese It—The Boss."

16. Jefferson, "Is There a Legal Solution to the Immigration Mess?"

17. "Holding the Line," *Economist*, March 16, 1996.

18. Lisa Corbin, "Recruiting Legal Workers," *Government Executive*, November 1995.

19. Ibid.

20. Immigration and Naturalization Service press release, U.S. Newswire, October 30, 1995.

21. Letter to the Editor, *Washington Post*, November 11, 1995.

22. Peter Kenyon, "Virginia Welfare and INS," National Public Radio, Morning Edition, December 4, 1996.

23. Kirsten Hallam, "Economic Refugees Dive into Labor Pool," *Nashville Banner*, December 9, 1996.

24. Yang, "Cheese It—The Boss."

8

SHARING TRICKS
TO PARE COSTS

DURING HIS 1980 presidential campaign, Ronald Reagan vowed to reverse what he termed "a decade of neglect" toward the U.S. armed services. In office he was as good as his word. Soon after his inauguration in 1981, Reagan launched what would become a $1.6 trillion effort to rebuild the U.S. armed services. The Navy was a major beneficiary of the surge in defense spending. In early 1981, Secretary of the Navy John Lehman announced plans to build a 600-ship Navy—a dramatic increase over the 479-ship fleet Lehman inherited when he took office. The Navy also received permission to develop dozens of major weapons systems— new aircraft, new classes of cruisers, new missiles, new armaments. By the mid-1980s, the largest peacetime military buildup in American history was under way.

The massive enterprise to upgrade America's armory, however, was (perhaps inevitably) plagued with problems. The new-generation weapon systems were often hugely complex. Attempts to rush new weapons from the drawing board to the field frequently resulted in missteps. Prototypes were often delivered late and over budget. Once in full-scale production, some weapon systems turned out to be unreliable and difficult to maintain. The Navy endured a string of embarrassing setbacks, such as the 1985 revelation that an early version of the F-18 fighter jet manufactured by the McDonnell Douglas Corporation and the Northrop Corporation

---

This chapter was researched and drafted by John Buntin.

featured a "design error that could cause failures in the structure holding the wings to the aircraft."[1] Not all weapon acquisitions efforts went badly—but those that did drew disproportionate attention. As the buildup steamed ahead, the Navy and the other branches of the armed services were beset by a seemingly endless series of stories about high costs and disappointing performance. The result was a widespread loss of confidence in the Defense Department's procurement system.[2]

Quality Control

Nobody was more exasperated by these problems than the Navy's Office of Naval Materiel. The prevailing view within the office was that the trouble was not with the average level of quality, but with unacceptably wide disparities in the quality of goods and services procured from contractors throughout the United States. Military contractors operated at very different levels of sophistication and efficiency. If production practices could somehow be leveled up, so that all the companies doing the Navy's work would be operating at the state of the art, the Navy could limit its procurement costs and avoid some of the headaches and bad press it was encountering.

But the suppliers were disinclined to disseminate details about their production techniques to the Navy and even less inclined to share that information with other contractors working on the same or similar weapons systems. The idea of sharing information was at odds with the intensely competitive culture of weapons producers. In most civilian industries, moreover, sharing data with competitors could invite unwelcome scrutiny from antitrust authorities. Producing for the Navy was different, to be sure: there was only one customer, and much of any efficiency gain brought about through information exchange—as long as the information concerned nuts-and-bolts production techniques, rather than design or pricing plans—could be expected to filter through to the Navy. Nonetheless, corporate officials tended to be conditioned to shun coordination with competitors and other outsiders.

As early as the late 1970s, Willis Willoughby, the respected head of the Reliability, Maintainability, and Quality Assurance Directorate in the Office of Naval Materiel, had watched with frustration while two Navy contractors developing a Navy radar system refused to communicate with each other during the production stage. One contractor was working on a particular production process that the other contractor had already attempted and abandoned as a technological dead end. To curtail what he saw as simple waste, Willoughby brought the two contractors together and told them that if they did not start working together the contract would go on hold, and Navy payments to both contractors would cease. Both companies initially protested that Willoughby was asking them to reveal proprietary information. Ultimately, however, Willoughby's argument that he was merely asking the two companies to share *process* data (and his threat to suspend payments) prevailed. The two contractors agreed to work together.

This ad hoc intervention led Willoughby to speculate on the potential for the Navy to reap cost savings and performance improvements through some systematic way of pooling manufacturing wisdom among contractors. Over the next few years, Willoughby visited more Navy contractors and became increasingly convinced that the lack of information exchange among Navy contractors was imposing significant costs on the Navy. Other senior executives came to share this conviction. In 1982 the Department of Defense (DOD) formed a Defense Science Board Task Force to determine why the weapons acquisition process took so long and was so dogged with quality and reliability problems. Three years later, the Defense Department published "Transition from Development to Production,"[3] which articulated a number of templates for identifying critical engineering processes and control methods. "Transition from Development to Production" also provided contractors with a rough roadmap for moving a weapon system into full-scale production.

This technical Pentagon publication turned out to have far-reaching significance. For the first time, the Defense Department had identified the major pitfalls (in terms of cost, schedule, performance, and readiness) associated with specific manufacturing practices. And while "Transition from Development to Production" dealt primarily with the problems associated with practices in common use among defense contractors, it suggested a further possibility. It was only a short logical step from highlighting flawed manufacturing approaches to identifying those manufacturing practices that had helped companies circumvent the most common problems.

Best Manufacturing Practices (BMP)

The Navy launched a pilot program in 1985 to advance this agenda in an organized way. The initiative, dubbed the Best Manufacturing Practices (BMP) program, was designed to serve as the mechanism for disseminating information on best manufacturing practices. These were defined as any "process, technique, or innovative use of equipment or resources that has a proven record of success in providing significant improvement in cost, schedule, quality, performance, safety, environment, or other measurable factors which impact the health of the company." Since its creation, BMP has helped more than a hundred corporations document and disseminate some 4,000 tested manufacturing practices. In 1997 alone, BMP estimates, the public savings flowing from this information-pooling exceeded $2 billion. Beyond the scale of the cost savings is the remarkable fact that BMP has become a federal program that private corporations clamor to work with.

In the 1980s, before BMP could get off the ground, it had to resolve several thorny problems. How would a federal program induce defense contractors—conditioned by "compliance audits" to dread too-close contact with government officials—to open their doors to curious public employees? How could BMP overcome ingrained habits and basic instincts on the part of private firms and persuade companies to share valuable knowledge? These challenges fell to Ernie Renner, whom Willoughby hired in the spring of 1985 as BMP's first (and for many years, its only) full-time Navy employee. His job was to translate the pooling of best practices among Navy contractors from a concept to a program.

Willoughby's instructions to Renner were at once straightforward and daunting: Go out and survey companies with top-flight manufacturing practices that other Navy suppliers could use to good effect; describe and document the technical wisdom; then publish the results. From his years of work in this area, Willoughby had a list of companies and divisions, primarily in the field of electronics, that he thought were good candidates for a survey. That was the mission. All Renner had to do was implement.

Any hopes Renner might have harbored that weapons producers would automatically embrace this notion were promptly dispelled. His first contact was with one of the producers on Willoughby's list, Litton's Guidance and Control Systems Division. Litton responded warily to Renner's overtures, which started in the summer of 1985. After BMP representatives made several visits to the company's California facility and met with the president of the division, Litton finally agreed to open its doors to the BMP team. One obstacle was overcome—but no BMP team yet existed. With no staff (and little budget to hire staff) Renner had to borrow one.

Fortunately for BMP, most of the Navy units and commands Renner approached proved willing to lend their best engineers to the enterprise.

Participating in the kind of survey Renner envisaged struck senior managers as an excellent opportunity to season their personnel through broader exposure to cutting-edge technology and manufacturing processes. Renner soon had a pool of nearly twenty engineers, on loan from various Navy organizations, ready to work on surveys.[4]

BMP's first survey was a modest affair. Renner himself and a handful of other Navy engineers constituted the entire team. Reports of the first survey were distributed to a mailing list of roughly 250 people. But Litton, luckily, was pleased with the results. Renner had his toe in the door of the military contractor community. As he tried to gain entrée to other contractors, Renner could now tell wary companies that they should talk to Litton to learn about what a survey would mean in practice and what participation would entail. Word spread gradually within the defense-supply world as companies began to realize that a BMP survey was in effect a free (if remarkably public) report from a team of highly qualified consultants. The list of companies willing to participate lengthened. Eventually companies began taking the initiative, contacting BMP to see about scheduling a survey.

BMP quickly developed a standard survey procedure. Once a company identified areas in its operations that it considered state-of-the-art and indicated openness to a visit, BMP selected a team chair for the on-site survey. The team chair would consult with managers at the target company and work out an agenda for a three- to five-day site visit. Before arriving, the chairman would vet the roster of intended team members with the company. Once on site for what was usually a Monday-to-Friday sojourn, the team followed a tested protocol. The first day typically was devoted to an overview of the facility, to acquaint the team with its products and processes. Days two through four were spent on the factory floor examining equipment, observing procedures, interviewing employees, and analyzing data. Toward the beginning of the last day of the site visit, the team presented a rough draft of the written report. In this draft, the survey team identified which of the processes and techniques the company had presented as exemplary really rated the label "best practices."

The most valuable part of the process, from the company's perspective, often turned out to be learning why those items it had considered best practices failed to make the grade. BMP survey teams frequently spent much of the final day explaining where practices fell short. This afforded BMP teams the opportunity to point out companies with similar practices that did rise to the top level. As time went by and BMP's catalog of best practices grew, BMP teams were increasingly able to provide companies with reports that actually documented the state of the art. Participating in surveys thus allowed companies to benchmark their own approaches against BMP's growing catalog of best practices.

BMP's survey process did not end with the site visit. A few weeks later, the team chair sent a second draft of the report to the company for comments. The company retained the final say on what could be published. Any findings, issues, or technical matters the company did not want made public were excised. When the content of the final report was agreed on, the document went to BMP for publication and distribution.

All of the members of BMP's survey teams were volunteers from other branches of the Navy and from other agencies. As the team members' home agencies learned that a stint on a survey could both augment a worker's expertise and improve the quality of Navy equipment, they became increasingly ready to lend staff, and even to cover their travel costs. The home agencies were willing to provide their experts for surveys because BMP limited their staff's participation to a single work week, thus making it imperative to get as much as possible done during those five days.

Before arriving for a site visit, the BMP team would be divided into smaller teams of three or four people, each with its designated area of concentration. At the end of each day, each team would huddle to rough out language describing the exemplary practices (or, as the case may be, problems) they had observed during the day. If the recording was put off for even a day, Renner had learned, recollections dulled as new observations piled up. Once the site visit ended, only the team chairman and BMP staff would be involved in working on the final report, and the rest of the team members scattered back to their home organizations.

The word about BMP spread within industry, and its distribution network grew. Whenever a company participated in a survey, the program would ask the company to designate a single "point of contact." BMP stayed in touch with these contact people, who were the first circle of recipients for subsequent survey results. Gradually, a network of interested and informed customers grew up around BMP. By the mid-1990s, units of AT&T, Boeing, GE, Hewlett-Packard, IBM, Lockheed Martin, Motorola, Polaroid, and Raytheon had participated in BMP surveys. As the central survey-and-disseminate mission matured, BMP learned that the connections it helped orchestrate could generate far broader benefits. Motorola—an early participant in BMP—made a presentation on its quality control methods and "the metrics of measuring" at a BMP workshop in the early 1990s. After the presentation, Ray Currens, from Motorola's Scottsdale-based Government Electronics Division, was approached by a representative of Texas Instruments' Defense Systems and Electronics Group. The two technicians got to talking, and the conversation led to further, more formal contacts between the two companies culminating in the decision by Texas Instruments (TI) to join Motorola's Six Sigma Research Institute.[5] In 1992, TI's Defense Systems and Electronics Group won the Commerce Department's prestigious Malcolm Baldrige National Quality Award, an honor it credited in part to its work with BMP. In March 1993, TI reciprocated Motorola's earlier advice by inviting Motorola representatives to tour its facilities and witness the fruits of its involvement with Six Sigma. According to Motorola's Currens, as a result of its participation in BMP, "We learned very quickly that manufacturing is a science; propriety is in the design."[6]

In the early 1990s, Willoughby came to Renner with a proposal for a new BMP initiative. Program managers, argued Willoughby, need a better way to organize their special requirements. Designers have workstations that allow them to model their products and anticipate problems; managers need to have something similar—a suite of tools that will help them sequence and orchestrate their decisions. Though this notion involved a different level of productive activity than the technical best practices BMP was organized around, it had the same basic logic—stepping in to accelerate high-level standardization that would ultimately benefit the Navy. Renner was intrigued by Willoughby's idea and quickly committed BMP to developing what came to be known as the Program Manager's WorkStation.

The WorkStation Initiative

In 1992, after months of consultation with government and industry program managers and engineers, BMP rolled out a suite of software tools designed to give manufacturers access to technical advice and risk management information. The software suite had three major components: KnowHow, a searchable electronic library; the Technical Risk Identification and Mitigation System (TRIMS), a tool for pinpointing and circumventing program risks; and the BMP database, which contained descriptions of the best manufacturing practices catalogued through BMP surveys.

The WorkStation initiative represented a sharp extension of the BMP franchise. The program had previously focused almost exclusively on improving the state of practice among Navy contractors. But KnowHow and TRIMS were potentially useful to almost any manufacturer. This was no coincidence. BMP increasingly saw eventual, if indirect, benefits to the Navy from broader improvements in the U.S. industrial base, and it deliberately sought to leverage its special capacities in the service of the larger agenda. In 1992, BMP reached beyond its traditional customer base to conduct a survey of Tandem Computers, a California-based company that specialized in producing fault-tolerant computers and networks. Tandem Computers was not a defense contractor, but it had heard of BMP and welcomed a survey team.

Over the next few years BMP took several steps toward reaching a wider audience. In 1993 it teamed up with the National Institute of Standards and Technology (NIST) and the Engineering Research Center at the University of Maryland to create the BMP Center of Excellence. The partnership with NIST gave BMP, which had worked primarily with large defense contractors in the past, entrée to NIST's network of business centers serving small and medium-sized companies. BMP's partnership with Maryland's Engineering Research Center let the program promulgate its principles to an academic audience and into engineering schools' curricula. A year later BMP opened its first satellite center at the Department of Energy's Oak Ridge National Laboratory. Oak Ridge, responding to a presidential directive instructing the Department of Energy's laboratories to ease the transfer of government technologies to the private sector, designated one of its employees to help familiarize businesses with BMP tools and resources. Within four years of Oak Ridge's launch, BMP had nine satellite centers in seven states and in the District of Columbia.

BMP aggressively developed partnerships with other organizations as well, including professional organizations such as the Aerospace Industries Association and the Society of Automotive Engineers; with universities, such as Ohio State University, the Massachusetts Institute of Technology, and the University of New Orleans; and with publications such as *Industry Week*. The result, as Linda Kaboolian of the John F. Kennedy School of Government observed, was the creation of the basis of a "network" organization where the broad enterprise was carried forward by the spokes (the partners) as well as the hub (BMP).

BMP itself also grew. In 1995, Anne Marie SuPrise was detailed to BMP from the Federal Emergency Management Agency and two years later became the program's second full-time Navy employee. While its official work force (albeit doubled by the new addition) was still tiny, BMP's de facto work force had grown considerably. In addition to Renner and SuPrise, BMP also had three associate directors who were on other Navy programs' payrolls but were allowed to devote much of their time to BMP. BMP was supported by approximately thirty contractor personnel. Several students at the University of Maryland also worked at the BMP Center of Excellence, and each satellite center also had someone working part-time on BMP. The size of the pool of volunteers from which BMP could draw survey team members had also swollen to about 120 people. Moreover, for the first time BMP survey teams began to include representatives from other private companies (subject to the approval of the company being surveyed).

In May 1995, BMP set up a web site (http://www.bmpcoe.org) that effectively put the Program Manager's WorkStation on line. Software tools like KnowHow and TRIMS could now be downloaded from BMP's web site for free. Users could also access the BMP database, which by that date contained descriptions of more than 2,500 best manufacturing practices identified during surveys by BMP teams.[7] If a manufacturer could not find what it was looking for with KnowHow or with the BMP database, it would turn to one of BMP's Special Interest Groups, on-line bulletin boards where users could post papers or pose questions. Network users are linked to these resources by BMPnet, which allows users to run and download BMP programs and to communicate with other BMP users. By 1997, BMP's web site was receiving roughly 35,000 hits from approximately 7,000 visitors a day.[8] More than 50,000 survey reports and other publications were distributed to over 6,000 people representing 3,600 companies.

At the end of 1997, BMP set out to calibrate the scale of the savings achieved using BMP tools and products. The estimate, for that year alone, came to $2.1 billion. Given the fact that BMP's annual budget was in the 2-million-dollar range—and even allowing for some quibbling about the actual scale of the savings—this suggested a rather impressive rate of return.[9] That year both the Maryland Center for Industrial Energy Efficiency and the Army asked BMP to train their staff so that they could begin to identify and promulgate best practices within their own field of operations.

In 1998, BMP conducted its most ambitious survey to date—a visit to Raytheon that involved a team of twenty-seven technicians and technical writers. That survey examined 129 manufacturing techniques and pronounced 84 of them "best practices." By the end of that year, 100 U.S. firms had participated in BMP's survey process since the program's inception.

Yet even as America's armed services settled into a post–cold war environment sharply different from the Reagan-era buildup in which it was born, BMP demonstrated staying power. Not only had it expanded its network beyond traditional military contractors, but the demand for its services among its traditional clientele was showing renewed urgency at century's end. In February 1999, President Clinton unveiled a year 2000 budget proposal that called for a $12 billion increase in the defense budget, the largest increase in military spending since the Reagan administration. President Clinton's proposal included roughly $4 billion in funds for new weapon systems alone, such as an updated variant of the F-18 for the Navy, new amphibious assault vehicles, and the new Virginia-class of attack submarines, as well as an increase in the rate of shipbuilding. Early congressional reactions pointed to an eventual increase in defense spending even larger than the president proposed and suggested that a new era of weapons modernization was about to begin.[10] As long as the Navy has new weapon systems in the works, and as long as the manufacturing prowess of the Navy's suppliers matters for defense readiness and for the federal budget, BMP's mission promises to retain its relevance.

Notes

1. Philip Geyelin, "Aircraft Whose Wings Will Not Fall," *Washington Post*, October 24, 1985, p. A23.

2. This chapter draws heavily on information gathered by Linda Kaboolian, associate professor at Harvard University's John F. Kennedy School of Government, during several days of site visits and research, as well as her insights.

3. DOD 4245.7-M, September 1985.

4. Three Navy offices—the Naval Surface Warfare Center in Crane, Indiana; the Naval Avionics Center in Indianapolis; and Naval Industrial Resources Support Activity—gave critical early assistance by providing the first teams of technical experts that allowed BMP to conduct surveys.

5. Six Sigma was Motorola's ambitious program to limit its defect rate to no more than 3.4 per million.

6. Letter from Ray Currens, Motorola Government Electronics Group, to Ernie Renner, director, Best Manufacturing Practices, February 15, 1993.

7. In addition, BMP frequently winnowed its database to ensure that the best practices documented continued to be relevant to potential customers.

8. This number was somewhat inflated by the fact that it counted hits by a considerable number of users who were not actually using the BMP database. A year later, BMP refined its methodology and concluded that the BMP database itself was getting about 7,000 hits a day. BMP also discovered that the average user checked in on the BMP database once a week to look for new surveys.

9. This 2-million-dollar budget figure counted only the Navy's cash contribution to BMP's budget. In-kind contributions effectively doubled BMP's budget.

10. "The President's Budget Proposal: The Details—Freeze on Medicare Money to Hospitals Would Pay for Health Care Initiatives, Military Spending," *New York Times*, February 2, 1999, p. 17.

9

RECLAIMING RELEVANCE

THE AMERICAN WEST remained mostly unworked and lightly populated at the turn of the twentieth century, with much of the land too
parched for even the most determined homesteaders. In 1902, anxious to
fulfill the vision of continental settlement sparked a century earlier by the
Lewis and Clark expedition, Congress created the Bureau of Reclamation. The bureau, an agency within the Department of the Interior, was
given an audacious mission: to harness the West's awesome rivers, bend-
ing their flows to water the desert and to render the arid vastness fertile
and fit for human habitation.

Water Projects

The bureau proved up to the task. The massive dams and reservoirs,
humming hydroelectric power plants, and thousands of miles of irrigation canals created under its auspices have provided Americans in seventeen western states with electricity, shielded communities from devastat-
ing floods, and delivered trillions of gallons of water to transform what
had been barren land into some of the most productive farms in the
country. The land irrigated by reclamation projects produces 60 percent
of the vegetables and 25 percent of the fruits grown in this country. The

---

This chapter was researched and drafted by Dalit Toledano.

Hoover Dam (arguably the most imposing of the bureau's engineering feats), 1,244 feet long and 660 feet thick, stands at the base of the Black Canyon on the Colorado River. Since its completion in 1936, the Hoover Dam has increased crop production in the region tenfold.[1]

For decades the Bureau of Reclamation's accomplishments stood as both a testament to human determination and ingenuity and as a symbol of national progress. But by the mid-1980s, the agency that had worked its will on the western landscape was facing a serious threat to its future. While Reclamation's prolific dam building had earned it the ardent support of western agribusiness, the agency's activities had not won universal acclaim. Environmentalists protested that concrete-worshipping Reclamation engineers had dried up wetlands and undermined natural ecosystems. Fishermen complained that the dams were depleting fish reserves and wiping out some salmon and trout habitats. Native Americans began to sue the government for water diverted from their lands. As population growth soared in the West, urban and suburban residents began to resent competing with farmers for water.

Perhaps the most significant threat to the agency, paradoxically, was that it had pursued its founding mission with such stunning success. It was only a little exaggeration to claim that every major dam worth building had already been built. Like Alexander the Great lamenting the lack of new worlds to conquer, Reclamation found itself essentially a construction agency with little left for its 8,000 employees to construct.

The political setting was also in flux. The bureau had traditionally fared well with western politicians, who understood the advantages of large-scale public works projects that in the short term provided residents with construction jobs and over the long term provided farmers with cheap water and saved residents from flooding disasters. But the nation faced newly severe fiscal constraints, and even the bureau's biggest supporters in Congress knew that this engineering powerhouse had some notable financial shortcomings.

In theory, the money the bureau spent to construct, operate, and maintain its facilities was to be recovered from the beneficiaries, through user fees and capital cost repayments. But the agency had historically been unaggressive about cost recovery; for example, bills for the capital cost of irrigation projects usually ignored interest expense. A Department of Interior study found that federal subsidies for one set of irrigation programs ranged from 85 to 99 percent.[2] Even users who could afford to do so rarely paid anything approaching the full freight. And, as the bureau exhausted the list of top-priority dams, it had taken on some projects where it was far from clear that the benefits, accurately reckoned, outweighed the costs. A series of well-publicized controversies concerning dam siting had hurt Reclamation's standing with Congress and sparked escalating charges of economic inefficiency.

The bureau's critics, meanwhile, were gaining political clout. Many westerners had come to think differently about the region's natural resources. Decades of dredging and digging and diverting had taken a visible toll, and Reclamation's massive construction projects came to be seen less as heroic technological triumphs and more as meddling with Mother Nature. Skeptics gave the agency the galling nickname Bureau of Wreck-lamation.[3] As the environmental lobby grew in stature, Native Americans, fishermen, and recreationalists had also grown more sophisticated at organizing and making themselves heard. They found an audience for their water complaints among new-generation western politicians who owed their elections to the residents of the growing urban centers and sprawling suburbs—residents who chafed under tough water-use restrictions during drought years and resented farmers' access to low-cost irrigation water.

Mounting pressure led to an agency-wide self-assessment in 1987. The resulting report was the first formal acknowledgment that the agency had done what it set out to do—it had completed its original mission "to reclaim the arid West." Commissioner C. Dale Duvall declared that the bureau had to cross the divide from the old mission to a new one. The erstwhile mover of mountains would become the steward of America's water resources.

This proposition was initially met with considerable skepticism. Many mocked the notion of the bureau's engineers and technicians retooling themselves into experts in salmon spawning, for example. But the cynicism was overdone. There were early indications that the agency's management was serious about transforming the bureau. The relocation of its headquarters from Washington, D.C., to Denver, Colorado, so that personnel could be closer and more responsive to those most affected by their policy decisions, was a major down payment on reinvention. And Reclamation had potent incentives to embrace the new approach. The alternative was to acquiesce in organizational decline as Congress slashed the bureau's construction budget by more than half between 1986 and 1992.[4]

Still, these first steps toward accommodating new demands fell short. The bureau, which had excelled at customer service when its "customers" were narrowly defined, found itself ill prepared to deal with diverse and divisive water issues. The agency's internal organization, with its many layers of management and its top-down structure, echoed a military chain of command. This was not in the least surprising, given the core mission—building big dams—pursued during its glory days. With vast sums of money and citizens' physical safety hinging on each major decision, relentless reviews and built-in checks made enormous sense. But attempts to deal with new water issues—issues that often required flexibility and speedy resolution—were too often put through these same endless paces. Plans to alter California's Shasta Dam so that it would release colder water for salmon and trout reportedly were reviewed more than 450 times.[5]

The Bureau of Reclamation, which had reshaped the continent's mighty rivers, was stumbling in the face of more mundane modern challenges. It was dismissed by some as a "New Deal bureaucracy in an e-mail age."[6] Calls for the agency's dissolution grew louder and more insistent in the 1990s. One critic summed up a popular sentiment: "When the mission of an agency is complete, it should have a self-congratulatory party and vanish."[7]

In early 1993, one of the most spirited challengers of the bureau's old mission was sworn in as the new secretary of the interior. Bruce Babbitt, a former governor of Arizona, had once somewhat famously referred to the agency as a "dinosaur." Just the year before his appointment, Babbitt had summed up the bureau as "a bunch of dam-builders . . . unable to adjust to the new reality." And as for their new efforts to accommodate environmentalists, Babbitt had scoffed, "Conservation just isn't in their genes."[8]

In May 1993, the secretary chose Dan Beard to head up the Bureau of Reclamation. As the former staff director for the House Natural Resources Committee, Beard had spent nearly as many years as had Babbitt observing the bureau with a jaundiced eye. Representative George Miller (Democrat from California), the chair of that committee, had worked with Senator Bill Bradley (Democrat from New Jersey) to shift water in California away from agricultural users to urban areas.[9] Babbitt and Beard began almost immediately to draw up plans for transforming the agency.

There is no evidence that either of the men set out to abolish the bureau. "It's like that old adage," conceded Beard; "where you stand on an issue depends on where you sit."[10] From where Beard and Babbitt were now sitting, powerful bureau supporters (in Congress and beyond) formed a prominent part of the landscape. The prospect of shutting down Reclamation faced some formidable logistical objections as well as political impediments. "The Bureau of Reclamation is the largest wholesale water supplier in the United States," Beard said. "We're not going away [because] we can't."[11]

Indeed, not even the bureau's harshest critics questioned the need for some federal oversight of western water policy; environmental and resource issues have a way of ignoring state boundaries. Both Beard and Babbitt wanted to succeed where others had failed, bringing environmentalists, fishermen, Native Americans, and urban populations to the table in deciding the disposition of the West's water. They wanted the bureau to orchestrate the accommodation of diverse imperatives in the new West. If they could pull off this transformation, then in a very real sense the old bureau would fade away. Reclamation would not be shut down, but its capabilities would be reconfigured and redeployed to serve sharply different missions.

Developing a New Identity

It would require much more than pronouncements from the top, however, to accomplish such a rebirth. The bureau's employees had seen reform campaigns wash over the organization in the past, leaving little lasting change in their wake. "We had ninety years of history to overcome," Beard once commented. "Convincing employees that we were serious and that this was not just a paperwork exercise was not easy."[12] Reclamation policies would not change until the culture of the bureau changed—and the culture would not change unless the agency's employees wanted it to.

Soliciting employee input was a crucial first step. Beard asked seven mid-level and lower-level employees to sit on an advisory board that would review and report on all of the bureau's programs and operations. All employees were urged to send comments to Beard—signed or not, as the workers wished—on widely distributed feedback cards. The commissioner probed bureau employees. Where can our performance be improved? How can costs be cut? Could what we do be accomplished just as well without us? Where are opportunities to share expenses with others? All signed cards were answered with a note or a phone call from Beard, and in November of 1993, after weighing the hundreds of responses he received and the advisory board's report, Beard published a "Blueprint for Reform."

The document underscored that Reclamation would have to be fundamentally restructured to pursue its new priorities. Budget categories would have to be reworked, personnel reassigned or positions eliminated, responsibilities altered. Those programs within the agency that had been devoted exclusively to the construction of water impoundment facilities would dwindle, and resources would be shifted to new programs designed to arbitrate water disputes, improve wetlands, and restore fish and wildlife resources.

The agency's intricate organizational layers and bureaucratic hurdles had generated the loudest complaints from employees. The project managers in charge of individual dams or other facilities had traditionally been required to navigate an arduous system of reviews before making any significant moves. As Beard noted, "People (had been) operating in a system where there was little trust in the employee's ability to do a job."[13] This was not only demoralizing, he thought, but inefficient. Beard set out to demonstrate his confidence in the bureau's employees, using management tactics starkly at odds with the bureau's traditional top-down culture. Staffers recall that one of Beard's favorite phrases, in conversations with subordinates, was, "I don't know; you figure it out."[14] When he decided to move decisionmaking authority out of Denver to the twenty-six field offices, he also issued each project manager what he called "forgiveness coupons," which read: "It is easier to get forgiveness . . . than permission." A coupon is cashed in when a manager makes a mistake. Managers were told that doing their jobs right would require them to run through a minimum of two coupons a year. "If you do something bold and innovative, and it's controversial, and people start yelling at you," Beard told his front-line personnel, "then you whip this sucker out and wave it, and then they have to shut up."[15] The coupons were an important signal from the top: creativity was in; inertia was out.

Other management changes were more conventional, if no less important. Beard eliminated several top executive positions in the agency, decreased the number of supervisory personnel, and reduced a seven-tiered decisionmaking structure to two or, at most, three levels of authority. This meant more than a simpler organizational chart for the bureau. It allowed faster action on key projects and grants. Approval for a 5-million-dollar bureau contribution toward the construction of a southern California wastewater treatment plant intended to reduce pollution in the Santa Monica Bay came through in one week. Under the old system, the process would have taken six months—and cost $250,000.[16] Designing the ladders that allow fish to migrate past dams could now be done in eight steps requiring six months, instead of twenty-one steps and three years. As Vice-President Al Gore put it, "Reclamation cut the approval time for a fish ladder down from a fish's lifetime to a single spawning season."[17]

All of this was by no means painless. Despite shrinking construction budgets, the bureau's work force had remained relatively stable, and a degree of downsizing had now become inevitable. Beard called the conversion of the Denver office from a headquarters into a technical service center "gut-wrenching . . . you take 25 to 30 percent of the staff and eliminate them."[18] Within two years of having taken over, Beard had overseen a reduction of the work force from 8,100 to 6,600.[19] He made efforts to have employees with relevant expertise transferred to other government agencies, such as the Department of Energy. Outplacement counseling was offered to cushion the blow to other workers. But the personnel fallout from reinvention was searing nevertheless.

Not just those downsized out of their jobs, but also those employees who stayed with Reclamation found their work lives in upheaval. Some of the agency's newly appointed top managers had been chosen specifically because of their skepticism about Reclamation's old way of doing business, and they were not shy about making sweeping changes. Some changes, of course, were welcome ones, like a new enterprise initiative fund that let managers use a certain percentage of their year-end savings for high-priority but discretionary activities.[20] Employees attended new training sessions to hone their problem-solving skills or toured private firms famous for their commitment to teamwork, such as Saturn and Herman Miller. A towering eight-foot stack of regulations was shrunk to a more manageable six inches of guidelines. And a new computer system let employees communicate directly with the commissioner.[21]

Many adjustments were tougher to accept. The technical specialists in the Denver office, who had lost much of their policy-setting authority, had to operate on a fee-for-service basis—much like private sector consultants. They had to hire out their scientific, engineering, and research expertise to customers, including external parties like state agencies, Indian tribes, or other federal agencies as well as the bureau's area offices. But area offices were no longer limited to Denver employees for many services and were free to choose other suppliers if headquarters let quality slip or costs escalate.[22] These new demands on employees, coupled with lost status, generated some internal resentment.

Some of the bureau's longstanding constituencies were dismayed at the passing of an old order that had served them well. A new directive required beneficiaries of traditional Reclamation projects to pay, through cash or in-kind services, at least 35 percent of construction costs up front.[23] Even as the customer share of costs increased, the number of such traditional projects dropped.

Eluid Martinez took over from Beard in late 1995. The new commissioner was the former state engineer for New Mexico, with twenty-four years of experience in water administration and management. He articulated the agency's updated priorities before a congressional committee in the spring of 1997. No new irrigation projects would be initiated, he promised—instead, federal funds would be used to maintain existing projects, with maintenance defined to include mitigating the projects' adverse effects. Almost 40 percent of Reclamation's 1998 budget was earmarked for operation, maintenance, and rehabilitation of existing infrastructure. The rest was for wrapping up uncompleted projects and promoting "an integrated approach to the management of water."[24] One of the most venerable maxims of bureaucratic behavior is that no agency willingly surrenders its turf. The Bureau of Reclamation provides a counterexample. The Small Reclamation Projects Act loan program issues cheap finance for small irrigation projects. The bureau had administered the loans since 1956. But when Congress decided to grant only the funding needed to complete grandfathered projects, the bureau responded enthusiastically: "In this era of budget constraints," Commissioner Martinez told Congress, "we believe it does not make sense for Reclamation to be the 'banker' for the development of small water projects. Reclamation should not be in the business of providing loans or loan guarantees; [we] should not compete with private sector financing."[25]

The bureau's readiness to stick to its knitting and let somebody else make the loans, however at odds with the conventional wisdom about federal agencies, becomes less remarkable in light of the scale of Reclamation's remaining mission. It is the second largest water supplier in the United States, delivering an annual 10 trillion gallons of water to 31 million people. Its fifty-eight power plants turn out 42 billion kilowatt-hours each year. The 10 million acres irrigated with bureau-supplied water produce three-fifths of the nation's vegetables. Beyond these legacies of its founding responsibilities are the duties that come with its new, broader mission: maintaining salmon habitats in Oregon; arbitrating disputes over irrigation allocations in Corpus Christi; restoring damaged ecosystems in the San Francisco Bay; struggling to orchestrate workable deals among water claimants in the drought-ridden Southwest; forming new partnerships with Native Americans, municipalities, irrigation districts, and other federal agencies.[26]

There is little risk that the Bureau of Reclamation's rawboned heritage will give way to dull consensus over kinder, gentler new priorities. New Mexico's Senator Pete Domenici (while supporting many of the changes at Reclamation) cautioned in an appropriations hearing that while "we're moving rapidly away from any new development projects and more in the direction of ecosystem and environmental projects. . . . It does seem to me that there are still some developmental projects that are needed in this country. And we'll be looking to create a little more balance."[27] Such tensions are sure to remain; new ones are sure to arise.

When Bruce Babbitt took over at Interior, many thought he and Beard were naive to think that the bureau could change much. One reporter mockingly summed up the reactions to an early press conference unveiling Reclamation's reinvention plans: "The Bureau of Reclamation, the Department of Interior's muscular, earth-moving, concrete-pouring, environment-be-damned builder of such engineering marvels as the Grand Coulee and Hoover Dams—is going to become a 90s kind of guy."[28] However flip the metaphor, and however skeptical the sentiment behind it, this is not a bad account of the bureau's struggle to claim a new mission that fits both its own proud past and the imperatives of the future.

Notes

1. Lisa Corbin, "Going Leaner and Greener," *Government Executive*, November 1995.

2. Leslie Kaufman, "Reinvention Reality Check: The Bureau of Reclamation Finds It's Not Easy Going Green," *Government Executive*, April 1994.

3. Timothy Egan, "Can This Man Reinvent the West?" *Sacramento Bee*, August 15, 1993.

4. Russ Linden, "Engineering Reclamation: Former U.S. Dam-Building Agency Is Reborn," Gannett News Service, August 30, 1993.

5. Tom Kenworthy, "A Leaner and Greener Bureau of Reclamation; Water Management Policies Being Redefined," *Washington Post*, November 2, 1993.

6. Jackie Adams, "Agency Reinvention Saves $100 Million, Cuts Bureaucracy," *Daily Inter Lake*, Kalispell, Minnesota, November 5, 1995.

7. Lt. Col. David Clark, Department of the Army, letter to *Government Executive*, February 1996.

8. Carol Bradley, "Federal Water Agency Changes Its Direction," Gannett News Service, June 17, 1992.

9. Kaufman, "Reinvention Reality Check."

10. Ibid.

11. Mark Obmascik, "Banking on Rivers to Green Up Image, U.S. Dam-Builder Renames Conference Rooms," *Denver Post*, March 4, 1994.

12. Site visit report.

13. Corbin, "Going Leaner and Greener."

14. Site visit report.

15. Stephen Barr, "Agriculture, Reclamation Embrace Major Reorganization," *Washington Post*, April 14, 1994.

16. Ibid.

17. Vice president's remarks at Interior Department event, May 31, 1994.

18. Ibid.

19. Letter from Secretary of the Interior Bruce Babbitt to Bill Parent, May 17, 1995.

20. Linden, "Engineering Reclamation."

21. David C. Beeder, "Reclamation Bureau Chief Calls It Quits," *Omaha World Herald*, June 13, 1995.

22. Ibid.

23. Testimony of Eluid Martinez, Commissioner of the Bureau of Reclamation, Hearing of the Energy and Water Development Subcommittee of the Senate Appropriations Committee, May 6, 1997.

24. Ibid.

25. Ibid.

26. *Fact Sheet*, Bureau of Reclamation, Department of the Interior, April 1996 and March 1998.

27. Hearing of the Energy and Water Development Subcommittee of the Senate Appropriations Committee.

28. Kenworthy, "A Leaner and Greener Bureau of Reclamation."

10

MOTIVATING
JOB SAFETY

EARLY ONE SPRING not long ago, each employee of the Maine-based plastics maker Forster, Inc., received a gift in the mail—a pair of formidable boots, built to handle the ghastly winter and spring weather that Mainers endure as the price for their state's summer glory. The gift memorialized a distinctive occasion in a distinctive manner: Forster's employees had just logged a total of one million hours on the job without a single injury, an achievement realized only once before in the company's century of operations. This being Maine, management could think of no more fitting way to mark the milestone than with L. L. Bean boots for everyone. This being Maine—and March, with the muck ankle-deep from the melting show—the employees were touched by the sentiment.[1]

Meanwhile in Freeport, Maine's coastal retail mecca, L. L. Bean was itself setting records for workplace safety. Hundreds of employees—from shoemakers to telephone operators to warehouse workers—were serving on safety committees, one of the more visible manifestations of a company-wide commitment to root out hazards in Bean's sprawling complex of factories, offices, and stores. Their efforts, along with those of the ergonomics experts and other consultants the company hired, were producing dramatic reductions in L. L. Bean's rate of injuries and illnesses on the job.[2]

This chapter was researched and drafted by Dalit Toledano.

Indeed, nearly 200 businesses across Maine, employing more than 30 percent of the state's work force, were making unprecedented efforts to provide their workers with safer places to do their jobs. Why the stepped-up emphasis on worker safety? Was it due to a simultaneous, statewide surge of solicitude toward employees? Certainly many companies—in Maine as everywhere, that year as every year—were genuinely interested in keeping their employees safe and healthy. And no business likes the costs (to either the pocketbook or employee morale) that come with workplace injuries.

OSHA's Role

But in Maine, the renewed energy and attention were largely due to an experiment that had been launched by the Labor Department's Occupational Safety and Health Administration—known widely (though not always affectionately) by its acronym, OSHA. The experiment was meant to craft a model of détente in one of America's more dysfunctional business-government relationships with the hope that as goes Maine, so would go the nation.

This was a tall order. By the early 1990s, OSHA and U.S. business had settled into the domestic equivalent of cold war, with periodic outbreaks of open hostilities. Since 1971, when a series of gruesome workplace accidents led Congress and the Nixon administration to initiate federal regulation of workplace conditions, OSHA had pursued a mandate of breathtaking scope: to ensure safe and healthful working conditions for every laboring man and woman in America. Both its original legislation and subsequent amendments give OSHA the duty of translating broad legal requirements into specific rules and then enforcing compliance with those regulations. These include formidably precise instructions for limiting the hazards from industrial machinery, for protecting workers from workplace exposure to potentially dangerous chemicals, and for informing employees about specific dangers and (more generally) about their employers' obligation, enforced by OSHA, to keep the workplace safe. Friction with business is built into OSHA's mandate. Businesses that are inclined to cut corners on health and safety see OSHA rules as infuriating impediments. But even employers who want to do right by their workers often bristle at the maze of federal rules and bemoan the paperwork burden.

To monitor compliance with its regulations, OSHA maintains field offices across the nation. If an employee complaint flags potential problems at a workplace, OSHA sends inspectors to investigate. Even in the absence of tip-offs from employees, OSHA targets the most hazardous industries for periodic spot inspections, picking firms at random and monitoring their compliance with health and safety laws. And a fatality or major accident triggers an OSHA follow-up. These inspections, whether random checks or responses to complaints or catastrophes, can take several OSHA employees weeks or months to complete, depending on the size of the workplace. If the inspections turn up violations of OSHA regulations, the company is fated for citations, fines, follow-up monitoring, and often litigation.

However unpopular with business its standard procedures may have been, OSHA has had an impact. Since 1971, the annual toll of workplace fatalities has been slashed by nearly 60 percent.[3] Part of this improvement, to be sure, comes from changes in the economy that shrink the proportion of dangerous jobs; there are fewer fishermen to be dragged overboard by faulty gear, fewer lumberjacks to be crushed by trees or slashed by saws. But even *within* industries there is ample evidence that OSHA has made a difference in workplace safety, as rates of death, injury, and illness have declined, especially in the most hazardous occupations. The improvement has come at a price, however, and by the time OSHA was a quarter-century old it was facing conflicting pressures, from many different quarters, to change the way it did business.

There has always been a gap between OSHA's mission—to bring every workplace into compliance with its regulations—and OSHA's means. As Congress has passed new health and safety laws, as the economy has grown, and as budget pressures have constrained the agency's head count, that gap has widened. OSHA and its state-based partner agencies field fewer than 2,000 inspectors. This modest corps of safety experts is charged with protecting more than 100 million employees at 6 million workplaces.[4] From the perspective of organized labor, the problem with workplace safety is laws that are unduly lax and enforced too timidly by an agency that is preposterously short of staff. Labor leaders find it shameful that in the world's richest economy, 17 workers are killed and 16,000 injured on the job every day.[5] In testimony before a congressional committee, one labor leader spoke of a series of recent workplace accidents that ended in tragedy: "[These workers] died because OSHA is too weak, because there are too few inspections, because there are too many serious, but unregulated hazards in American workplaces and fundamentally, because too many employers think that they have too little to fear from OSHA."[6] Many business leaders, meanwhile, view OSHA as the grim archetype of big government—needlessly intrusive, deaf to the logic of economic efficiency, and always ready to believe the worst about business.

Since neither business nor labor much likes the idea of an OSHA inspector using his or her own judgment about what is or is not safe, procedures for enforcing workplace health and safety laws are rigidly formalized. Regulations are spelled out in meticulous detail. Each time an ambiguity has triggered a lawsuit, OSHA has added another layer of specificity to clarify the rules, and the pages businesses must peruse to learn their obligations multiply. Inspectors operate under the rule, "You see it, you cite it." They must cite and penalize employers for every code violation encountered in the course of an inspection, and they are not allowed to make distinctions between honest errors by well-intentioned employers and cynical corner-cutting by firms that would rather put workers at risk than spend a buck for safety.

Beyond the rules barring leniency has been a sense among OSHA staffers (as well as among labor leaders and sympathetic legislators) that strict penalties helped to counterbalance the rarity of inspections. Statistically speaking, employers have had an excellent chance of getting away with safety violations, at least until a death or serious incident moved them to the top of the inspection list. So the penalty for the violations that are detected has to outweigh the cost savings from scrimping on safety if firms are to find compliance rational. If the cost of a parking ticket was just a penny higher than the cost of feeding the meter, who would bother to park legally if the odds of getting caught were less than 100 percent? Tough sanctions may have been a reasonable application of game-theory logic—but the consequence was that the employers who did get caught suffered what seemed to them unfair penalties for safety shortcomings no worse than what other employers got away with every day.

The combination of sparse OSHA staffing, a growing list of laws and regulations, and by-the-book penalties meant that many businesspeople came to think of an OSHA inspection as something like being hit by lighting: not very likely to happen, but very bad news if it does. Even if an employer is scrupulously attentive to worker health and safety, even if managers spend time informing themselves about OSHA rules and regulations, once an OSHA inspector shows up, the odds are high that some violations will be found and that penalties will be paid and costly changes required. But if victims of a lightning bolt can only shake their fists at the unfairness of fate, employers who endure an OSHA inspection can complain to the press. And they can use their political influence to change health and safety laws or weaken OSHA's ability to enforce them.

In the years after OSHA's birth a folklore of OSHA outrages emerged. Some of the tales were simple inventions or wild distortions of reasonable rules. But applying cut-and-dried regulations to a complex economy has yielded plenty of accurate, or partly accurate, anecdotes that feed skepticism about OSHA. Ronald Reagan loved to tell a story about a small Iowa store owned by a husband and wife—who were also the store's only employees—forced to close its doors because it could not meet the OSHA requirement of separate bathrooms for male and female employees. Another favorite tale features the $400 penalty routinely awarded to those who fail to display a poster summarizing safety rules and telling workers how to report violations.[7] OSHA figured prominently in *The Death of Common Sense*, Philip Howard's best-selling assault on the "bureaucratic overkill" he sees as endemic to our government and legal system. Howard describes the woes of a brick factory in Reading, Pennsylvania, where OSHA inspectors stalk through the building with rulebooks and tape measures, determined to find violations: "They are especially interested in railings. [The brick factory] has been cited for having railings 39 or 40 inches high, not the regulation 42 inches, in older parts of the factory." OSHA regulations, Howard suggests, are not simply over-precise but just plain preposterous. "Warnings are posted everywhere. A large POISON sign dominates one side of a storage shed filled with bags containing something hazardous: it turns out to be sand."[8] OSHA and labor leaders maintain that there is a logic to seemingly excessive rules. Without posting information on how to blow the whistle, hazards might never be identified until too late. Workers tumble to their deaths over a railing that is a little too low, or damage their lungs by inhaling the type of fine-grained sand stored in that brick factory's shed. But these protests carried little weight with employers who felt themselves to be sincerely safety-conscious and victimized by silly, needlessly costly rules.

OSHA's reputation within the business community has not gone unnoticed by Congress. "Most employers would describe OSHA as the Gestapo of the federal government," according to one member of the House.[9] Business hostility made OSHA a tempting target as deficit reduction forced limits in federal spending. Congressional champions for workplace health and safety often succeeded in passing tougher laws, but were less successful in fortifying OSHA resources for additional inspections. So the gap between mission and means continued to widen, setting in motion a vicious circle: labor leaders and other safety advocates insisted on tough enforcement; resource constraints meant that most workplaces went years without an inspection. When bad luck or worker complaints did lead to inspection, the almost inevitable fines and requirements to change equipment or procedures inspired new OSHA folktales—thus intensifying political efforts to bridle the agency with budget cuts or legislated restrictions.

But as the list of businesses up in arms about OSHA inspections lengthened, each passing day also brought news of workers who had been killed, hurt, or sickened on the job by hazards that could have been prevented. It seemed to thoughtful people throughout business and government that there had to be a better way.

In Maine, amid the fishing fleets, lumber yards, low-slung factories and hardscrabble farms (and a world away, it seemed, from Washington's spin cycles and political positioning), Bill Freeman—the head of OSHA's Maine office—was struggling to find that better way. It was not that Freeman and his team lacked either the taste or the talent for the good old game of enforcement hardball: on Freeman's watch, OSHA Maine had racked up a record number of inspections, violations cited, and fines levied, and it had won awards for its record of tough, vigilant enforcement.[10]

Reassessing

Freeman was proud of his team. And yet, in spite of their efforts, Maine led the nation in workplace accidents. Its worker injury and illness rate was 63 percent higher than the national average; injuries serious enough to cause lost work time were 71 percent higher than the rest of the country.[11] All the citations, all the fines, all the hard work—not to mention the ill will generated and the political flak endured—and the state was *still* scraping bottom. Sure, Maine had more than its share of hazardous jobs, but Freeman did not seek the comfort of easy excuses. He asked himself how he could be doing everything right, or at least everything according to the OSHA play book, without doing better at making Maine's workers safe on the job. And then he had the courage to wonder if the OSHA play book might not be part of the problem.

Freeman had noticed that bringing a company into compliance with OSHA regulations did not necessarily guarantee safety. OSHA inspectors had visited a grocery store, for example, and fined the owners for some real enough electrical violations and for failing to properly instruct their employees in handling certain chemicals. And the store proceeded to fix these problems. But although a growing number of the grocery store's check-out clerks were suffering from carpal tunnel syndrome and tendonitis, OSHA inspectors—going by the book—had not suggested any modifications in routines that might lessen the severity (or lower the incidence) of these painful afflictions. Similarly, though produce workers were suffering a surprising number of sometimes serious falls caused by loose grapes on the floor, this source of injury went unmentioned by OSHA inspectors.[12] This particular hazard certainly did not appear in any regulation (and imagine the scorn that would be heaped on OSHA if it ever did). Still, Freeman knew that wherever OSHA put its emphasis, the safety director of any given company would be forced to follow. And these were troubling illustrations of how a thorough, by-the-book OSHA inspection could fail to address major sources of injury for employees. In fact, the most common injuries at many Maine plants were the sprains, strains, and other kinds of trauma known as soft-tissue injuries, which tend to occur when a worker repeats the same motion over and over again. And though these injuries were costing many workers time away from their jobs, OSHA rules were silent on the subject, beyond citing the "general duty" to maintain workplace safety.

The loose grape syndrome was not the only problem with the way OSHA was doing its job. Freeman had begun to wonder if fines and citations were really the best way to get management focused on safety. One experience had been particularly illuminating. After an initial inspection at a paper plant run by Boise Cascade had uncovered numerous violations, heavy penalties followed. When OSHA inspectors returned to the plant for a follow-up visit, they were impressed with how seriously the company was taking the safety issue. Almost 95 percent of the problems that had initially been identified were being fixed.[13]

The catch was that the five percent of problems that had not yet been remedied applied to so large a factory that, going by the rules, OSHA should have hit Boise Cascade with another half-million or so in penalties. But Freeman questioned the fairness of throwing the book at a management team that seemed to be working in good faith to fix the problems. Local managers had stuck their necks out with corporate higher-ups to get clearance for an aggressive safety campaign. If the payback was another round of heavy fines, the local managers (and some workers as well) predicted a backlash. "You'll send a clear message to corporate that there's no pleasing you," Freeman remembers their pleading. "No matter what we do, you don't care. And corporate is just going to take the attitude, 'The hell with them. Let's fight them from hence-forth.'"[14] The right thing to do, Freeman decided, was to stretch his discretion to the limits and lower the fines.

Freeman was also uncomfortably aware that the tough fines OSHA had imposed on companies like Scott Paper and Bath Iron Works had not deterred other Maine companies from violating the very same regulations, despite statewide publicity about the six-figure and million-dollar penalties. Worse, it seemed OSHA was having only a very temporary effect on the companies it was inspecting. When OSHA officers returned to a factory or a mill or a plant they had inspected just several years earlier, the same violations were often found. Apparently many of the adjustments made to correct violations had only been quick fixes.

Around the time Freeman was making these troubling discoveries, he received a new assignment from John Miles, the administrator of OSHA's New England regional office. Miles asked Freeman and Cindy Coe, his deputy director, to come up with a targeted enforcement program for Maine's toughest cases. Data on workers' compensation claims had revealed that around 200 companies, which collectively employed about 30 percent of Maine's work force, were responsible for a disproportionate share—nearly half—of the state's workers' compensation claims.[15] Focusing on these accident-prone employers seemed like a promising way of leveraging scarce resources. The companies included utilities, hospitals, shipyards, nursing homes, textile mills, health care facilities, insurers, retail chains, and paper mills. Freeman noticed, as Miles had earlier, that a great many of the companies on the list might go a long time between OSHA inspections under the normal procedures.

Yet even if Freeman had not been plagued by doubts about the payoff of standard enforcement techniques, his new assignment seemed beyond the bounds of the possible. The list contained far too many companies for his small staff to inspect. The goal of looking at the sources of the workers' compensation claims seemed sensible. But Freeman still had to respond to worker complaints at other firms. And even if he abandoned random inspections beyond the 200 target companies (and left the remaining 70 percent of the work force to fend for itself) it simply was not plausible that a handful of OSHA inspectors could root out the problems at all of these risk-prone firms. Moreover, what if there turned out to be major hazards—remember those grapes—where the lack of specific legal authority left OSHA with little power to force a fix? Freeman worried that the new assignment might mark an end to his reputation as a top enforcer.

But suppose there was another way to improve safety at the targeted firms—one that made better use of Freeman's small team of inspectors? What if, instead of dragging companies kicking and screaming down the path of compliance, OSHA could motivate voluntary safety improvements? Could the companies somehow be induced to deploy their own resources—including, crucially, the special expertise of managers and workers that no outsider could ever hope to match—in the service of safety improvements?

The Maine 200

Freeman and Coe decided to experiment with just such an approach, presenting the companies on the list with the opportunity to "choose your OSHA."[16] One choice, the targeted companies were told, was a standard inspection, with the citations and fines that normally follow. The other was for the firm to launch its own safety program, with OSHA experts operating more as health and safety consultants and less as health and safety cops. This may have been a bit of a bluff on Freeman and Coe's part; they would have been swamped if too many firms chose the first option. But, as it turned out, that did not happen. With only a handful of exceptions, the targeted firms—which came to be known as the Maine 200—opted for voluntary health and safety campaigns.

Beyond the prospect of a wall-to-wall inspection, there were other reasons the vast majority of companies were willing to participate. Many corporate safety officers relished the opportunity to design their own safety programs, and the "choose your OSHA" offer gave them the chance to make their case internally. Even many of the business people who railed against heavy-handed federal regulators had a grudging respect for OSHA's technical expertise. But in the past they had been reluctant to tap into that expertise, since letting an OSHA staffer in the door would trigger the "see it, cite it" routine and, almost inevitably, a torrent of fines and penalties. There was, of course, another reason for signing up: business people hate the bad morale and rising insurance costs associated with work-related injuries and illness. The "choose your OSHA" approach tapped a reservoir of latent willingness to get serious about workplace safety.

So began a whole new model of OSHA enforcement in Maine featuring a newly cooperative relationship between employers and OSHA, a relationship with more carrots, fewer sticks. Participating companies inspect their own premises for safety problems that include, but are not limited to, technical violations of OSHA rules. They write up and carry out an action plan to correct the problems, making mandatory progress reports to OSHA. Employees must be able to participate at all stages, and timetables are established for each obligation.

The assumption is that companies will stick to their plans, but the program is not premised on blind faith. Senior company executives attest to the truthfulness of any submissions to OSHA; criminal penalties are a possible consequence for filing false information. Random inspections are used to make sure that progress reports are accurate and that employees are being afforded the opportunity to participate. Random inspections are not used to root out code violations, but instead to verify adherence to the company's own safety plan. OSHA inspectors can set technical code requirements to the side and focus on helping a company eliminate its most serious problems—including those for which OSHA may not have any formal standards. Many OSHA officers welcome their new role. "It's a better use of our time," says one inspector. "We're finally getting the chance to be safety professionals."[17]

"Before, when OSHA came to our plant, we detained them at our gate and called our legal people," recalled Chet Manuel, an engineering project manager at a pulp and paper mill in Skowhegan. "Maine 200 gave us an excellent opportunity to work with OSHA as a friend."[18] The paper mill where Manuel worked was owned by S. D. Warren, whose management sat down with labor officials and agreed to establish health and safety steering committees and inspection teams that included many of the facility's employees. In six months, five in-house inspection teams found 18,000 violations, 300 of which were potentially life-threatening.[19] The human resource manager at S. D. Warren admitted, "By doing it (the inspections) ourselves, we were tougher" about identifying problems.[20]

This sentiment was echoed by many of the participants in Maine 200. "We fixed a lot of things OSHA inspectors would have walked right by," says Glenn Rondeau, the manager of safety services at Millinocket-based Great Northern Paper Co. Like other firms, the company organized and trained teams of employees to search for safety problems. They found thousands of them in the company's sawmill, hydroelectric dams, and paper mills, including deteriorating equipment and inadequate machine guards. And the company set about correcting them—with a $32 million price tag.[21]

Some businesses have introduced safety programs that include on-site visits from occupational and physical therapy experts. Therapists help L. L. Bean employees who have mild injuries stay on the job, and ergonomists design work stations that meet individual needs. The emphasis is not only on fixing that which has gone wrong in the past, but on preventing injuries in the future. Lewiston-based Cole-Haan has its own physical therapy room, with accompanying equipment and personnel. The firm reports a dramatic decrease in its annual workers' compensation costs.[22]

And Maine 200 has given new influence to safety advocates within businesses. Steve King (no, he's not *that* Stephen King of Maine, however much fun it may be to contemplate the notion), the human resource manager at New Balance, reports that Maine 200 helped him sell his ideas to the athletic-wear company. "We needed to justify our safety programs within New Balance, and OSHA helped."[23] And with senior management on board, OSHA officials are more confident that safety plans are actually being carried out. Of the nearly 450 monitoring visits conducted by late 1997, only three found employers acting in bad faith.[24]

The creation of Maine 200 was not met with universal acclaim, to be sure. Many in the labor community were initially concerned that a less combative relationship between OSHA and business would result in decreased vigilance on worker safety. Some of this early skepticism has evaporated as illness and injury rates drop. And the fact that employees have played such a crucial role in making their jobs safer has been important to winning labor support. "Our employees have become experts on what is and isn't safe," said a vice president from textile-maker Guilford of Maine.[25]

Some labor advocates remain unconvinced. "We're talking about really getting into the worst workplaces in the state and rewarding them for being the worst workplaces by giving them a second chance," scoffs Keith Mestrich, an AFL–CIO safety specialist.[26] But OSHA has not lost its teeth. In July of 1996, an egg producer that had been part of Maine 200 was fined more than $3.6 million by OSHA when inspectors found migrant workers living and working in squalid conditions. The publicity generated by the fine led several New England supermarket chains to boycott the company. And the terms of a 1997 settlement required the company to pony up $2 million in payments, hire an ergonomics consultant and a safety director, and employ an independent firm to verify compliance with regulations.[27] OSHA has not forgotten how to use its old moves when that is what the game calls for.

One obstacle to assuaging critics of Maine 200 has been the difficulties in reporting quantitative results. One seemingly obvious measuring stick would be the number of worker's compensation claims filed since the program's creation. But about the time Maine 200 was getting started, the state tightened the eligibility rules for workers' compensation, making before-and-after comparisons hazardous. Another factor complicating assessment of Maine 200 is the tendency of new safety programs to produce an initial surge of reported illnesses and injuries, thanks to increased awareness and decreased stigma, even if the underlying rate of workplace hazards declines.

But there are plenty of indications that the Maine experiment has made a difference. In 1995 alone, the 184 participants spent an estimated $100 million on safety investments for the 1,245 factories, mills, and farms where their 127,000 employees worked.[28] Seventy percent of these companies reduced their illness and injury rates, often by one-third or more.[29]

OSHA officials say they could never have engineered such far-reaching changes for so many employers in such a short period of time had they been confined to traditional enforcement methods. Consider: OSHA inspectors found 36,000 violations in Maine between 1983 and 1991. Under Maine 200, within a period less than half as long, participating companies found *180,000* violations—and quickly corrected more than 100,000 of them.[30] When the number of inspections and fines went down, the number of hazards found and fixed actually went up.

Maine is not the only state in search of new ways to prevent the workplace accidents that cost American businesses $112 billion each year.[31] And a massive increase in traditional enforcement is not in the cards. As Representative Christopher Shays acknowledged: "If it was ever true that OSHA could effectively inspect, monitor and improve safety conditions at all of the nation's workplaces, it is not a valid operational premise today."[32] Federal or state workplace-safety officials in fifteen states— from New Hampshire to California—quickly set out to adopt or adapt parts of the Maine 200 model, hoping they will be able to replicate some of the successes of that experiment.[33]

Leveraging OSHA's resources by catalyzing companies' capacity to find and fix their own workplace hazards is by no means a risk-free strategy. It could turn out that cooperative relationships between OSHA and business will end up making workers less safe, as some labor leaders warn. It could turn out that regulators will fail to follow through on the pledge to spare good actors from needless procedural burdens, as some managers fear. But the signs are that Maine is mapping a promising path for making a little OSHA go a long way.

Notes

1. Forster, Inc., news release, February 16, 1995.

2. Dan Wise, "An OSHA You Could Love," *Business & Health*, February 1996.

3. Secretary of Labor Robert Reich, Testimony, House Committee on Economic and Educational Opportunities, Subcommittee on Workforce Protections, June 28, 1995.

4. Secretary of Labor Robert Reich, Testimony, Senate Appropriations Committee, Labor Health and Human Services, Education and Related Agencies, Labor-HHS Budget Impasse, March 5, 1996.

5. Assistant Secretary of Labor Joseph Dear, Testimony, House Small Business Committee, July 26, 1995.

6. Michael J. Wright, Director of Health, Safety and Environment–United Steelworkers of America, Testimony, House Committee on Government Reform and Oversight, Subcommittee on Human Resources and Intergovernmental Relations, October 17, 1995.

7. "Common Sense Reinventing Government Is Hard to Dislike," *Columbus Dispatch* (editorial), May 16, 1996.

8. Philip K. Howard, *The Death of Common Sense* (New York: Warner Books, 1994), pp. 13–14.

9. David Maraniss and Michael Weisskopf, "The Hill May Be a Health Hazard for Safety Agency," *Washington Post*, July 23, 1995.

10. Russ Linden, "'Maine Top 200'—OSHA Shifts Its Focus from Regulations to Outcomes" (Charlottesville, Va.: Russ Linden & Associates, 1995).

11. State of Maine, "Occupational Injuries and Illnesses," Bureau of Labor Standards, 1990.

12. Harvey Simon, "Case Study: Regulatory Reform at OSHA," John F. Kennedy School of Government, 1996.

13. Ibid.

14. Ibid.

15. Meredith Falacci, "Maine's 'Top 200' Program," *Job Safety & Health Quarterly*, Fall 1993.

16. Simon, "Case Study: Regulatory Reform at OSHA."

17. Robert D. Behn, "Regulators to Consultants," *Government Executive*, November 1995.

18. "Cutting Workplace Injury and Illness" (editorial), *Chemical Engineering*, October 1995.

19. Behn, "Regulators to Consultants."

20. Innovations in American Government, 1995 Awards Program, Site Visit Report. A change of ownership at Warren has subsequently led to a retreat from the Maine 200 approach and safety problems have cropped up again, according to OSHA's Joel Sacks.

21. Mary Anne Lagasse, "Great Northern Safety Efforts Catch Federal Eye," *Bangor Daily News*, October 18, 1995.

22. Wise, "An OSHA You Could Love."

23. Innovations in American Government, 1995 Awards Program, Site Visit Report.

24. Memo from Joel Sacks of OSHA to Liz Rogers of the Council for Excellence in Government, October 1, 1997.

25. Mark A. Hofmann, "OSHA Touts Innovation in Maine," *Business Insurance*, October 9, 1995.

26. Ibid.

27. Hiawatha Bray, "Egg Farm to Pay $2 Million in Penalties," *Boston Globe*, May 20, 1997.

28. "Maine Top 200 Pilot Program," 1995 Annual Report, Occupational Safety and Health Administration, U.S. Department of Labor.

29. Assistant Secretary of Labor Joseph Dear, House Small Business Committee, July 26, 1995; memo from Joel Sacks to Liz Rogers.

30. Eric Blom, "OSHA Gets Award for New Safety Program," *Portland Press Herald*, October 27, 1995.

31. Secretary of Labor Robert Reich, Testimony, Senate Appropriations Committee, Labor Health and Human Services, Education and Related Agencies, Labor-HHS Budget Impasse, March 5, 1996.

32. Chairman Christopher Shays, Testimony, House Government Reform Committee, Human Resources and Intergovernmental Relations, October 17, 1995.

33. Acting Assistant Secretary of Labor for Occupational Safety and Health Administration, Gregory R. Watchman, Testimony, Senate Committee on Labor and Human Resources, Subcommittee on Public Health and Safety, July 10, 1997. In 1999 a federal court blocked OSHA from implementing a national version of Maine 200 without further review.

11

COLLABORATIVE STEWARDSHIP

THE 1974 BOOK (and subsequent movie) *The Milagro Beanfield War* portrays an embattled band of Hispanics in an arid and majestic western locale, fighting against autocratic government officials and greedy resort developers for access to the natural resources their livelihoods required. While there was a degree of artistic license in the way the story was told, it was rooted in a very real clash that occurred in the Camino Real Ranger District of the Carson National Forest in New Mexico.

The United States Forest Service (USFS)

While there was a centuries-long history of tension between citizens and government in New Mexico (as in other western states), Camino Real and local residents had in fact largely enjoyed a live-and-let-live relationship during the decades leading up to the incident depicted in the movie. U.S. Forest Service officials recognized that the local Hispanics and Native Americans had long regarded the forests bordering their villages as common lands, owned by all for the benefit of all. The locals depended on the National Forest for basics—including wood to build and heat their homes and cook their food—and considered open access to the forest a hallowed right. The Forest Service had accommodated this need by allowing residents to harvest the leavings from large commercial timber projects.

This chapter was researched and drafted by Kirsten Lundberg.

During the 1960s and 1970s, American society underwent a broad change in its attitude toward the environment. The Forest Service, however, did not alter its procedures to reflect the new passion for preservation or to make room for the locals' time-honored ways amid the new imperatives. By the 1990s, Camino Real was confronting an array of organizations with their own ideas of what environmental stewardship required. These new demands disrupted the equilibrium between the Forest Service and the people who lived around the Carson National Forest, precipitating a painful breakdown of the old modus vivendi. The large-scale timber projects on which the locals indirectly depended were tied up in lengthy and expensive court battles. Locals found themselves trapped in the middle, with little leverage over the Forest Service or the preservationists, cut off from the resources they required. The locals blamed Camino Real, and their relationship deteriorated into confrontation and rancor.

The Carson Forest Leadership Team, comprising district rangers, the forest supervisor, and staff, knew it had to devise a new approach to the difficulties besetting Camino Real—as well as other districts within Carson National Forest that were experiencing similar problems.

In 1996 an in-house brainstorming group known as the core team came to the forest leadership with a proposal. The team had developed a new strategy for ecosystem management that it thought would satisfy the growing number of Forest Service constituents. But the new approach depended heavily on collaboration and cooperation. It would need the right kind of leader to pull it off. Crockett Dumas, the ranger in the tense Camino Real district, volunteered to pilot the new model of cooperation. If he failed, Dumas knew it was only a matter of time before the cinematically picturesque landscape could erupt with very real-world ugliness.

Vast tracts of public land across the country (but especially in the West) are administered by the U.S. Forest Service. The Camino Real Ranger District comprises some 300,000 acres within the Carson National Forest, forty miles north of Santa Fe. Carson comprises 1.4 million acres of mountains, valley, and high grasslands, a substantial piece of public real estate. The Forest Service—the largest agency within the U.S. Department of Agriculture—employed 40,000 people nationwide in the early 1990s. Its mandate is to manage the nation's public lands—as its mission statement reads, "caring for the land and serving the people." The agency must maintain a delicate balance among historic, cultural, recreational, and environmental considerations, along with commercial uses of land and timber resources.

This means it wears a variety of hats, as environmental overseer, recreation director, and business manager. As environmentalist, the Forest Service is responsible for sustaining the quality of the forests by blocking the wrong kind of tree-cutting and orchestrating the right kind. Typically, the Forest Service contracts with the highest-bidding wood-products company to come into a selected segment of National Forest, harvest some trees for commercial sale, and clear the undergrowth. As recreation director, the USFS is in charge of leisure uses of the land, guiding hikers, campers, fishermen, hunters, and skiers to areas where they can pursue their activities without unduly degrading the land. Finally, the Forest Service is also a business. It is one of the few government agencies with products to sell—timber, mineral rights, and recreational services. For this reason, it is expected to generate revenue for the federal coffers rather than just spend taxpayers' dollars.

Like other western states, New Mexico has a long history of conflict over land and water rights, a history that still resonates today. The first settlers of the land that would become the Camino Real Ranger District were the Pueblos, who founded settlements more than a thousand years ago. Today the Picuris and Taos Pueblos remain as descendants of the once-dominant culture. Important archeological sites lie within the Carson National Forest. Native Americans, writes Carson Forest archeologist Maria Teresa Garcia, have a distinctive relationship with the land. "American Indian world view fostered then, as it does now," she writes, "a holistic sense of place and reliance upon one's surroundings. More important, it ascribed little difference between people and the natural world."[1] A similarly complex relationship with the land applies to the other major group of Camino Real residents—descendants of the Spanish colonists in Mexico who arrived around 1700. While the Spanish settlers recognized private property rights, they also created common lands outside their settlements, which all members of the community had the right to use for timber and game, water and pasture. These Spanish land-ownership arrangements were affirmed by Mexico when it achieved independence in the early 1800s.

During the Mexican-American war of 1848, the land changed hands yet again. After a hiatus of private ownership, the U.S. government took possession at the turn of the century. Government agencies, such as the Bureau of Land Management and the newly created Forest Service, became the local administrators. The Hispanic and Native American communities established earlier were absorbed into the national lands or continued to live on their borders. Their traditional reliance on the land

and their conception of common use endured. Some of the Hispanic residents, moreover, insisted that their ancestors' land grants remained valid and had been brushed aside illegitimately during the nineteenth century. Their conviction that much of the land within Carson was by rights *their* land exacerbated sensitivities about access to the forests.

The Camino Real district surrounds or abuts thirty-two unincorporated communities and two Native American pueblos with some 20,000 residents. For decades Camino Real and its neighboring Hispanic and Native American communities coexisted with only occasional episodes of antagonism. The residents of these remote mountain communities depended on the common lands established under Spanish colonial rule to sustain their families. Wood from the forests was critical to survival. Wood provided building materials for homes, farm buildings, and fences; it heated houses and fueled the wood-fired cooking stoves. Around two-thirds of the local population used wood for heating, and about a third cooked with wood. "You know what happens [in the city] when the electricity goes off for several days?" Camino Real Ranger Crockett Dumas explained. "Here, the electricity goes off, it's no big deal. But if you're out of firewood, you're hurting."[2]

Forest Service officials around Camino Real understood local attitudes toward the surrounding forests—after all, many of them, especially the less senior officials, were locals themselves. In a largely informal accommodation, the Forest Service had long allowed residents to go in after a commercial lumber harvest and help themselves to the "slash," or "dead and down"—the small wood products left behind. The residents had "free use" permits, which allowed them to collect the wood at no cost but their labor.

Benevolent as this arrangement may have been, it was clear who was in charge. Historically, Forest Service personnel—many of them trained as scientists—were "quite autocratic and authoritarian," says Dumas. Forest rangers were individually responsible for generating the plans governing forest use in their districts. In the 1960s and 1970s, this meant drawing up a "Multiple Use Area Guide" as mandated by the 1960 Sustained Use Multiple Yield Act. With the passage of the 1970 National Environmental Policy Act, rangers also had to prepare environmental assessments of any proposed project. The 1976 National Forest Management Act required elaborate "Forest Plans" with more ambitious environmental goals.[3] But the ranger worked alone. "He might ask a few questions," recalls Dumas, "but nobody else was really involved." After all, notes Dumas with a touch of irony, "we were the ones that had the education and the science. We knew what was good for the land, and we knew what was good for the people. This worked well for a long time."

From the 1960s to the 1980s, broader changes in American society began to have a practical impact on the Forest Service. Information technology took off and Forest Plans, for example, were transferred to computers. This proved time-consuming and hugely costly—the Carson Forest plan was finalized fully ten years after the legislation requiring it. But other challenges came from the outside. The same era that brought the computer into the mainstream also saw the arrival of environmental awareness and the emergence of activist groups such as the Sierra Club and the Wilderness Society.

In the Camino Real district, new kinds of people arrived, with new priorities for the land. Some lived in communes, replicating the locals' subsistence economics but pursuing a very different culture. Some of the newcomers were professionals who liked the rural life. Some arrived to settle (often as seasonal residents) in newly developed resort communities. The recreation industry boomed. Outfitters and guides suddenly became players in the local economy, with considerable political influence.

The Forest Service was unprepared for the cacophony of new interests demanding a role in what had been a technical planning exercise firmly controlled by USFS professionals. As the ranger tried to draft a Forest Plan for the district, dozens of interests fought for control of the pen, including a local group called Carson Forest Watch, the Forest Guardians in Santa Fe, the Southwest Forest Alliance, and a strong local chapter of the Sierra Club. Where a group was unsuccessful at influencing the plan, it often turned to the courts. Camino Real found itself pitted against a wide variety of groups, often hostile to one another—some wanted more commercial logging; others emphasized hunting and hiking; others celebrated pristine wilderness—but all were united on at least one point: resentment against the Forest Service. Reminisces Dumas:

> All of a sudden, there were a lot more people who wanted to use the National Forest. We'd been going along great here for years. In 1984, the Forest Service was recognized as one of the top ten business organizations in the United States. We were on top of the world. We had convinced people the world was flat and we were headed west. And about 1985, '86 we fell off the face of the earth. We lost a lot of respect.

By the 1980s, trouble erupted. USFS vehicles in the Carson Forest were vandalized. At one point, USFS personnel were advised to enter certain areas only when traveling in pairs. These incidents, while relatively minor in themselves, reawakened a healthy fear in those Forest Service employees who remembered an outbreak of real violence in the 1960s. That episode, during which the Penasco headquarters of Camino Real was bombed, had taught the USFS that it would pay a price if it came to be seen as an alien presence disrupting the local way of life.

These tensions came to a head with the announcement that Camino Real would issue a contract to remove some of the trees on 15,000 acres of land—the so-called Alamo-Dinner (A-D) parcel—to a major timber company. The parcel included ancestral land-grant areas long worked or grazed by the local residents. Under the terms of the commercial deal, most of the felled trees would go to the timber company. The locals would derive only minimal benefit from the project. With fewer and fewer large contracts going through—thanks in part to the increased litigation from environmental groups—it was becoming increasingly difficult for residents to obtain the wood products they needed.

In August 1988, the Forest Service scheduled a public meeting to discuss the A-D timber sale. The Service hoped that the meeting would be a formality, because the A-D project had already suffered significant delays since it was first proposed in 1986. Officials expected a turnout of a dozen people. But one Forest Service employee, concerned over the project design and the lack of community involvement, anonymously got the word out to local residents. More than 150 people arrived at the public gathering, which was forced by the overcrowding into the adjacent parking lot. Tempers ran hot. The crowd shouted down the Forest Service personnel as they tried to discuss the proposed project.

The public uproar captured wider attention, and the A-D project was sent back to the drafting table. Meanwhile, in February 1990, Camino Real acquired a new district ranger, Crockett Dumas. Dumas had been district ranger on the Avery Ranger District in the Idaho Panhandle National Forest. He took charge with the hope that he would be able to calm local fears and anxieties. Nonetheless, he says he had no idea what a hornet's nest he was walking into. "If I'd seen the video [of the Alamo-Dinner meeting] I probably wouldn't even have tried to get the job," Dumas recalls.

Listening

The regional leadership knew how difficult the situation had become at Camino Real. The Camino Real district office faced three overriding problems: a demoralized staff; bad relations with the community; and legal threats from environmentalists. Carolyn Bye, director of public affairs for the USFS regional office in Albuquerque, suggested to Dumas a novel way to improve at least one difficulty: mending relations with the community. She proposed conducting a door-to-door survey of area residents. Getting the staff out to meet with the locals promised both to provide a richer pool of information on what community priorities actually were and to reconnect Forest Service employees to the community. Early in 1991, the Camino Real staff of forty-two, including technicians, foresters, and wildlife biologists, got their marching orders to get out there and *listen*.

The staffers were not uniformly enthusiastic about the idea at first. (Their colleagues in other areas of the Carson Forest reinforced any preexisting reluctance by asking uncomfortable questions about how the staff would ensure their own safety.) Bye gave each staff member a pocket-sized card to carry, printed with the sentence, "I'm going to people's homes to listen." To downplay the official nature of the enterprise, personnel did not wear their uniforms (although they did travel in their distinctive green trucks). The Forest Service scientists and administrators sat at kitchen tables over countless cups of coffee and discussed the problems of individual residents. They visited nearly 1,500 homes. Gradually, with each mundane human encounter, Forest Service staffers and local residents gained a better understanding of each others' histories, goals, dreams, and anxieties. Max Cordova, head of the local Truchas Land Grant environmental group, says the survey "was a movement in a new direction. Basically, the people had always come to the Forest Service and the Forest Service had acted from a position of authority. By the Forest Service's going to the people, I think it started a new system of management."[4]

In the past, a small number of groups had represented themselves as the voices of the overall community. What the survey revealed was that the range of views within the community was in fact much wider than the Forest Service had ever before been able to uncover. The Penasco Area Community Association, for example, developed a new relationship with Camino Real as a result of the survey. The Forest Service team was gratified, if not surprised, that the survey uncovered a diversity of community voices. Indeed, Dumas later acknowledged that a subsidiary objective of the survey was "to show these other people that they really didn't speak for the community." The community at large, it became clear, did not so much object to the Alamo-Dinner project in itself as to the prospect of diminished access to the firewood and other resources on which they depended.

So A-D was redesigned to accommodate the newly recognized local priorities. This did not deter one environmental organization, with few apparent community ties, from appealing the project all the way to the chief of the Forest Service. But a decision to proceed was upheld and, in October 1991, Alamo-Dinner got under way after a five-year delay. In the event, the Forest Service harvested 5 and one-half million board-feet of timber out of the parcel, the same amount that had been projected in 1986. While some of it still went to a timber company as had been specified in the original plan, most of the wood went to the community for fuel, *vigas* (house logs), and other "personal use" forest products.

Dumas, for one, felt the whole Alamo-Dinner experience had yielded an important, if somewhat uncomfortable, lesson: large-scale timber sales, while cost effective, could be counterproductive where relations with the community were concerned. But for the moment, he could see no alternative. Orchestrating large timber sales was the only routine on the table for governance of the forests. As one insider put it: "The learning curve was slow and the next several planned timber sales reverted to business as usual."[5]

In June 1992, Camino Real published an initial notification ("scoping letter") of plans to sell timber in the La Cueva parcel, a 9,500-acre area in the Rio Pueblo watershed. It proved controversial, guaranteeing delays and frustration. La Cueva, in its early days, had ominous similarities to an earlier sale called Ojos-Ryan. The Forest Service had first proposed a timber sale on the Ojos-Ryan parcel of 11,595 acres in the Rio Grande del Rancho watershed in May 1990. But the project was tied up for three years by appeals under the National Environmental Policy Act, and only in December 1993 was the district able to proceed with the sale. Similarly, in August 1993, Camino Real submitted a draft environmental impact statement for a proposed timber sale in what was known as the Angostura analysis area. Public response was overwhelmingly against every alternative, and Dumas dropped the proposal.

The Carson Forest leadership decided it was time to reexamine USFS policy on large-scale timber sales. It had created in 1994 a core team, whose assignment was to speed up the environmental analysis process for large timber sales. Now the leadership asked the four-person core team to analyze the La Cueva project. In February 1995, the La Cueva project was dropped from further study when the core team concluded that it was not only draining Camino Real staff resources, but that it would not help the community obtain wood products nor improve forest conditions. But core team recommendations did not stop there. The exercise of reviewing La Cueva had inspired the team to explore how it might design a wholly new procedure for forest management that could serve the communities, the Forest Service employees, and the needs of the forest.

The fresh thinking was well timed. It was clear that the escalating hostilities among the local residents, environmental groups, and the Forest Service had resulted in the worst possible world for all parties. Forest Service employee morale was at an all-time low. Trying to develop proposed projects forced staff members to invest hundreds of hours in environmental analysis, only to be confronted once they were done with huge loads of paperwork associated with appeals and litigation. Popular feelings ran high against the Forest Service, not only in Camino Real but throughout Region Three, comprising New Mexico and Arizona.

At least as upsetting to the staff members was their awareness that they were not accomplishing their bottom-line goal of keeping the forest in good shape. The Camino Real region was not virgin forest. During the early part of the twentieth century, heavy logging of the district for railroad ties, plus intensive livestock grazing, had virtually denuded many of the area's original old-growth forests. But as new growth emerged in the ravaged areas, the trees came in so densely that individual shoots struggled to compete for available water and sunshine. The trees were stunted and unhealthy. Max Cordova of Truchas Land Grant says the land was able to support 120 trees per acre; but density in the Carson had reached 1,200 trees per acre. Forest fires were not unusual—and were costly to contain. Area streams had run dry because the trees each absorbed from twelve to twenty gallons of water a day and, because of their unnatural density, took all the water.

Within Camino Real, more than 200,000 acres required thinning. Moreover, the monogrowth—similar varieties of trees growing on broad tracts of land—affected wildlife. Ben Kuykendall, the district wildlife biologist, explained that with dense stands of mostly identical trees, the forest becomes like a desert for wildlife. Without variety, animals must forage over many more acres to find the food they require. As a result, many species leave the area altogether. Wildlife diversity plummets.

Local residents found themselves the victims of the tension between the USFS and the environmentalists. Max Cordova likens the stand-off to a neighborhood brawl.

> It was like two kids on the block—the Forest Service on one side and the environmental community on the other. The new kid on

the block, the environmental community, was telling the Forest Service, "You don't know what you're doing." And the old kid on the block was saying to the environmental community: "You're overreacting. You don't know what *you're* doing." As a result, there was a stalemate.

As the Carson Forest timber projects were held up in litigation, local communities found themselves cut off from their wood supplies. Camino Real officials, in their efforts to cope with the legal challenges, initially gave short shrift to local priorities. Cordova recalls that the Forest Service limited the number of free use permits issued to residents—despite the clear benefits of thinning the forests. On occasion, 200 people would stand in line from 2 a.m. to receive what turned out to be an allocation of fifty permits. Remarks Cordova: "What we thought was, if you had 200 people lined up, there should be permits for 200 people. Because there was work that needed to be done in the forest. If we got the people involved, we could thin out those trees and the people could use the product in return to heat their homes and build their homes and stuff."

The community was also angry with the Forest Service because there was almost no "dead and down" to be had, thanks to controlled burns of the forests. Instead, residents were allowed to cut greenwood, which required at least three months to dry before use.

Matters came to a head in 1995, when an environmental group called Forest Guardians led a coalition seeking a court injunction to block the taking of all timber from the National Forest on the grounds that the logging imperiled wildlife habitats. The U.S. District Court granted the injunction and, in August 1995, prohibited indefinitely all tree cutting in any of the national forests within Region Three. Subsistence users fell under the same prohibition as commercial loggers.

This was a potential calamity for the Camino Real residents. Local leaders, including members of the Truchas Land Grant, met informally with environmental groups, asking them to have their lawyers lift the injunction and substitute a new one that would recognize time-honored subsistence uses. Couldn't the locals be left out of the fight between loggers and environmentalists by making an exception for cooking and heating fuel? But the coalition of environmentalists proved unwilling to complicate their legal strategy by making such an exception. As fall turned the high elevations chilly and winter loomed, the Hispanic and Native American communities warned that their wood supplies were inadequate to get them through the season.

As the Camino Real staff scrambled to shield the locals from becoming innocent victims of the legal skirmish, the Carson Forest core team set out to lower the odds that this kind of impasse would happen again. Spurred on by the stalemate imposed by the court injunction, the core team proposed a new formula for ecosystem management. As the core team saw it, the problem with current project design and analysis was that the USFS put all its eggs in one basket. Or, to use the metaphor the team crafted, "we loaded everything up in a large dump truck and drove down the highway. If there were any roadblocks, everything came to a halt." The team's goal, says core team member John Shibley, became to "get out of the dump truck and get into sports cars—a lot of them. If some got stopped, so be it; others got through."[6] The core team proposed a simpler planning process, one that would develop solutions through collaboration rather than confrontation. The Forest Service's own employees, the team pointed out, were an untapped source of expertise and ideas. In late 1995, Dumas agreed to let them try out their ambitious concept at Camino Real.

In January 1996, in the Camino Real Penasco office, the core team brought together every one of the district employees. They pledged to keep at it until the group had devised a workable formula. This marked the first time that Camino Real employees below the level of ranger were involved in planning. The staff spent two weeks intensively brainstorming. They discussed all they knew about the forest—its history, its communities, its ecosystem. Many employees were also long-time local residents. Front office staffers Suzie Romero and Evelyn Gallegos, the "voice of the Forest Service" in Camino Real, added considerable community perspective. Henry Lopez, a local resident and Camino Real staff member, adds: "I live with these people. I realize how hard their lives can be. I will be buried with them." Wilbert Rodriquez, another resident-employee, regularly contributed "Wilbert's words of wisdom," says core team member Audrey Kuykendall. "He cut right to the chase and wrapped up what all were saying."[7]

The core team posed four questions to guide the process:

—What are existing conditions in the 300,000 acres of the Camino Real Ranger District?

—What would desired future conditions look like?

—How do we get from here to there?

—What are the priorities for the next five years?

The staff began by taking a big-picture view of the district. They formally identified four elements: ecosystem management units, social influence zones, existing conditions, and desired conditions. The social influence zones were a new concept in forest planning. The zones reflected historic and contemporary claims and uses of the forest and abutting land. Laid out in a map format, planners were able to see where social concerns overlaid other, more conventional resource needs related to watershed, wildlife habitat, and ecosystem conditions. Combining these four elements in a single plan helped target projects (to improve forest health and provide forest products) where they were needed most: at the points of greatest disparity between actual and desired conditions.

Never before had the Forest Service so explicitly engaged the question "why here and why now?"—for themselves or for the public. Putting aside the formal hierarchy, the staff took a vote on the most important work facing Camino Real over the next five years. Throughout this process, Dumas took a back seat, playing a subtler leadership role than his predecessors. Explains Forest Planner Carveth Kramer: "Now the ranger sat in the group, just as another employee—listening to what was being said. He was spending less time talking and more time listening to what his employees told him about the forest and the communities. This was a team process."[8]

By March 1996, Camino Real had ready a draft of the new ecosystem management plan. Then they sought comments from any and all parties concerned about the future of the National Forest. Their questions, says Kramer, included: "This is what we have heard from you and this is what we intend to do. Does this make sense to you? Any suggestions?"[9] Instead of holding meetings to discuss the resulting suggestions, Forest Service agents took all interested members of the community, from farmers to hunters to skiers to environmentalists, out into the forests to look at the areas they were talking about. "This 'at the Round Table' stuff doesn't work," according to Dumas. "You meet at the table, and you can go round and round forever. It's actually getting out on the ground" that produces results.

For Max Cordova and the nonprofit Truchas Land Grant, this new approach was welcome—if long overdue. Truchas had been promoting better communication with the Forest Service for years. Truchas contributed constructive comments on the plan and encouraged others to do likewise. Individual citizens also had their say. The final blueprint reflected many rounds of talks and abundant compromises. "We incorporated the public to where they had ownership in what was going on," summarizes Dumas. "They felt like they were part of the decisionmaking process."

The team initially called its novel planning procedure ecosystem management. But Forest Service officials in Washington told the Camino Real team that what they had stumbled on was really collaborative stewardship. That label was just fine with the team members. Whatever it was called, the core of the change was a shift from an "authoritarian, autocratic type management to more convening and facilitating," in Dumas's words. "Instead of me, the great authoritarian ranger, saying this is good for you, this is what we're going to do, we turned that around. What that did is it let the community have its say, and it got the [nonmanagerial] employees involved, two key things that had never happened."

By the time the court lifted its injunction against timber harvesting in December 1996, sixteen months after the ban had been imposed, Camino Real was ready to run with collaborative stewardship.

With the plan in hand, local people proved willing to help the Forest Service with its mission of safeguarding the health of the Carson Forest. Instead of paying contractors $150–$200 an acre to thin overgrown forest, for example, residents were systematically invited in to harvest the trees for firewood. After initial thinning, the leftover slash was carefully burned to improve the forest ecology. From 1996 to 1998, Camino Real sponsored six forest health projects, which yielded more than 3,000 cords of wood to local residents.

The Forest Service was no longer working alone to produce such results. District forester Carol Holland, for example, began to train the Picuris Pueblos in skills that would preserve the forest. Before collaborative stewardship, a Forest Service employee would grab a chainsaw and shovel and head for the woods to do what thinning or other task needed doing. Once collaborative stewardship was in place, Holland taught the Pueblos to do the thinning themselves. This provided income to the community, and it strengthened the tie between the people and the land. Says Holland: "We are discovering that when we work together and both understand the reasons for doing things, we both grow and understand the needs of the forest better."[10]

Instead of establishing a formal administrative procedure, there evolved a wide range of formal and informal ways to trigger the collaborative stewardship process. Camino Real invited initiatives from any interested party—a small rancher wanting to improve his grazing allotment, a large forest products company in search of timber, a native community protecting an archeological site. Moreover, following their instincts that formal meetings were often a waste of time, staff members substituted monthly "ranger's day out" field trips. All who wanted to participate in forest planning were invited to hike together through the forest parcel in question. As they walked, they discussed such topics as tree health, undergrowth density, fire hazards, water supply, and wildlife. The walks changed the social and political dynamics of a project, bringing together—outdoors and on the ground—timber-company representatives, environmental activists, and local residents.

Collaborative stewardship allowed the Forest Service to build cooperative relationships with a wide range of local groups. One of these was the nonprofit Forest Trust, which had long promoted environmentally conscious resource management. Camino Real also won over the Rio Pueblo–Rio Embudo Watershed Protection Coalition, whose members were once outspoken adversaries of the Forest Service. The Santa Fe chapter of the Sierra Club joined with the Forest Service in working with those who graze their animals on National Forest lands to minimize the impact on fragile ecosystems.

The new planning process led to joint ventures between the Forest Service, local entrepreneurs, and community groups. Together the Forest Service and the Truchas Land Grant won a small grant in May 1997 to start the Truchas Community Forest Products Yard. The yard harvested and marketed small-diameter trees from the National Forest, using local labor. That same month, the Picuris Pueblo won another grant of $12,000 to inventory the natural resources on Pueblo land and to establish a trained crew to evaluate vegetation and watershed improvement projects, including those planned for National Forest land. In November 1997, Camino Real won a Forest Management Program Reinvention Pilot Project grant to implement a three-year stewardship contract jointly with the Truchas Community Forest Products Yard, the Picuris Pueblo, and Forest Trust to improve forest health through projects that would contract with local businesses.

Collaborative stewardship could also point to more conventional measures of success. The Forest Service regularly measures volume of timber harvested per district. For 1998, Camino Real's lumber harvesting target was 2.4 million board-feet. But using collaborative stewardship, the district actually produced 5.1 million board-feet. Furthermore, this was accomplished despite a cutback of 60 percent in the district's personnel since 1991, from forty-two to seventeen employees.

Camino Real and the USFS regional leadership were aware, however, that collaborative stewardship had a cost. Although the district still had a forest plan, it had traded a focus on large-scale, money-making projects for reduced sales on parcels as small as ten acres. The district was no longer generating the revenues it had under standard forest plans. For example, the outstanding 1998 lumber harvest went largely toward personal uses, which garnered little revenue compared with the commercial timber sales of earlier years. Promoting community cooperation does not necessarily produce significant revenue for the U.S. Treasury, and the budget system still tied funding to results as measured by revenues. "This makes sense," wrote a Camino Real spokesperson, "if you are in the business of selling a product. It creates problems when you are in a stewardship role, maintaining a healthy, fully functioning ecosystem."[11]

But collaborative stewardship yielded other rewards that the Forest Service budget officers would be more likely to appreciate. Since 1993 no Camino Real small forest ecosystem project had been challenged or appealed. The savings in court costs and staff time were significant. By turning its attention from large timber sales to small forest improvement projects, the Forest Service fostered good relations with the community and helped the ecosystem—but also helped the local economy. Instead of sending value-added timber work out of the community, small family businesses did the logging, generating jobs and income. The economic benefits showed up less on the ledger of Forest Service revenues and more in the form of local economic vitality.

In addition, Camino Real discovered early ecological dividends from collaborative stewardship. Instead of allowing loggers to "treat" or remove a large proportion of trees as before, Camino Real started insisting on a more selective approach. Individual tree-harvesting parcels became smaller. The wildlife began to return as other types of vegetation had a chance to take root and grow. Elk, for example, were on the increase.

Collaborative stewardship affected Camino Real staff's working relationships and routines as well. Kuykendall, the wildlife biologist, and Lopez, the forester, redefined how they do their jobs. Instead of the forester's marking trees for harvest, with the biologist submitting comments afterward, the two men turned to surveying the forest together. Now it was often Kuykendall who suggested the areas to cut, while Lopez's skills helped make it happen. The two men also cleared acre-sized openings in the forest, which allowed for the growth of grasses and browse for animals. "These become the grocery stores for wildlife," Kuykendall notes. "The deer will be able to have lunch without walking all day searching for something to eat."[12]

The district found it could apply the collaborative strategies of its forest programs to other activities as well. In 1997, Camino Real completed nine wildlife and fisheries projects, including prescribed burns, reseeding, and restoration of native fisheries without appeal or litigation. Collaborative stewardship principles were also used in reducing wildfire hazards near urban forest communities. Two hundred homeowners in three communities agreed to controlled "fuel-reducing" blazes near their houses once they understood how that would protect them against major fires. A dispute over whether skiers could bring their dogs along on USFS trails was resolved according to collaborative stewardship principles of cooperation and discussion among the interested parties rather than the old-style method of arm's-length advocacy by competing interests culminating in top-down decisions.

The program's reputation spread quickly beyond Camino Real. Customers wanting personal-use forest products proved willing to drive more than 100 miles, past other Forest Service offices, to do business in the Camino Real Ranger District. The customers seemed eager to support a program with a reputation for working with the community to promote the environmental health of the Carson Forest. In 1997, Camino Real and the core team won a "Hammer Award," a trophy for successful government reinvention, from Vice President Al Gore.

This approach found its ultimate vindication in the sense of involvement residents acquired in Forest Service projects. Citizens who had bridled at the top-down large-scale forest projects proved eager to implement "their" plan. The new approach yielded an unquantifiable sense of civic engagement. Understanding the biological necessity of thinning stands of trees, for example, allowed residents to take personal satisfaction in seeking out unhealthily overgrown areas when harvesting the wood they needed. As a Camino Real publication put it: "The people now feel like they are a part of accomplishing something good for the Forest instead of just taking something from it." Max Cordova puts it simply: "It's very easy to point out problems. It's much harder to find solutions to those problems. That is the biggest [accomplishment of] the collaborative stewardship program between the Forest Service and the communities—that there was a problem-solving technique."

The Forest Service workers at Camino Real insist they did not set out to develop an innovative program. The team simply wanted to do its job—keep the forest healthy, give the locals a chance to stay warm in the winter, and steer clear of lawsuits and ugly scenes. The result was collaborative stewardship, an approach that worked, says Kramer, not least because of the public willingness to pitch in and make it effective. "Without the public," comments Kramer, "none of this would have worked.

Their willingness to get involved and expand their understanding is key. This story is about ordinary people in the community who became true leaders."[13] In graphic recognition of the community contribution, the core team presented its vice presidential Hammer Award to community leaders. The plaque hangs in the Truchas Land Grant office.

Notes

1. Maria Teresa Garcia, "Traditional Use of Pinon-Juniper Woodland Resources," address to symposium on Managing Pinon-Juniper Ecosystems for Sustainability and Social Needs, April 26–30, 1993, Santa Fe, N.M. Garcia is assistant forest archeologist with the U.S. Forest Service in Carson Forest.

2. Interview with Crockett Dumas, January 11, 1999. All further quotes from Dumas, unless otherwise attributed, are from this interview.

3. The 1976 act was an amendment to the 1974 Forest and Rangeland Renewable Resources Planning Act.

4. Interview with Max Cordova, February 18, 1999. All further quotes from Cordova, unless otherwise attributed, are from this interview.

5. Innovations in American Government, 1998 Awards Program, semifinalist application, p. 6.

6. Ibid.

7. Letter from Carveth Kramer, January 1999.

8. Ibid.

9. Ibid.

10. Ibid.

11. Innovations in American Government application.

12. Letter from Kramer.

13. Ibid.

12

REFORGING THE COMMUNITY CONNECTION

I N THE MINDS OF many Americans, paperwork and bureaucracy are the leitmotifs of the federal government. Virtually anyone who has been involved with a federal program—as a beneficiary or, even more so, as a worker or manager—harbors memories of dense thickets of documentation and Byzantine procedures. Coordination among programs, moreover (even programs with overlapping missions), is widely seen as one of Washington's weak suits. Even if every piece of red tape, when traced back to its origins, revealed a defensible or indeed indispensable motive, each encounter with bureaucratic complexity would still take a toll on the citizenry's esteem for the federal government.

Community Planning and Development (CPD)

This stereotype has often been invoked in reference to the sprawling Department of Housing and Urban Development (HUD), not least its Office of Community Planning and Development. This office is the nexus of an array of related but separate missions, pursued by a long list of public and private entities entwined in complex and shifting alliances. As the menu of HUD–administered programs lengthened over time, CPD evolved into an applications clearinghouse for many of these programs. Until recently, communities looking for assistance to help the homeless,

---

This chapter was researched and drafted by Kirsten Lundberg.

for example, or to promote urban redevelopment or build affordable housing, had to apply to separate programs, following inconsistent application formats and funding cycles, to tap each stream of federal support.

As Vice President Al Gore launched his "reinventing government" crusade in 1993, newly appointed HUD Secretary Henry Cisneros set out to explore how his department could get on board the reinvention bandwagon. A preliminary survey persuaded Cisneros that HUD's effectiveness was hampered and its reputation tarnished by the barriers of paperwork and bureaucracy that walled the agency off from the citizenry. HUD was widely seen by those it was meant to serve as a distant, forbidding domain.

Andrew Cuomo, who had just been confirmed as HUD's Assistant Secretary for Community Planning and Development, came to the job determined to make his mark by reestablishing communication (and thereby, eventually, trust) between HUD and the citizens and localities it dealt with. Cuomo championed a campaign to change the way CPD did business whose motto was "Putting People First." (The motto, echoing the title of the official Clinton-Gore campaign book, may have gained in memorability what it sacrificed in originality.) Beginning in March 1993, CPD launched an in-depth review of its program goals and procedures. The presumption was that CPD's diffuse institutional malaise would require a range of remedies, targeted to community complaints. Cuomo focused on a refreshingly direct question posed to the office's "customers": How could CPD do a better job? CPD officials fanned out from Washington to interview clients in state and local programs, asking them what they wanted from the department. The reinvention effort devoted special attention to exploiting the potential of new information technologies. The rationale was straightforward: to the extent paper was part of the problem, the emerging alternatives to old-fashioned paperwork ought to be part of the solution. The two core questions—What are clients' priorities? How can information technology help?—dominated the internal review.

As answers to both questions began to crystallize, an unglamorous but compelling common theme emerged: comprehensive planning. HUD officials and local program directors found they shared the view that better, more effective targeting was impossible unless communities were allowed—and expected—to evaluate their needs and resources from an integrated point of view. To accomplish that would, however, require a reexamination of CPD's mission, its culture, and its procedures. It would mean undoing years of HUD–CPD practices.

The Department of Housing and Urban Development is one of the federal government's smaller cabinet agencies—with fewer than 10,000 employees—but its mission is more complex than its size might suggest. Its Office of Community Planning and Development alone administers around $8 billion annually in federal grants to communities nationwide. CPD programs affect millions of people who live in subsidized housing, who are fighting AIDS, or who are homeless. Over the years, the four major enterprises within CPD's jurisdiction had each evolved into its own programmatic parallel universe. These programs were HOME investment partnerships, community development block grants (CDBG), emergency shelter grants, and housing for people with AIDS (HOPWA). Each operated autonomously, with separate authorizing statutes, regulations, staff, professional orientation, constituencies, counterpart agencies at the state and local levels, grant cycles, application processes, planning requirements, and reporting procedures. To receive funding from these programs, HUD mandated twelve separate planning, application, and reporting documents. This meant that a local government doing business with HUD might have to produce 1,000 pages of federal forms or more each year.

Beyond the wear and tear the paperwork burden inflicted on local government's good will toward HUD, these parallel processes also stymied efforts to forge coherent strategies at the local level. Program-specific regulations made it hard for localities to link their housing and community development activities, for example, or to coordinate either category with services for the homeless.

Despite the massive documentation required, moreover, it proved frustratingly difficult for federal administrators to judge whether the CPD–funded programs were successful, by the ultimate metric of better lives for citizens. Simple numbers—of applications processed, housing units constructed, clients encountered—all these could be, and were, counted and recorded. But the information generated by CPD documentation was usually too coarse, and too inconsistent in its format, to support any nuanced assessment of a program's impact. Critics said the federal government cared only about process, and nothing for performance. But the problem was subtler. The stewards of federal funding, aware that they were poorly equipped to monitor real-world impacts, focused on procedure in the hopes that fastidious processes would serve as a proxy for effective performance. But the substitute all too often proved flawed.

For their part, the state and local recipients of federal funds lamented the tangle of red tape. Most muddled through, coping with the requirements as best they could. Some jurisdictions—frustrated and angered by what they considered unreasonable restrictions imposed by federal regulations—simply broke the rules and hoped they would not get caught. A very few policy entrepreneurs assembled funds from a variety of sources to create integrated programs in spite of the procedural impediments. But these enterprising individual efforts were, not surprisingly, rare. More commonly the procedural fragmentation had predictable consequences. Communities received more funding than they needed for some categories of operations and too little for others. Substance abusers among the homeless might have access to abundantly funded services, while the mentally ill homeless went underserved. Or the reverse.

This multilayered and regulation-bound system imposed costs in several different currencies. The most obvious burden was the equipment, staff, and material devoted to paper processing. But subtler costs may have been more serious. The lack of coherence in HUD grant programs discouraged careful planning and offered ready excuses for muddle at the local level, frustrating good managers and shielding bad ones. The most pervasive cost, perhaps, came in the form of diminished citizen involvement. The complexity of the procedures made it nearly impossible for anyone—from mayors to city council members to ordinary citizens—to understand how individual programs operated or how they interconnected. As the programs became less comprehensible, both accountability and public support eroded. This was the spiral of institutional dysfunction that Assistant Secretary Cuomo, with the vigorous support of Secretary Cisneros, set out to disrupt.

Cuomo was exasperated that even as every commentator trumpeted the information age, HUD remained for many Americans as bafflingly inaccessible as some bureau from the days of quill pens. HUD's mission, moreover, was more directly centered on service to the citizen than other departments, such as Defense or Interior, making its communications shortcomings all the more lamentable. When citizens can interact with their banks through ATMs on virtually any street corner, their expectations for institutional accessibility and responsiveness escalate. What excuse could there be for government to remain aloof? As Cuomo put it: "The burden is on government to speak the citizen's language, not require the citizens to learn our acronyms or read 1,000-page documents. This means we must give information in the way other institutions do— quick, informative, concise. On computer, in the home."[1]

Consolidating programs could catalyze that process. But consolidation alone was too narrow a strategy, as CPD knew from its own experience. Over and over, in the past decades, HUD had been the battleground for campaigners brandishing the banner of consolidation. Two waves of "new federalism," one during Richard Nixon's presidency and a second during the Reagan administration, combined individual programs into broader block grants. The goal was to restore greater discretion over programs and spending to the local level, reducing programmatic clutter, easing evaluation, and augmenting accountability. Prominent among these earlier consolidation efforts was the 1974 community development block grant (CDBG) program. The CDBG swept together a wide variety of single-purpose grant programs that had sprung up since the 1954 Housing Act. Yet as experience with CDBG accumulated, concerns intensified that the block grants suffered from purposes that were too broadly defined, diffuse measures of success, and monitoring procedures too feeble to enforce accountability.

The block grant reforms depended on integrated planning at the local level, but they included few provisions to promote such planning. Indeed, HUD had retreated over time from its efforts to encourage comprehensive strategies. Before CDBG, communities could draw on so-called 701 planning grant funds.[2] But that program was phased out by 1981 as CDBG expanded. In line with the themes of local discretion and restricted federal meddling, the block grants required only two planning documents—a citizen participation plan demonstrating how citizen input was sought and used; and a community development plan. The citizen participation plan was widely regarded as a bureaucratic nuisance, and its recommendations were rarely followed. There were no criteria for what the community development plan should contain, and so it was not even submitted to HUD for approval. Federal micromanagement remained out of fashion. But the presumption that local officials would spend federal funds efficiently and accountably, if only they were left alone, appeared flawed as well.

Decades of disappointing efforts to address the problems of distressed communities had promoted something approaching consensus that urban problems had to be attacked in a coordinated way. Isolated programs targeting homelessness, housing, and economic and community development had not worked. Nor had it proven realistic to expect local officials to do the coordination on their own, in the face of HUD procedures that neither required nor encouraged coordination. The concept of comprehensive planning was given new vitality with the 1990 Cranston-Gonzalez Affordable Housing Act, which reestablished some federal responsibility for monitoring state and local authorities' spending of federal dollars. Among other things, the Housing Act required a comprehensive housing affordability strategy (CHAS) from jurisdictions taking part in the HOME program. CPD issued regulations for HOME in 1991, and some 400 jurisdictions submitted a CHAS in 1992.

When Cuomo took over CPD in 1993, he judged the CHAS concept a sound one, but he felt it did not go far enough. If it made sense to ask communities to demonstrate that their housing policies hung together in a rational way, why not solicit an integrated strategy for all CPD–financed programs? But, wary of simply triggering a new cycle in the ever-shifting tide of HUD paperwork requirements, Cuomo went one step further: why not have just one planning document to cover all the programs? This single form, which might be called, simply enough, a consolidated plan, could inform the whole array of CPD services.

However appealing this might be in principle, Cuomo knew that he could not implement such a change overnight. He would have to enlist the support of HUD employees, customers, and overseers alike. Cuomo decided to begin with the customers. His first step was to solicit suggestions from those who would be asked to produce, and then to use, such a planning document. Unless it was taken seriously and, more to the point, seen as useful at the local level, a consolidated plan would quickly degenerate into pro-forma paperwork. Once suggestions from the field began to coalesce into a reform proposal, Cuomo could worry about selling the new procedures internally.

CPD launched nationwide consultations with local and state agency representatives in March 1993. The meetings continued for nine months, into December. Conferences were held with more than 10,000 individuals and groups, while nearly 1,000 state and local governments also had their say. The regional hearings uncovered deep-seated dissatisfaction with HUD rules and procedures. This unhappiness, unfortunately, did not suggest any uniform mandate for change. Indeed congressional committees, executive branch program specialists, and interest groups that had helped construct the separate programs or insert procedural requirements had a vested interest in their continuation. One person's red tape is another's vital safeguard; common-sense consolidation can feel like a simple loss if your program is the one losing its independent status. Cuomo's early soundings of Congress yielded little promise that lawmakers would endorse statutory changes to promote a comprehensive approach to program application and reporting procedures. For their part, Washington-based interest groups objected to giving up regulatory requirements that served to protect their concerns.

Meanwhile, as word spread within the agency that far-reaching procedural changes were under consideration, resistance surfaced in several quarters. CPD headquarters staff in Washington who administered the separate programs were often unenthusiastic about any reforms that might water down requirements and diminish their own influence. Nor were field officers uniformly happy at the prospect of new procedures. However unremarkable it may seem to ask local officials how they plan to use grant money, this notion clashed with an entitlement mentality within some precincts at HUD, which resisted the idea of making federal assistance conditional on submission of a plan. This sentiment could arise from quite different biases. Some whose views were formed in the Great Society era felt that the more resources deployed against urban ills the better, with few questions asked. New federalism enthusiasts within the bureaucracy felt local officials should not have to convince the feds that their plans made sense. There was also the inevitable bureaucratic reluctance to complicate life by coordinating with other offices on a comprehensive approach.

To help convert internal and external skeptics, Cuomo and his like-minded deputies assembled working groups composed of local or at-large representatives of relevant interest groups (rather than delegates from the national office), workers from HUD's field offices, and senior headquarters staff. The task forces were charged with cutting across programmatic boundaries to map out what kinds of data would be generically useful. Field staff members, who were used to dealing with a broad range of issues, proved to have greater influence on the evolving policy than headquarters staff members, who were more accustomed to thinking in terms of segmented programs. Once the HUD leadership was convinced of what should and should not be included in a comprehensive plan, the new procedures were formalized administratively—rather than attempting to get Congress to write new legislation—and Cuomo's attention turned to promoting the revised approach to HUD grant recipients and other constituencies.

Procedural changes implied a good deal of painstaking, unglamorous organizational rewiring. For example, Cuomo established a single data processing unit within the newly created Office of Executive Services to support the new planning system. The Office had line authority over CPD employees in the field, allowing comments and concerns from those dealing with HUD customers to be quickly incorporated into the new system design. As the original working groups disbanded at the end of the start-up phase, their functions were shifted to a consolidated planning task force with day-to-day responsibility for implementation.

Cuomo hosted a national conference in March 1994 to launch CPD's new consolidated planning process. Among the guests were Vice President Gore, cabinet officers, and more than 2,000 community leaders. At the Washington, D.C., conference, CPD distributed draft guidelines and a new publication, *From Vision to Reality*, making the case for an integrated planning system and explaining how CPD could work with communities to ease the transition.

A Consolidated Plan

The basic idea of the consolidated plan was to radically simplify procedures for tapping the funding streams flowing through CPD. These included the four flagship enterprises—HOME, CDBG, emergency shelter grants, and HOPWA—as well as empowerment zones and enterprise communities, and a number of homeless programs. Taken together, these operations accounted for roughly $10 billion in congressional appropriations, serving nearly 1,000 cities and counties.

The new approach at once deregulated much of CPD's planning, application, and reporting process and intensified expectations for the requirements that remained. CPD's process asked communities to submit a single planning document and application instead of applying to separate programs operating on different calendars. The hope was that, armed with a single plan, communities could better map a path for their own development and better deploy HUD resources to speed the journey. Concentrating attention on a single plan promised to reduce paperwork, improve accountability, and generate citizen involvement.

CPD articulated three goals for the consolidated planning process, geared to the underlying missions motivating the federal grants: decent housing, a livable environment, and economic opportunity. To advance these goals, CPD required communities to provide in each consolidated plan full information in six areas. The plan included:

—an assessment of a community's housing needs, as well as the extent of homelessness within its borders;

—a housing market analysis, including an inventory and report on housing conditions;

—a description of strategies for using federal funds to meet the community's most urgent needs;

—an annual action plan, demonstrating how the proposed economic development, housing, and homeless activities would work together;

—certification that the community would involve citizens, promote fair housing, and comply with other overarching mandates; and

—a description of monitoring procedures for projects funded under the plan.

The monitoring provisions included the establishment of performance measures. But in an important departure from past practice, these measures were to be specified not by the federal government, but by the grant recipient. Thus the planning document itself would define, from the very beginning of a project, the achievement benchmarks its own directors considered reasonable. HUD then stipulated that a program would have to meet these performance goals to trigger the release of further program funding—a built-in mechanism for ongoing program evaluation. This design, CPD officials hoped, would promote both overall accountability and stewardship of individual projects based on results.

CPD published a "Proposed Rule for the Consolidated Plan" in the *Federal Register* in early 1994—a procedural step mandated by federal administrative rules, establishing a formal open season for commentary and critiques. Not all CPD communities were enthusiastic. Some were still recovering from the effort of assembling their first CHAS under the 1990 Housing Act, and the prospect of a super-CHAS, as the consolidated plan could be characterized, was unnerving. The objections turned out to be moderate in scope and intensity, however, and that August CPD took the next step toward closure, issuing draft regulations (informed by constituents' comments) for consolidated planning. Starting in 1995, a consolidated plan would become standard practice for communities applying for any of CPD's four major funding programs. The new process emphasized consultation between the grant recipient and HUD field offices as plans took shape, and CPD hoped and expected that most applicants would segue smoothly to the new streamlined system. In the late months of 1994 the agency reviewed more than 1,000 comments from some 120 individuals and groups and refined the system in light of these reactions. And by August 1995, more than 900 grantees had submitted and received approval for their first consolidated plan.

But streamlined planning was only the first tactic in CPD's strategy of procedural reinvention. The second tactic involved using information technology to break through the barriers separating HUD from the citizens it was meant to serve. The leading edge of the information technology effort was closely tied to the planning reforms. To make it easier for communities to draft their inaugural plans, CPD went shopping for software. Early in the process, CPD contracted with a firm producing commercial mapping software, but soon found the product could not be cheaply adapted to the special needs of HUD's client communities. CPD then cast a wider net, assembling an advisory group from among major computer firms to develop a low-cost, user-friendly software system for integrating and organizing the information that underlay strategic planning. On the advice of the advisory group, CPD formed a product development partnership with a commercial firm to create two versions of the tool CPD envisioned.

One version, designed for jurisdictions seeking HUD funding, was essentially an administrative management tool that integrated mapping, word processing, and database software. This consolidated planning software let local officials sweep together data originating in multiple sources, mix and match and manipulate the data, and channel it into reports, displays, charts, and maps to illustrate the plan. Once the software was developed, CPD shipped it, free of charge, to the communities working on their consolidated plans—equipping them to display, in graphic detail, how resources were being deployed against needs. They could trace how different projects overlapped, geographically and financially. Local officials were invited to customize maps and data to highlight their own issues and problems. The software was ready by June 1994, and within a month CPD held the first of forty training sessions on how to use it.

A second software package was tailored for use by citizens and local nonprofits, in line with Secretary Cisneros's theme of citizens as customers. It was a simplified version of the consolidated planning software, made widely available at HUD's wholesale cost. This version equipped individuals and groups to look under the hood of their community's consolidated plan. Like the consolidated planning software local officials used, its star feature was a mapping capability that allowed users to array data to highlight their particular interests and concerns. Citizens could call up a highly detailed map of their area and trace the flow of federal dollars across districts and neighborhoods. They could pinpoint an individual project and almost instantly display the economic and demographic characteristics of the surrounding area. A citizens' group could see how the location of a proposed park, for example, related to the concentration of people likely to use the park. As one CPD document put it: "These maps replace bureaucratic verbiage with specific projects in identifiable neighborhoods." CPD marketed the software to community groups, housing authorities, libraries, and other local institutions.

A special edition of the software, released shortly after the standard package, was an even more powerful tool. The advanced version let users import other relevant information, such as crime statistics or social services, into the basic program. Using the mapping function, for example, citizens could highlight neighborhoods with the highest crime rates, or the slowest job growth, or the lowest average income, or the greatest concentrations of single mothers and children. As a brochure describing the new program put it: "Now citizens 'see' those characteristics of their community that can be the source of new beginnings and new strategies for economic growth."

If knowledge is power, the software catalyzed a quietly revolutionary dispersal of power over urban development. CPD officials hoped it would make federally funded programs more accessible and transparent to the citizens with a valid, but heretofore frustrated, interest in joining the conversation on their communities' future. Alternative strategies for solving local dilemmas could be easily mapped and tried on for size. Better informed citizens and groups could more readily debate and challenge program specialists and elected officials. Communities would be able to perceive more clearly the needs of individual neighborhoods, the allocation of taxpayers' money by current and planned programs, and the implicit priorities embedded in both the status quo and alternative visions.

The two parallel tactics in CPD's reform strategy—the consolidated plan and the suite of planning software—were packaged and promoted together under the banner of "community connections" and harnessed to the engine of the government-wide reinvention crusade. HUD's community connections echoed core reinvention themes—cutting and simplifying process; empowering front-line workers with information and authority; and focusing on results rather than process. To raise the profile of what might otherwise be dismissed as humdrum administrative changes, Cuomo and Cisneros trumpeted goals for community connections that were ambitious to the point of audacity. The declared objectives were to:

—restore civic society, by restructuring relationships and communication between government and people;

—reinvent government, by redesigning relations among federal, state, and local government, moving focus from process to performance;

—revitalize urban policy; and

—advance academic and policy-oriented research.[3]

Cuomo and his deputies envisaged the parallel pursuit of all these goals energized by access to a common pool of data. The new software and the integrated planning process around which it was organized would promote both more rationality and more participation in state and local policymaking. By making results more realistic, more specific, and more readily measured, it would make performance-based assessment an achievable ideal. It would stimulate creativity by liberating states and localities to become policy laboratories. And it would accelerate policy research by opening these laboratories to scholarly scrutiny through a national database on the needs, plans, and actual performance of nearly 1,000 communities. This integrated disbursement and information system, when fully operational, was meant to allow anyone who was interested to track the expenditures and accomplishments of all CPD–funded projects. CPD also placed summaries of each community's consolidated plan on its world wide web page, http://www.hud.gov.

By 1996, CPD was able to evaluate one full cycle of community connections, with broadly encouraging results. Costs for program administration went down, relative to the status quo ante, and staff efficiency went up. In 1992, a staff of 1,088 had administered a program budget of $5.5 billion. In 1995, only 918 staff members (20 percent fewer) administered 82 percent more in federal funds ($10 billion). Putting the major CPD programs on the same administrative calendar, one of the simple procedural changes embedded in community connections, turned out to have major benefits. It liberated HUD's own field staff members from much of the paperwork drudgery they had previously endured, allowing them more time to work on problem-solving and technical assistance for grant recipients.

State and local officials applauded the consolidated plan as a less burdensome and more useful process than the comprehensive housing affordability strategy it superseded. The new system had both a wider scope and fewer fixed requirements, and it was easier to tailor to a community's particular planning needs. Many jurisdictions welcomed the expanded opportunities for citizen participation in community planning and the greater clarity about the proposed use and distribution of federal funds. Cameron Whitman, senior legislative counsel at the National League of Cities, told CPD the consolidated planning process was a "fantastic planning tool. It really has made things easier." Detroit mayor Dennis Archer, initially skeptical, came to consider it "a valuable experience, with or without the possibility of federal funds. The community believes in what we're doing now." Wisconsin governor Tommy Thompson credited the plan with "reducing paperwork and duplication of efforts and encouraging greater coordination between various state and local agencies."[4]

Early experience suggested that the consolidated plan was indeed making it easier for local officials to map the interconnections among complex urban dynamics and thus pinpoint where interventions could have the broadest impact. For the homeless, for example, local strategies now led from providing emergency shelter to counseling, job training, and mental health services, as well as providing transitional and permanent housing. One study reported that the number of people moving off the streets and into housing had multiplied fourteen times since 1992, with only three times the funding.[5] CPD officials felt comprehensive planning could take considerable credit for the efficiency gains. The more transparent process also made possible program integration beyond HUD itself, embracing enterprises anchored in other federal agencies as well as state and local initiatives. For example, HUD launched a joint endeavor with the Department of Transportation to coordinate several regional transportation planning efforts with the consolidated plans of the relevant communities.

Community connections found favor on Capitol Hill as well as in urban streets. The oversight panel to which CPD was answerable, the House Subcommittee on Housing and Community Opportunity, reacted positively to the innovation. Republicans on the panel liked community connections' emphasis on deregulation, performance management, accountability, and the application of technology. While some of the Democrats at first worried that consolidation would slight the interests of key urban constituencies, they came to endorse the initiative as those very constituencies saw the merits of more transparent planning and wider access to data. These benefits quickly took concrete form in more inclusive conversations in community after community. In Muncie, Indiana, for example, 700 people showed up for forums organized around the drafting of the city's consolidated plan. Some 250 local groups participated in the development of Spokane's plan, while the process in Burbank involved more than 189 agencies, 24 county departments, and 108 community groups. In North Carolina, local governments used cable TV to encourage community participation, while Harris County, Texas, put its consolidated plan on the web for wide-open public comment.

Press reaction, too, was unexpectedly positive. Syndicated columnist Mary McGrory wrote in the *Washington Post*: "No longer are great behemoth programs wheeled out of Washington and planted in some locale that doesn't particularly want them, except for the money. . . . Localities have to have plans that dovetail with the plans of other organizations."[6] *Federal Computer Week* wrote that "the system . . . is an early hit among lower governmental units that work with HUD."[7] And even the big-picture political glossy *George*—not generally known for its preoccupation with procedural reforms within the bureaucracy—depicted Cuomo's dream for community connections in terms that must have gratified the assistant secretary: "One day, he [Cuomo] imagines, such maps will document every dollar the federal government spends—enabling the public to ignore the tricky math of politicians and finally figure out for themselves what they really get for their taxes."[8]

Notes

1. "Community Connections: A Context for Consolidated Planning," undated CPD fact sheet.

2. At its height in the mid-1970s, the 701 grants provided $100 million to communities nationwide for planning purposes.

3. "Community Connections."

4. Innovations in American Government applications.

5. Ibid.

6. Mary McGrory, "The Homeless and the Heartless," *Washington Post*, April 7, 1996.

7. *Federal Computer Week*, March 4, 1996.

8. *George*, March–April 1996.

13

GETTING NEW DRUGS ON THE MARKET

THE EARLY 1960s were glory days for the U.S. Food and Drug Administration (FDA). Resisting pressure from consumers and the pharmaceutical industry alike, the FDA had refused to approve for sale in the United States a new drug called thalidomide. The sedative had proved enormously popular, particularly in Europe, as a treatment for morning sickness during pregnancy. By the time it was discovered that thalidomide causes profound birth defects such as missing limbs, it was too late for thousands of European newborns.[1] But the FDA—notably medical officer Frances O. Kelsey, Ph.D., M.D.—was a hero. Kelsey's tough-minded scrutiny of the marketing application had saved countless American babies from deformity.

Safety First

The thalidomide experience dramatically reinforced the FDA's commitment to caution on drug regulation. But over the years, this bedrock institutional value became a source of vulnerability as public priorities shifted from safety alone to both safety and rapid access to new medications. Scientific advances led to the discovery of dozens of new drugs, eagerly awaited by patients and the advocacy groups that formed to sup-

---

This chapter was researched and drafted by Kirsten Lundberg.

port them. Yet scores of these breakthrough medications backed up in the FDA approval pipeline, hostage to painstakingly slow reviews.

As the AIDS epidemic swept the country in the 1980s, the vague feeling of discontent with the FDA drug approval process crystallized into organized lobbying to force faster action. Reformers sought ways to make expeditious work compatible with conscientious work. Patients and the drug industry wanted to reduce dramatically the average twelve years it took for a drug to go from first discovery to market—two and a half years of that spent waiting for the FDA to give its stamp of approval.[2] But successive waves of reform, reorganization, and redefinition failed to produce any noticeable transformation of FDA operations.

But 1990 marked a watershed. President George Bush appointed David Kessler administrator of the FDA. The former director of New York's Albert Einstein Hospital quickly made his mark as a maverick who did not mind making policy waves. By 1992, Kessler thought he saw a way to forge common cause with the pharmaceutical industry to accelerate the rate of new drug approvals in a way that would benefit both the industry and the FDA.

Until the twentieth century, doctors and patients alike regarded drugs as inherently risky. There were no scientific standards for their development or use, and medicines as frequently caused illnesses as cured them. The image of the doctor as quack—an unqualified practitioner administering fantastical potions—had firm foundations in popular experience. It took a series of public health scandals, however, before the U.S. government established a watchdog over the drug industry.

Congress created the Food and Drug Administration in 1906 after a number of widely publicized tragedies (including the deaths from a defective diphtheria antitoxin of children in St. Louis). Its first director was Harvey Wiley, a crusader for more than a quarter century for government regulation of food and drugs. The 1906 Food and Drug Act required that drugs meet certain standards of strength and purity and gave the FDA responsibility for establishing those standards. The legislation did not, however, mention any obligation by manufacturers to prove the safety of a drug before putting it on the market.

That changed in 1938 with the Federal Food, Drug and Cosmetic Act—which had been five years in the making. Unfortunately it, too, became law only after a calamity: the deaths of 107 people from a poisonous ingredient in a product named "Elixir of Sulfanilamide." The 1938 law gave the FDA considerably more teeth than it had possessed before. The agency was charged with approving all drugs as safe before

they could be sold to the public. The FDA was not responsible for conducting its own research of proposed medications; instead it reviewed
tests carried out by the drug companies that developed the products. The
law also authorized FDA inspections of drug-production facilities and
allowed court injunctions (in addition to existing powers of seizure and
prosecution) as new weapons against threats to public safety. In 1951 the
FDA created the category of prescription (as opposed to over-the-
counter) drugs, to be taken only under the supervision of a physician.

The early 1960s thalidomide affair, however, propelled the FDA to
new heights of public legitimacy and policy clout. In October 1962, Congress passed the Kefauver-Harris Drug amendments. This law required
the FDA to find a drug not only safe, but effective, in its intended use
before granting approval for marketing. The law stipulated that the FDA
review process was to take no longer than six months, but there was no
provision to enforce that timetable.

Subsequent drug laws sought to address public health needs, expanding the FDA's oversight duties and adding to its workload. A 1983 bill,
for example, gave companies incentives to develop cures for rare diseases; another in 1984 eased the marketing of generic drugs. Additional
regulations (as distinct from laws) set standards for the use of human
subjects in clinical trials of new drugs (1981); strengthened monitoring of
adverse reactions from available drugs (1985); and encouraged the industry and FDA to speed the availability of new drugs for life-threatening
and debilitating diseases (1988).

By the early 1990s the FDA had become a powerful agency employing
some 8,000 people in more than 150 cities across the country. The FDA
regulated commerce worth an estimated 25 cents out of every consumer
dollar. Its six centers had wide-ranging responsibilities for food and drug
safety. FDA employees monitored the safety of most foodstuffs;
researched and approved medical devices from tongue depressors to
heart defibrillators; and regulated the labeling of food on the nation's
grocery shelves. Its annual budget was more than $900 million.

The most controversial divisions within the FDA were those responsible for the regulation of drugs: the Center for Drug Evaluation and Research (CDER) and the Center for Biologics Evaluation and Research.[3]
Scientists at the two centers were responsible for the safety of all drugs,
meaning traditional chemical compounds, vaccines and other biologics
(medicines made from living organisms), and the products of biotechnology. Their mandate extended to every aspect of the drug industry, from
development to drug labeling, marketing, and advertising. The centers'

decisions had literally global impact, as drugs approved by the FDA often received automatic approval in other countries. Anyone using a prescription drug—in the United States alone some 2 billion prescriptions are filled every year—was an FDA client.[4]

The two FDA centers reviewed for approval not only new drugs—so-called new molecular entities—but also novel formulations, combinations, or applications of existing drugs. While the procedure for obtaining approval differed slightly among these categories, they were all time-consuming both for the FDA and for the sponsoring drug company. For new drugs, for example, a company typically submitted to the FDA an "investigational new drug application" after it had completed laboratory and animal tests of its new product, but before conducting clinical trials using human subjects. FDA scrutinized the trial design and its hoped-for results before giving clearance to begin human trials. Only after successfully completing tests with human subjects did the company file an application for final FDA approval.

To analyze the hundreds of applications a year for new or improved drugs, the FDA employed a small army of scientists. Chemists reviewed how a drug was made and whether it met standards of strength, quality, and purity. Pharmacologists evaluated the effects of the drug on laboratory animals. Physicians looked at similar results in trials using humans and probed the accuracy of proposed labels. Pharmacokineticists analyzed the drug's chief ingredient and tracked its progress through the human body. Statisticians examined the designs of the studies as well as their conclusions.

After these exhaustive reviews, the FDA had to be able to answer two questions: did well-designed and controlled studies provide substantial evidence of the effectiveness of the proposed drug; and did the results show the product is safe if used as instructed? Once it had reached conclusions on these points for a particular drug, the FDA sent action letters to the sponsoring company. An approval letter meant the company could commence marketing; an approvable letter indicated minor issues remained before final approval; a not approvable letter described important changes to be made. Only an average 20 of every 100 drugs proposed for review made it through three prescribed phases of testing and were approved for marketing. But the FDA had to review all 100 to determine which 80 failed its standards.

With the years, the growing demands on the time and expertise of the FDA had far outpaced its resources. The visible result by the 1990s was a paralyzing backlog in new and revised drug approval applications. The backlog meant that work on an application routinely began only a year or so after submission. The average time required for the FDA to approve a drug was twenty-two months.

The backlog's cost to the drug industry was clear—millions of dollars of forgone revenue as it waited for word from the FDA. Consumers also suffered, and horror stories abounded. One drug for arthritis was approved in 1991 after nine years under FDA review; a drug treating angina took eight years to win approval.[5] As for the FDA, the backlog contributed to declining morale and a deteriorating reputation.

Some observers blamed the 1962 legislation—the Kefauver-Harris amendments—for the added burdens of extensive laboratory analysis, animal tests, and clinical human trials, which added time and expense to drug development. By 1990 elapsed time to launch had reached a twelve-year average for approved drugs, and development costs had risen almost tenfold since the 1960s.[6] Even factoring in inflation, that was a stunning increase. While the law clearly cut risks, critics charged that it also inhibited innovation; the introduction of new drugs fell by more than two-thirds after the 1962 law, from an average of fifty-four a year to sixteen.[7]

The $100 billion drug industry—fairly or not—laid the blame for rising costs and declining innovation squarely on the FDA. To bolster its argument that waiting times did not have to be so long, the pharmaceutical industry pointed to Europe. Britain, industry spokesmen noted, could vet new therapies in as little as eighteen months. Moreover, averred drug companies, American producers were losing the edge on new drug therapies. An increasingly smaller proportion of new drugs gained first approval in the United States; many had been available abroad for an average of six years before they could be bought in the United States. Although FDA approval was widely considered the "gold standard," which would often ensure automatic approval overseas, the converse clearly did not hold true.

The FDA, for its part, countered that the drug companies themselves were partially to blame. As approval times grew longer, the industry became sloppier in the applications it submitted, knowing that the earlier the application got in the agency's door, the sooner it would reach the front of the line for FDA attention. The results were applications that had to be literally delivered by the truckload, comprising thousands of pages of often incomplete, undigested data.

In a vicious circle, such onerous paperwork contributed to declining productivity but increased defensiveness among FDA staffers. A 1990 advisory committee report characterized the FDA staff as overwhelmed and demoralized, incapable of coping with increased duties and an inadequate budget. The six-month deadline for reviews was seen as a bitter joke. Employees reacted to the stress by adopting an "us versus them" mentality, rallying around the unofficial FDA motto: "Do you want it fast, or do you want it right?" As the notion of working down the backlog came to seem increasingly futile, many staffers throttled back to a nine-to-five schedule, regardless of the workload. Even the physical plant was sadly deteriorated—one manager arrived in 1989 to find his division staff of sixty-six had no fax machine and, for computers, only two elderly Wang word processors.

In November 1990, President George Bush appointed David Kessler administrator of the FDA. A thirty-nine-year old doctor and lawyer who also held an advanced business degree, Kessler quickly made headlines with a frontal assault on the accuracy of food product labeling. He cracked down on drug companies that advertised drugs for uses not approved by the FDA. He imposed a voluntary moratorium on the sale and use of silicone breast implants. And from the start, Kessler took seriously complaints that the sluggish FDA drug approval process was keeping life-saving drugs from new patients and driving up the costs of those drugs that did finally get approval.

No longer were the loudest complaints from business. Consumers by 1990 had become newly vocal, inspired in large part by the epidemic of AIDS (acquired immune deficiency syndrome) sweeping the United States and the world. While patient advocacy groups had long existed for a variety of illnesses, the fight against AIDS enlisted almost unprecedented support across a broad spectrum of society. As the number of diagnosed AIDS cases rose steadily in the 1980s, the stricken, their friends, and their families placed their remaining hope in the ingenuity of the scientific and pharmaceutical community to produce a cure, a vaccine, an antidote—anything that might save lives. A thriving black market developed in contraband drugs smuggled in from Canada, Mexico, and Europe. Why, activists demanded, was the FDA stalling on making these same drugs available to desperate patients?

In fact, well before Kessler's time the FDA—under the doctrine of "compassionate use"—had allowed doctors to obtain unapproved innovative drugs for terminally ill patients. During the mid-1970s, thousands of heart and lung patients were given beta blockers before they won FDA approval. Some 20,000 patients used amiodarone—for heart arrhythmia—before its 1985 approval as the drug Cordarone.

In 1987 the FDA rolled out some new tactics for speeding drugs from laboratory to bedside. The new regulations grew out of the testing of a pioneering AIDS drug, AZT (zidovudine). In early tests, patients on AZT had demonstrated a clearly higher survival rate than those taking a placebo. The study was halted in September 1986 and, within a week, the FDA authorized treatment with AZT. More than 4,000 AIDS patients were treated before AZT received formal FDA approval in March 1987—in a record 107 days.

As a result, the FDA adopted a formal new category of drug: treatment INDs, or medicines authorized for use (by seriously ill patients) at the earliest "investigational new drug" stage of FDA review. These are drugs still in the approval pipeline, but provisionally available before the clinical trials are formally complete. Treatment INDs have included drugs for Alzheimer's, Parkinson's, various advanced cancers, and respiratory problems in premature infants.

User Fees to Accelerate Review

But Kessler recognized that, with its current management structure and—equally important—with its current budget, the FDA could not accelerate new drug approvals on a routine basis. He resuscitated an idea which, while it had failed in earlier iterations, seemed to hold the most promise for bringing noticeable change to the agency: user fees to fund faster review. The concept was simple. Industry would pay the FDA a set fee when it submitted new drugs for approval. In exchange, the FDA would guarantee closure within a limited time period.

Earlier proposals for user fees had foundered on the politics of mutual suspicion. The FDA first considered drug review fees in 1966, on the recommendation of the Bureau of the Budget (the precursor of the Office of Management and Budget.) In that instance, however, the Department of Health, Education and Welfare (HEW), in which the FDA resided, vetoed the measure on the grounds that drug regulation yields broad public benefits and is thus properly funded by general revenues. HEW also worried that fees would burden small businesses or be passed on to customers in the form of higher drug prices. Subsequent attempts to introduce user fees in 1971, 1982, and 1986 likewise failed.

Considerable opposition came from Congress, where some Democratic leaders feared such financing would erode the FDA's integrity as it became fiscally dependent on the industry it was supposed to be regulating. The drug companies, in turn, feared that their fees would substitute for taxpayer support of the FDA when Congress came to look for easy spending cuts. Periodic efforts by the Office of Management and Budget to impose user fees and reduce appropriations in other areas only served to fuel their anxiety. Most industry players felt that, even if the money were reserved for FDA operations, it would do little good in speeding review. Besides, the notion of boosting the FDA's resources was at odds with industry efforts, through public relations and political means, to limit the agency's authority.

But by the early 1990s, the sides had reached a stalemate. FDA supporters despaired of increasing appropriations, while agency detractors despaired of weakening its regulatory power. A lucky confluence of circumstance and individuals led to renewed examination of the user fee option. A senior Bush administration FDA official with a corporate background, for example, learned informally from friends in the venture capital industry that the financial burden of user fees would be swamped by the expected profits from faster approval of drugs. At the same time, the head of the Pharmaceutical Manufacturers Association had served as an assistant secretary of commerce and was familiar with other successful examples of user fees.

The result was renewed negotiations among industry, Congress, and the FDA. While early discussion included fees on numerous FDA–regulated products, a compromise proposal applied fees only to new prescription drugs and some biologics.[8] An initial draft created by the FDA and Congress did not include performance goals for the FDA. After industry objections, the proposed bill included an FDA commitment to improve the drug review process. The industry also demanded that fees be purely supplementary to existing FDA appropriations; that they be dedicated to reviewing new drugs and biologics; and that they be reasonable.

With the eventual support of former opponents such as Senator Edward Kennedy (Democrat of Massachusetts), Representatives John Dingell (Democrat of Michigan), and Henry Waxman (Democrat of California), and the cooperation of Gerald Mossinghoff of the Pharmaceutical Manufacturers Association, draft legislation on user fees was presented to Congress. The bill satisfied industry by guaranteeing that user fees would go exclusively toward improving FDA approval times. It linked the fee payments to enhanced performance, accountability, and predictability. Government appropriations to the FDA would not be reduced.

The fees were relatively light burdens for most of the roughly 175 drug companies covered by them, especially in comparison with the extra earnings at stake. There were three classes of fees. To submit a new product application, the sponsoring company would pay $100,000—50 percent at the time of application and 50 percent when it received an FDA "first action" (approval or request for additional information) letter. A second class of fee—$6,000—was to be paid yearly for the period of time the drug remained on the market under patent protection. A third fee of $60,000 a year was charged to the 250 drug establishments manufacturing drugs covered by the user fee law.[9] (Each of these fees was slated to rise over time, but even when fully phased in, the burdens were modest.) Businesses with fewer than 500 employees were charged half the application fee, due only one year after submission. Waivers were granted if necessary to protect public health, if the fee constituted a barrier to innovation, if the new drug was similar to a generic not subject to user fees, or if the fee charged exceeded the cost of the review.

The House of Representatives passed HR 6181, which became the Prescription Drug User Fee Act (PDUFA), on October 5, 1992. The Senate passed essentially the same version on October 7, and President Bush signed it into law on October 29, 1992. The legislation was valid for five years, after which it would have to be renewed. Congress agreed that drug-review appropriations would remain at 1992 levels for the life of the law.

As its share of the user fee bargain, the FDA undertook to review applications for "standard" drugs (those similar to existing drugs) within twelve months. It would vet priority applications (for drugs with important new therapeutic possibilities) within six months. On the grounds that such a radical change could only come about gradually, the PDUFA phased in the tough new timelines: 55 percent of applications would have to meet the accelerated schedules in FY1994, 70 percent in FY1995, 80 percent in FY1996 and 90 percent in FY1997.[10]

Concurrent with passage of the bill, the FDA implemented long-overdue management changes. While Kessler set the tone, management and staff took responsibility for the details. The FDA put in place formal project management procedures, with a systematic setting of priorities, formal timelines, and tracking. It promoted more intensive interaction with the drug companies at all stages of the review process. It established continuing training programs, designed and initiated a week-long new reviewer's course, instituted a formal process for identifying and publishing key policies, initiated a leadership development fellowship program, and worked to improve transparency, consistency, and accountability at all levels. An outside management consultant retained for the transition predicted that transforming the agency culture enough to fully meet the target drug review goals would take five to seven years.

The PDUFA fees provided $28.5 million in FY1993 and nearly $54 million in FY1994. With those funds, the FDA was able to hire new personnel—spending $23 million more on salaries alone—and to upgrade key equipment. The results astonished even PDUFA proponents. In the second year that PDUFA was in force, the FDA met the performance goals for the *final* year, reviewing on time 95 percent of new-drug applications. By November 30, 1994, the FDA had cleared all but nine applications from the long-looming backlog.

At the same time that the FDA implemented the provisions of the PDUFA, it also adopted a streamlined drug review process for breakthrough drugs treating fatal diseases. The accelerated approval approach, established in 1991 regulations, allowed companies to present surrogate endpoints as acceptable substitutes for proving the long-term effectiveness of new drugs. Under the old rules, drugs could be ruled effective in saving lives or providing cures only after a lapse—often of years— showed the patients had recovered or were still alive. A surrogate measure was an interim result—such as increased T-cell production in an AIDS sufferer, or lowered blood pressure in a heart patient—which could reasonably indicate that a recovery or remission would follow. Accepting surrogates meant that the FDA could grant early marketing approval based on laboratory results until so-called clinical endpoint data became available. The result was that sick or dying patients got promising treatments more quickly.

The 1994 pattern of overfulfillment of PDUFA goals continued through 1997, when the legislation came up for renewal. The FDA calculated that during the five years since passage of the PDUFA, the FDA had collected a total $331.6 million in fees, of which $70.2 million went to hire some 600 additional scientists to review applications. During this period, the agency's review time of new drug applications had fallen steadily, from a median 26.7 months in 1992, just before the PDUFA came into force, to a median 15.4 months in 1996. Of the new drug and license applications entering the pipeline and subject to the PDUFA time limits, the FDA was able to review 98 percent on time in FY 1995, and it maintained a similar pace in 1996. The backlog on new drug applications had been pushed to zero.

This decline in approval times continued despite a rise in the absolute number of new drugs cleared for marketing, from 91 in 1992 to a record high of 131 in 1996.[11] Fifty-three of these were new molecular entities, products with an active substance never before approved for marketing in the United States. Drugs to fight HIV led the way in early clearance. On March 1, 1996, for example, the FDA approved Ritonavir—one of a new class of AIDS drugs called protease inhibitors—in a record seventy-two days. The agency accepted surrogate endpoints as indicators of Ritonavir's effectiveness. Two weeks later Indinavir, another protease inhibitor, won approval in just forty-two days. Meanwhile, the median development time—from the first application to marketing approval—for the new molecular entities approved in 1996 was less than nine years. Twelve drugs, including three for AIDS, came from the laboratory to pharmacy shelves in less than six years.[12]

To those who had criticized the FDA for lagging behind Britain and other European nations in approval times for new drugs, the agency could now point to evidence that it had outperformed Europe. For 1996, said FDA Associate Commissioner for Policy Coordination William K. Hubbard, researchers compared approval times for fifteen new drugs reviewed in the United States and by the centralized European Union drug authority. The FDA reviewed those fifteen in a median 5.8 months, compared with 12.2 months in the EU. Moreover, the United States was first to approve eleven of the fifteen.

The FDA was particularly gratified that the expedited reviews had resulted in improved applications from the drug companies. The combination of FDA willingness to confer with drug sponsors early in the application process to ensure that tests would yield the information the FDA required, plus the evidence that the FDA was willing to move quickly, had motivated the drug industry to submit more complete and higher-quality applications. FDA Commissioner Kessler publicly lauded his agency's performance not long after he announced in November 1996 that he would be leaving the job after six controversial years. "Whether you are a critic of the agency, or a supporter," Kessler says, "whether you are a consumer or a pharmaceutical manufacturer, everyone can take pride in a 95 percent performance record."[13]

Meanwhile, the beleaguered FDA began to reap some good press. The *Washington Post* reported on February 28, 1997, that deaths from AIDS had fallen sharply, from 24,900 in the first six months of 1995 to 22,000 in the first six months of 1996, and it gave some credit to the new therapies rushed to market.[14] The *New York Times* on March 15, 1997, reported that the FDA had cleared new drug therapies for children with AIDS, even though "there are no conclusive studies of the effectiveness of protease inhibitors in children." The formal approval (some doctors had already used the drugs for children on an experimental basis) "means wider use and more guidance about dosage and adverse effects," the newspaper reported.[15]

Not all observers gave the FDA much credit for these developments. Henry I. Miller, for example, an FDA employee from 1979 to 1994 who had moved to the conservative Hoover Institution as a senior researcher, wrote in 1997 that "the FDA's so-called improvements are little more than pseudo-reforms intended to mollify the agency's critics. . . . The FDA is fudging the numbers. It now reports median approval times instead of mean, for example."[16] A 1997 study found that, while drug companies felt the FDA was improving, criticisms remained. "In general, the companies felt that the FDA impeded the process less but had done little to expedite it," according to the study's director, Bill Otterson. "Qualifications of the reviewer, turnover and clarity of requests for additional data remain major problems."[17]

Some medical experts cautioned the FDA against losing sight of its overall goal. Thomas Moore, a writer on medical issues, told the *Washington Post* that the emphasis on expediting drugs for a relatively small number of critically ill patients should not obscure the broader aim of ensuring the safety of drugs taken by millions of "essentially healthy people."[18] In an editorial, the *Washington Post* questioned whether the pressure to reform the FDA, to push its approval rates even higher and faster, constituted overkill. "The most avid reformers do not appear to be giving enough attention to the risks involved. . . ," opined the *Post*. "Even when time is of the essence, is speed ever more important than safety?"[19]

But despite these concerns, and inevitable criticism with every report of drug recalls or other problems, the reforms at the FDA, centered on the PDUFA, garnered wide endorsement. The pharmaceutical industry was outspoken in its praise of the PDUFA program. The faster approvals meant substantial financial benefits for the industry, which is estimated to save $25 million in research and development costs for every year's reduction in the FDA review time. Robert Ingram, president and CEO of Glaxo Wellcome, congratulated the FDA on the success of the PDUFA reform, including the management reforms that accompanied it. "What you have accomplished at the FDA is truly extraordinary. In looking back over the years, there have been dozens of initiatives to improve the efficiency of the drug review and approval process in the United States. However, the Prescription Drug User Fee Act is really the only one that has had a positive impact."[20]

William C. Steere Jr., chairman and CEO of Pfizer, Inc., praised the FDA for its enhanced communication with the drug industry. "The quiet process of improving dialogue between regulators and regulated may ultimately yield greater benefits to patients [than any specific reform]," he wrote.[21] In fact, when the PDUFA came up for renewal in October 1997, drug companies took out full-page national ads in support of the legislation. In what many saw as an incongruous turn of events, the drug industry vehemently opposed efforts by the Clinton administration in its 1998 budget proposal to decrease federal appropriations for the industry's long-time whipping boy, the FDA. The drug companies lobbied intensively for level funding for the agency. Said Peter Teeley, vice president of a biotechnology company: "The great irony is it will be the industry that will save the FDA in this budget process."[22]

In 1997 both FDA supporters and detractors had plenty of opportunity to voice their views as Congress debated a broad-based FDA reform bill. On November 21, 1997, President Clinton signed into law the FDA Modernization Act. The legislation was at least a partial victory for the Republican-dominated Congress, which had sought for three years to reform what it considered one of the most bloated and interventionist federal agencies. In what some might interpret as diluting the FDA's primary commitment to consumer safety, the act circumscribed FDA authority over experimental drugs and allowed independent reviewers—instead of the FDA—to vet lower-risk medical devices. But while it did not garner the headlines, there was a clear win for the FDA in the 1997 legislation. The act reauthorized the PDUFA for five more years.

Notes

1. Thalidomide was approved for use in some twenty countries, including Germany, England, Canada, Australia, Japan, and Brazil. The FDA had not specifically suspected teratogenicity in thalidomide, but the effect emerged in Europe while the drug was still pending approval in the United States.

2. Chris Warden, "The Prescription for High Drug Prices," *Consumers' Research Magazine*, December 1992, p. 10.

3. Others operations within the FDA include the Center for Devices and Radiological Health, the Center for Food Safety and Applied Nutrition, the Center for Veterinary Medicine, the National Center for Toxicological Research, the Office of Regulatory Affairs, the Office of Science, and the Office of Orphan Products Development.

4. The FDA also monitors over-the-counter drugs for safety and effectiveness.

5. Carolyn Lochhead, "'Deadly Over-Caution'; FDA Assailed for Slow Testing of New Drugs," *San Francisco Chronicle*, October 26, 1992, p. A1.

6. Warden, "The Prescription for High Drug Prices." The study was led by Joseph DiMasi, Ph.D., at the Tufts University Center for the Study of Drug Development.

7. The average yearly number of drugs approved was 13.7 in the 1960s, 17.3 in the 1970s, and 21.7 in the 1980s. Innovations in American Government application.

8. Exemptions included whole blood products or blood components for transfusion, some human therapies from bovine blood products, allergenic extract products, and in vitro diagnostics.

9. An establishment was defined as a business making at least one prescription drug at one location.

10. Similar goals were set for processing resubmissions (applications rejected the first time), for efficacy supplements, and for manufacturing supplements. Efficacy supplements are a request to add a new ailment or a new group of patients to be treated with an already approved drug; manufacturing supplements are requests to change the way an approved drug is made or to use new production facilities. The new drug applications received by far the most public attention, however.

11. The numbers of approved drugs were smaller in the intervening years, reaching seventy in 1993, sixty-two in 1994, and eighty-two in 1995. This can also, of course, reflect the number of applications being submitted to the FDA. There is always confusion between calendar year and fiscal year numbers. In FY1996, for example, the FDA approved forty-six new molecular entities (NMEs).

12. Figures from an FDA position paper, "FDA Approvals in 1996 Set New Records," January 14, 1997.

13. John Schwartz, "In Swan Song, Kessler Croons of FDA Progress," *Washington Post*, December 11, 1996, p. A23.

14. David Brown, "U.S. Deaths from AIDS Fall Sharply," *Washington Post*, February 28, 1997, p. A1.

15. Warren E. Leary, "AIDS Drug Is Approved as Therapy for Children," *New York Times*, March 15, 1997, p. 9.

16. Henry I. Miller, "Biotech's Meager Record," *Journal of Commerce*, February 6, 1997, p. 6A.

17. Thomas Kupper, "FDA Improving, Drug Firms Report," *San Diego Union Tribune*, September 26, 1997, p. C2. The article quoted from a study sponsored by the University of California at San Diego's Connect program (which works to get drugs approved more quickly) and carried out by Price Waterhouse.

18. John Schwartz, "FDA Reforms Have Momentum as Hearings Open," *Washington Post*, May 1, 1996, p. A08.

19. "Reform Isn't Risk-Free," *Washington Post*, July 17, 1996, p. A18.

20. Report by John D. Donahue cited in Innovations in American Government application.

21. Innovations in American Government application.

22. Cindy Skrzycki, "User Fees Bring Speedy Relief; The Dose Is the Question," *Washington Post*, May 30, 1997, p. G01.

14

REBUILDING DISASTER MANAGEMENT

HURRICANE ANDREW slammed into Florida on October 24, 1992, scouring the coastal communities southwest of Miami with winds reaching 140 miles an hour. Andrew was the worst hurricane to hit Florida in sixty years. More than 300,000 people fled their homes or huddled in fear as the raging winds wreaked major damage around them. Thirty eight died during the storm or in its wake. Two and a half million were left without electricity, and the water in two counties was pronounced undrinkable.

The Federal Emergency Management Agency (FEMA)

But Andrew's damage reached far beyond South Florida. It brought down a hurricane of criticism on the Federal Emergency Management Agency, which was responsible for managing disaster relief. As the hurricane swirled toward Florida, official FEMA estimates had predicted that only 2,000 people would be affected by Andrew. Roughly 150 times that many found themselves in harm's way. And once the storm passed, FEMA had proven unable to cope with the devastation Andrew wrought. Thousands of citizens were left unaided for days, and they directed their well-publicized scorn at FEMA.

This chapter was researched and drafted by Kirsten Lundberg.

This was not the first time the public had found FEMA's performance wanting. But for many, Andrew was the last straw. Critics lambasted FEMA's disaster relief efforts as too little, too late, and they condemned the agency itself as anachronistic and ineffective. Opponents in Congress and elsewhere called for FEMA's elimination. If it were to survive, FEMA would have to find new ways of doing business. In particular, it had to improve dramatically its capacity to calibrate risks and to orchestrate recovery efforts.

Yet deep within FEMA, a creative new way to predict and prepare for disaster damage had already been conceived. As Hurricane Andrew approached, FEMA official Paul Bryant had an insight that would transform FEMA. The discovery came too late to help deal with Andrew. But Bryant's flash of understanding would quickly translate into a new set of tools for anticipating disasters: the consequences assessment tool set, or CATS. With the help of CATS, FEMA would rethink its mission and rebuild its reputation.

The Federal Emergency Management Agency had its origins in the military. As the United States and the Soviet Union settled into their long thermonuclear stand-off in 1950, Congress passed the Civil Defense Act and founded the Civil Defense Administration, which later became the Defense Civil Preparedness Agency, a branch of the Defense Department. Its job was to oversee and manage civil defense programs for use in the event of nuclear attack—distributing food and medicine, arranging shelters, fighting fires, and organizing rescues.

"Civil defense," however, came to include coping with natural disasters as well as military attacks. (In the United States, happily, virtually all of our practical experience with civil defense has involved acts of nature rather than war.) Traditionally, responsibility for peacetime civil defense lay with state and local governments. Over the years, however, the federal government assumed a more prominent role in disaster recovery efforts, particularly the costs of rebuilding. From the 1950s to the late 1980s, the typical federal share of natural disaster costs rocketed from about 5 percent to as high as 90 percent.[1] Among other services, federal agencies paid for repairs to public structures, subsidized emergency services, provided housing for those who lost homes, and paid subsistence grants to people unable to qualify for low-interest government loans.

Responsibility for disaster relief was scattered among a bewildering array of federal agencies and departments by the late 1970s, inspiring a classic consolidation reform in 1979. Emergency management functions throughout the federal government were swept into a single new agency—

FEMA. The old Defense Civil Preparedness Agency formed the institutional core. But FEMA also absorbed the Federal Disaster Assistance Administration; flood, riot, and crime insurance programs from the Department of Housing and Urban Development; the U.S. Fire Administration and National Academy for Fire Prevention from the Department of Commerce; and the Federal Preparedness Agency from the General Services Administration.

The new agency retained the mandate for dealing with the consequences of a nuclear attack. But it also assumed responsibility for coordinating the response of twenty-eight federal agencies (plus the Red Cross) to all manner of natural disasters: hurricanes, tornadoes, earthquakes, floods.[2] By the early 1990s, FEMA had 2,600 full-time employees at its Washington, D.C., headquarters and at ten regional and area offices across the country. An additional 4,000 personnel remained on standby and could be rapidly activated in the event of a disaster. Its budget ran to almost $900 million, and it controlled an average annual disbursement of nearly $7 billion in disaster aid.

FEMA organized itself around four aspects of emergency management: response, recovery, mitigation, and preparedness. Response and recovery took place at the time of disaster. Mitigation referred to efforts, through public education, building codes, and financial incentives, to limit damage in the first place.[3] "Preparedness" was a broad term for equipping public workers and volunteers to swing into action effectively once disaster struck.

In the event of an emergency, a network of organizations ranging across the governmental hierarchy took a hand in the national response effort. At the top stood the president of the United States and his cabinet. The president could declare an event a federal disaster or emergency, triggering the release of federal assistance funds. The emergency support team was a federal-level group representing the twenty-eight agencies and Red Cross involved in disaster management. Beneath them were the emergency response teams, regional squads that sped to the scene of the disaster to set up operations. Disaster field offices operated as joint state and federal centers to manage response and recovery efforts. State emergency operating centers directed the emergency response activities at the state level. Local communities often operated corresponding centers. Combined, the state and local centers employed some 11,000 emergency managers nationwide, many more than FEMA itself.[4]

Yet despite the superstructure of federal involvement, on the day Hurricane Andrew careened toward the Florida coast, disaster preparedness remained (as it had been throughout U.S. history) a decentralized public-sector enterprise, with the first moves up to state and local officials. FEMA could not send assistance to a state until formally requested to do so by the governor. This bottom-up approach also applied to information. Most of the critical data used to orchestrate disaster management originated with local and state operations. Although the National Weather Service provided meteorological predictions, FEMA depended for its physical damage predictions, as well as for postdisaster assessments, on the expertise and first-hand accounts of local officials. The federal government usually entered the picture only in the recovery phase of a disaster, offering technical and financial support. FEMA's was a reactive, relatively passive, role. The summer of 1992 revealed the downside of this arrangement.

In late August, reports of an early-season tropical storm gathering force in the Caribbean began to trickle into FEMA. As the storm became a full-fledged hurricane and was named Andrew, the flow of incoming reports suddenly surged into a flood of data. On the ground in southern Florida, where the hurricane was expected to make landfall, local officials braced themselves as best they could. At FEMA headquarters, analyst Paul Bryant was frustrated in his efforts to estimate how much damage Andrew would cause, and in particular how many households might need disaster assistance. Customarily, he would call local officials to discuss the implications of the latest National Weather Service storm track predictions. But the local communications system was disrupted by the approaching storm, and Bryant could not get through.

Bryant, who had worked on civil defense since the cold war, had spent much of his career assessing the possible consequences of nuclear attack on civilian populations. FEMA and its predecessor agencies had routinely thought through the unthinkable. If a nuclear attack hit New York, or Los Angeles, or Miami, what would be the shape and scale of the devastation? Only by preparing in advance a detailed picture of the likely damage could FEMA mount a response. As Bryant, cut off from local reports, chafed at the lack of data by which to gauge Andrew's impact and structure a recovery plan, he had a flash of insight: Why not use the nuclear-attack scenarios as a rough guide to the hurricane's effects on the Miami area? His computer model, after all, did not care if it was simulating nuclear blast or natural wind. Quickly entering what he knew about Andrew's speed and approach, together with existing data on the target area of Florida, Bryant came up with an estimate that something more than 260,000 people were vulnerable to the storm.

This startlingly high figure was presented to FEMA director Wallace Stickney—and dismissed. After all, the methodology was untried. The model was ad hoc, an improvisation with no track record. Who could tell whether the figure Bryant obtained had been skewed by unintentionally omitted information or irrelevant components of the nuclear modeling program? Anyway, in the meantime, local officials had been contacted, and there was now some real, if incomplete, data on Andrew's likely impact. The standard procedures generated an estimate that Andrew threatened around 2,000 people—two orders of magnitude lower than the figure Bryant's method suggested. FEMA, and the local emergency officials, went with the lower number in making their preparations. And Andrew closed in on Florida's coast.

The hurricane struck hardest at Dade County, where it made landfall in the predawn hours of Monday, August 24, but its effects were felt in many parts of southern Florida. The number of Floridians requiring federal assistance eventually reached 310,000 (130,000 households). It took four days—an eternity in the eyes of those affected—after Andrew struck before federal forces mobilized to relieve the area.[5] As images of devastation filled the media and recriminations mounted, FEMA became the poster-child for distant Washington's incompetence. In what was widely seen as vote of no confidence, President George Bush put the Secretary of Transportation, not the head of FEMA, in charge of the Florida recovery effort.

South Florida recovered from Andrew faster than did FEMA's reputation. The Center for Strategic and International Studies called for dissolving the agency. A *Wall Street Journal* front-page article in early 1993 quoted disaster assistance experts who called the agency beyond repair. FEMA was put under internal and external review. Both the FEMA inspector general, in a performance audit of Hurricane Andrew, and the General Accounting Office (GAO), in five separate reports to Congress, concluded that FEMA could have made much greater use of predictive modeling technology in preparing for Andrew. A National Association of Public Administration report drew similar conclusions. The inspector general's recommendation was typical of the three assessments. FEMA, it said, should "adopt models employing appropriate technology to project disaster damage." It should also "establish a system and procedures for converting damage projections into a scaled Federal Disaster response."[6]

In April 1993, FEMA gained a new director with a high-level mandate to resuscitate the beleaguered agency. James Lee Witt was the first FEMA head with previous experience in emergency management, having served four years as director of the Arkansas Office of Emergency Services. Early in his career Witt had launched and run a construction company before being elected an Arkansas county judge at age thirty-four (making him the youngest elected official in the state). After being reelected six times to the judge's office, he was tapped by Governor Bill Clinton to run Emergency Services. When Clinton moved to Washington, he asked Witt to take on FEMA.

Witt inherited an agency burdened with poor morale among the career staff. FEMA had a disproportionate number of political slots and a reputation as a haven for well-connected appointees without much taste or talent for civil-defense work.[7] Witt declared his intention of turning FEMA around and remolding it into a professional organization responsive to customer needs. He encouraged the creative application of computers, communication technologies, and information sharing. Witt found FEMA's professional staffers receptive to the new directions. Indeed, he was gratified to discover that low-profile progress on improving and applying modeling technology was already under way.

Disaster Modeling

Federal disaster-response experts had used computer models since the 1960s, but most of the modeling efforts, and all of the funding, was related to national security. In 1989, FEMA applied modeling technology for the first time to a natural disaster. Following the Loma Prieta (California) earthquake, a model helped identify Santa Cruz as the area of greatest damage. The model helped FEMA allocate its resources to where they could do the most good. This application of computer models was not institutionalized, however, and there was little progress before Bryant's high-pressure tinkering in 1992. Bryant's prediction for Hurricane Andrew suggested that well-developed nuclear-wind models could be adapted to hurricane winds. FEMA decided to see whether it could systematically convert the military's nuclear attack model to an operational hurricane wind damage model for civilian use. This effort marked the birth of the CATS program, a joint venture between FEMA and the Defense Special Weapons Agency.

On December 14, 1992, FEMA contractor Science Applications International Corp. started building the hurricane model. CATS engineers incorporated data from a variety of sources, including the Defense Mapping Agency, the Census Bureau, the U.S. Geological Survey, and the credit analysis firm Dun & Bradstreet Corp.[8] Costs were minimized thanks to the extensive work the Defense Special Weapons Agency had already done on the model and its readiness to lend its expertise to help FEMA with the infant program. Within a month, a functioning hurricane wind damage model was complete.

But the CATS developers realized that this was only a first stage. The program they had created had exceptional scope. Once the door had been opened to integrated information systems, potential applications multiplied. The next stage of development would seek out other military technology that FEMA could redeploy.

Time for preliminary research and development, however, turned out to be shorter than the specialists could have predicted. Well before they felt entirely ready, the engineers and scientists had a chance to show what the new tools could do. During the summer of 1993, heavy flooding swept across the Midwest as the Mississippi River rose over its banks. The infant CATS program was able to receive and process images from meteorological satellites every few hours. Using satellites for emergency management was a new concept, and it resulted almost immediately in novel procedures. With such up-to-date estimates of the extent of the floods, the Department of Education, for example, was able to accelerate its preparation of grants to schools in affected communities. The Center for Disease Control used the same information to send medical assistance to the communities at greatest risk of health problems.

In late August 1993, almost a year to the day after Andrew bore down on Florida, Hurricane Emily approached the coast of North Carolina. FEMA's response this time was markedly different. First of all, Witt made sure the nation saw FEMA in action. He put the agency on twenty-four-hour alert. He himself went on national television to describe the emergency preparations: twelve tractor-trailer loads of tents, cots, plastic sheeting, generators, chain saws, and other supplies. Witt was seen consulting with his catastrophic disaster response group to prepare for the storm. He briefed both President Clinton and Vice President Al Gore.

But ultimately more important than heads-up public relations was the evolving CATS program. As Emily approached, a CATS task force used computers both to track the storm and to predict damage. Direct phone hookups fed National Weather Service updates into two FEMA desktop computers to revise scenarios continuously. Another PC connected to the National Weather Service electronic bulletin board posted advisories on which areas should be evacuated.[9]

Emily dissipated most of its force before arriving at North Carolina. But CATS had proved itself. The final prediction of damage to homes was

674; the actual number affected was 683. FEMA enjoyed an unaccustomed spate of favorable press, thanks in large part to CATS. Louise Comfort, a disaster-management expert at the University of Pittsburgh, said FEMA had experienced a "fundamental shift in attitude" since Andrew. "It's as though they finally are listening," she said.[10] FEMA was no longer waiting passively for requests for aid from governors but was putting the means to respond to those requests in place well ahead of time by anticipating what would be needed. Said FEMA spokesman David Martin: "We're just on the ground faster. We're not waiting around." James Kellett, assistant associate director of FEMA's Office of Systems Engineering, gave a thumbs-up to CATS's debut. "This was the first time the system gave us wind damage estimates for hurricanes," he told a reporter after the storm. "The bottom line is that the sucker worked." North Carolina's emergency management director Billy Cameron added his own endorsement: "It's a completely new ball game. I have nothing but praise."[11]

Building on this early success, the Defense Special Weapons Agency and FEMA formalized their collaboration and intensified the effort. In July 1994, the hurricane wind model was expanded to accommodate storm surge damage and to assign varying probability estimates for how much damage areas in a hurricane's track might suffer. That same month, emergency managers entered the number and location of water treatment plants in the path of a tropical storm into the CATS mix so they could steer fresh drinking water supplies to where they were most needed.

In 1995, FEMA expanded the scope of CATS to cover all manner of natural disasters. It adopted a five-year development plan that would transform computer simulation programs created for national security purposes and apply them to the civilian management of natural hazards. The CATS plan called for integration into a single database of a number of existing tools such as remote sensing systems, geographic information systems, and catastrophe models. CATS merged data on storm damage predictions with information about citizens with special needs: children under two, the elderly, prisoners, nursing home and hospital patients, and low-income populations. Businesses were ranked by annual sales, numbers of employees, products, and industry. Once the models had run, the system prepared lists of what resources were needed where. While FEMA technicians monitored CATS regularly during hurricane season, it was designed to begin its analysis automatically.

As CATS became more comprehensive, its integrated database could project with uncanny accuracy where disasters would occur, how severe they would be, how many people would be affected, which hospitals and roads would be closed and which could provide safe staging areas for a rescue operation. FEMA could produce its analysis within hours. Moreover, the information was presented in clear, easy-to-understand color-coded maps that captured the attention of decisionmakers at every level of government.

When FEMA expanded its complex of CATS–integrated databases to analyze floods, chemical and nuclear accidents, and fires, the Defense Department incorporated the new models into its operations worldwide. What had been a military-to-civilian technology transfer was now able to flow in the other direction as well.

CATS's development brought other cooperation in its wake as well. To develop its flood model, FEMA worked closely with the Army Corps of Engineers, while the U.S. Geological Survey provided crucial data for the earthquake model. Thanks in large part to this kind of interagency cooperation and sharing of resources, CATS had proved a relative bargain. From 1993 to 1995, the Department of Defense and FEMA spent about $3 million developing CATS. In 1996, fifteen full-time staff operated the CATS system. Their salary expenses ran about $940,000 annually, while hardware and software maintenance costs reached $509,000 a year. Considering the scale and the stakes of the mission it served, CATS was dead cheap.

As CATS progressed toward full deployment, its organizational home changed several times. In November 1993, a FEMA reorganization put CATS in a newly created Operations Support Directorate. Then in January 1995, the predictive modeling unit in that directorate was transferred to the Information Technology Services (ITS) Directorate, which contained the Applications Division. By 1996, CATS was ensconced in two branches of the Applications Division, the Modeling Branch and the Geographic Information Systems branch. Within the FEMA hierarchy, the chief of applications reported to the associate director for ITS, who in turn reported to the FEMA director.

In February 1996—in what was interpreted as a broad gesture of confidence in the agency—Clinton made FEMA director Witt a member of the cabinet. FEMA, said Clinton in making the announcement, "had been regarded almost universally as an agency not up to the job. . . . FEMA is now a model disaster relief agency."[12]

By 1996, CATS was proving its worth at each stage of FEMA's emergency management program. In the response phase, CATS was able to gauge the likely pattern of damage in advance (for hurricanes, tropical storms, and other disasters that tend to telegraph their punches) or shortly after the fact (for earthquakes and other sudden events). It estimated the number of households likely to be affected and categorized them as severely, moderately, or lightly damaged. It gave their locations so assistance teams could be quickly deployed. Accurate predictions allowed the government to stockpile supplies more strategically, allowing a speedier response without additional expense.

In the recovery phase, CATS was able to categorize essential resources such as hospitals, airports, and roads by the probability that the assets would be in operation after the disaster. The agency or team coordinating the rescue effort could then identify bottlenecks and move aid into the hardest-hit areas as quickly as possible. In the mitigation phase, CATS was able to identify and prioritize key structures such as bridges, which could be strengthened in preparation for possible disasters.

For the preparedness phase, CATS proved to be an invaluable training tool. In 1994, there were five requests for CATS–generated scenarios as the basis for training exercises. In 1995 officials prepared scenarios for use by twelve states and two interagency trials. One of them was the June 1995 "response 95" national exercise—a large-scale emergency management practice drill. All federal departments and agencies, two federal regions, and four states with their local communities took part in the exercise.

The CATS–integrated information system would have been of only limited use without the speedy relay of its products to those who needed it. This was a taller order than might at first appear. The job includes ferrying data between twenty-eight departments and agencies and fifty-six states and territories, so the designers had to take into account differences in organizational structure, hardware, software, display formats, and communications protocols. From the beginning they adopted three guiding principles:

—to the extent possible, all FEMA information systems would be based on an open systems standard;

—FEMA would convert all information to a format convenient to the end user;

—FEMA would use the widest possible communications bandwidth.

The agency approached the information challenge in stages. First it developed standard information products. Basic scenarios were published as a book and updated as refinements were added or requirements changed. FEMA created common standards for office systems, as well as for geographic information systems. In mid-1995, FEMA assembled the first comprehensive state contact book for use during an emergency. The 160-page contact book stipulated who would receive what information, which products would be transmitted, in what format the information would be sent, and what means of communication would be used. The contact book was published twice a year, was continually updated, and eventually metamorphosed from plain old paper to a node on the FEMA Internet site. It could also be found on the State and Local Users Group electronic bulletin board, where updates could be posted immediately.

The design and implementation of this complex information distribution system made a significant contribution to another of FEMA director Witt's strategic goals: strengthening local partnerships. FEMA made a substantial investment in adapting CATS so state and local officials could access it on their own computers. In response, the state and local managers enhanced their own analytical capacity, incorporated local information sources into the CATS model, and shared databases with FEMA.

As its communications network grew and evolved, CATS benefited from FEMA's close links to the Department of Defense. Thanks to FEMA's national security responsibilities, CATS had access to emergency communications systems unavailable to state and local governments and even to most federal agencies. This access allowed CATS to bypass communications bottlenecks during emergencies to obtain the most up-to-date information available from satellites and other sources.

At first there was considerable skepticism that a computer-based information system could really do much to improve the nation's emergency response system. Most doubters were, however, won over by the system's results. CATS's usefulness during earthquakes, for example, was given a dry run at the 1993 annual conference of the Central United States Earthquake Consortium. After the meeting, participants recommended that the model be made operational nationwide. Shortly after this simulation came a real-life test. In January 1994, the Northridge earthquake struck the Los Angeles area. Within hours of the U.S. Geological Survey's identification of the earthquake's epicenter, CATS estimated that 560,000 households would require assistance. In fact, 600,000 applied for help. The model showed which areas had suffered severe and which moderate damage. FEMA was able to project, among other things, what kind of foreign-language interpreters would be needed in which sectors. It also isolated areas where the probability of damage was so high that the government—flooded with damage reports and critically shorthanded—could begin to process claims even before sending in trained assessors.

Similarly, when Hurricane Marilyn struck the Virgin Islands in 1995, FEMA teams sped to St. Thomas, and CATS quickly produced projections of wind and water damage, site by site. "We were the first operational team to arrive," recalled Louis Wofsy, chief of FEMA's Applications Branch. "We were producing maps while other field offices were getting their computers up and running."[13] CATS predicted that 5,100 households would require assistance. Authorities eventually received 5,300 applications for help. By 1996, CATS had been used in more than twenty hurricanes and tropical storms, five major floods, the Northridge earthquake, and a number of large brush fires. The core technology had been replicated beyond the United States, by both military and civilian agencies. When Hurricane Georges swept through Central America in 1998, for example, equipment descended from CATS played major roles in the recovery efforts of several countries.

President Clinton became an avid user of CATS maps and relied on them to help decide whether an area merited federal disaster relief. Governors, members of Congress. and others came to expect graphic analysis of natural disasters. Departmental and agency emergency coordinators found CATS sufficiently useful that they redesigned their internal analysis systems around it. Federal coordinating officers who run disaster field offices, as well as state emergency managers, quickly found they could depend on CATS models for early information on the scale of a disaster.

FEMA has implemented a wide range of reforms to improve its operations and rebuild its standing, and no single innovation explains it all. But CATS played a significant role. Its predictive capacity made possible a fundamental change in FEMA's role in national disaster relief. Instead of simply reacting to states' requests for assistance, FEMA can now anticipate what will be required. Forewarned and forearmed, FEMA is equipped to be a more pivotal participant in the complex ballet of intergovernmental recovery efforts. As Adrian Linz, chief of FEMA's modeling branch, put it: "This capability has allowed the nation's emergency managers to move from acetate maps, grease pencils and telephones to accurate, rapid computer systems . . . from cumbersome and chronically delayed field reports to highly sophisticated modeling, remote sensing, and geographic information system capabilities to determine quickly and accurately the extent of damage and the demographic characteristics of the victims."[14]

The bulk of this transformation took place between 1993 and 1996—a remarkably rapid change, by the standards of the past. FEMA innovators, guided by their military counterparts in the Defense Special Weapons

Agency, redeployed national security resources into an all-hazard damage estimation and assessment system available on the ground and in real time.

Notes

1. Kenneth J. Cooper, "$2 Billion Fund for Disaster Relief Recommended," *Washington Post*, December 15, 1994, p. A17. Federal law limited federal participation to 75 percent of the overall cost of recovery, but exceptions were made.

2. FEMA also monitored and responded to breaches in dam safety or nuclear power plants and assisted after terrorist incidents.

3. Homeowners and businesses were, for example, given financial support to relocate out of flood plains or to rebuild using earthquake-resistant materials and methods.

4. In addition, the military retained some responsibility for disaster relief both at home and abroad. The Defense Nuclear Agency coordinated these efforts through units at Forces Command, European Command, Pacific Command, and the Army Corps of Engineers Emergency Operating Center.

5. In fact, the federal government could not act until formally requested to do so by Governor Lawton Chiles (Democrat), and the governor initially reckoned that the problem could be handled by Florida's National Guard.

6. Innovations in American Government application.

7. For a year after Bush won the presidency in 1988, it had been without a director altogether. In the months before Hurricane Andrew, FEMA had suffered unusual turmoil. A number of top officials resigned over personnel disputes. As for fulfilling its mission to serve the nation in emergencies, a disgusted Senator Ernest F. Hollings (Democrat of South Carolina) spoke for many when, in the wake of the disastrous 1989 Hurricane Hugo, he called FEMA "the biggest bunch of bureaucratic jackasses I've ever seen." Chris Lavin and others, "Florida Disaster Plan Wasn't Ready for What Hit It," *St. Petersburg Times*, August 29, 1992, p. 1A.

8. James M. Smith, "Hurricane Damage System Passes Test with Flying Colors," *Government Computer News*, vol. 12, no. 21 (September 27, 1993), p. 76.

9. Ibid.

10. Marshall Ingwerson, "FEMA Is Not Waiting for the Winds to Die Down," *Christian Science Monitor*, September 1, 1993, p. 6.

11. Seth Borenstein, "FEMA: Hurricane Andrew Taught Us Lesson," *Sun-Sentinel* (Fort Lauderdale), March 10, 1994, p. 3A.

12. Innovations in American Government application.

13. Judith Silver, "FEMA's GIS Coordinates Disaster Aid Efforts among Various Helpers," *Government Computer News*, June 10, 1996, p. 62.

14. Innovations in American Government application.

15

KEEPING PENSIONS SECURE

NOT SO LONG AGO, a company's promise of pension benefits was just that—a promise, whose fulfillment depended on the continued earning power and good faith of a worker's former employer. When the tottering automaker Studebaker shut down its South Bend, Indiana, auto plant in 1963, for example, thousands of employees lost not just their jobs, but also any hope of collecting the pension benefits they had earned during their years with Studebaker. Millions of other working Americans faced the same vulnerability. There were no rules governing employer contributions to pension plans and there was no requirement to back up pension promises with earmarked funds socked away in solid investments.

Keeping Promises

Businesses were thus tempted to cut corners on their pension plans. Firms often failed to pay enough into pension funds to meet realistic predictions about future benefit claims, and sometimes they even raided pension resources for ready cash. As wage rates soared in the booming economy of the early postwar years, many firms had seen the pledge of rich retirement packages as a cheaper alternative to wage increases, since the cash was not required up front. But as workers retired and sought to

This chapter was researched and drafted by Dalit Toledano.

collect, some employers could not or would not make good on their pledges, leaving former employees facing hard times in their old age. By the early 1970s, the difference between what employers had promised in retirement benefits and the funds they had invested to back up those promises was $100 billion and growing.[1]

This began to change in 1974, with the passage of the Employee Retirement Income Security Act, a pathbreaking and intricate piece of legislation that would become known to many—but fully understood by very few—under its acronym, ERISA. Pension promises could be hollow no longer. Any company offering a traditional defined benefit plan as part of a compensation package now had to keep pension funds separate from other assets and use objective assumptions about future payouts and investment earnings in calculating how much had to be paid into pension funds to keep pace with requirements. In defined benefit pension plans, the employer pledges to pay retired workers a specified benefit. This differs from defined contribution plans, where employers make a specified investment, and the size of the monthly check depends on how well the investment pays off in the years before retirement.

For the first time in the nation's history, private pensions would be backed by government guarantees—the newly created Pension Benefit Guaranty Corporation (PBGC) would insure basic retirement benefits for millions of American workers and retirees. This independent public corporation, funded by insurance premiums from firms sponsoring pensions, would stand as a second line of defense for retirement security.

Within ten years of ERISA's passage, pension underfunding had plummeted to $20 billion, even as the private pension system had expanded.[2] The first line of defense—requirements that employers take their pension promises seriously—turned out to work for most companies and most retirees. Once ERISA mapped out prudent provisions for delivering on pension promises, most firms proved able and willing to do right by retirees. But not infrequently, the second line of defense came into play. During that first decade, the corporation took over more than 1,300 pension plans when sponsoring companies folded or failed to fund their plans: nearly 55,000 retired Americans counted on the PBGC, not their former employer, for their pension checks.[3]

But it was not long before the PBGC began to feel the strain of shoring up the pension system. It was in the business of providing insurance, not orchestrating taxpayer-funded bailouts. As a self-financing operation, the PBGC covers the costs of pension rescues with its revenues from insurance premiums (with terms and rates determined by Congress), its own investment income, and the assets remaining in the failed pension plans it takes over. The viability of the PBGC as an insurance system depends on premium and investment income's staying ahead of the net liabilities incurred from terminated plans. In principle, bad years—with weak investment earnings, heavy rescue requirements or both—should be balanced by good years, keeping the corporation on a sound financial footing. In practice, the math failed to work out so happily. The PBGC was well into its second decade of operation without ever posting a surplus; instead, deficits accompanied each year of operation.

In response to these chronic deficits, premiums were raised, collection procedures improved, and additional fees imposed on underfunded plans. These reforms were important, but ultimately insufficient. Throughout the 1980s and into the early 1990s, the PBGC's mounting liabilities pushed it deeper and deeper into deficit. A sober look at economic and demographic trends offered little reason to believe that relief was on the horizon.

The Pension Benefit Guaranty Corporation is a very special kind of insurance enterprise, with limited control over the factors that most powerfully shape its financial status. The difficulties inherent in demographic or financial forecasting even ten years down the road are immense. The strength or weakness of the national economy will drive trends in bankruptcies among plan sponsors, the ability of employers to make adequate contributions to their plans, and the PBGC's own investment results. Today's worker—tomorrow's retiree—is likely to live longer than today's pension beneficiary, but just how much longer is unclear. The scope of the PBGC's responsibilities shrinks or expands depending on how labor force trends influence employers' decisions to offer defined-benefit pensions instead of making contributions to individual retirement plans—or cutting back altogether on retirement benefits. Judicial interpretation of the PBGC's mandate and powers plays a crucial role in defining the nature and extent of the corporation's authority.

Risk and uncertainty are by no means unique to the PBGC. Any insurer rolls the dice, as a basic of the business. But the PBGC, unlike private insurers, is obligated to underwrite everybody—even if past experience reveals that underwriting a particular industry or segment of an industry is unprofitable. As one Arthur Anderson principal succinctly put it: "They have to take the dogs."[4]

To balance these special burdens, the PBGC commands powers not available to private insurers. Under ERISA, Congress gave the PBGC one big stick—the threat of involuntary termination. The ability to initiate termination of a pension plan when "necessary to protect the interests of the participants or of the insurance program" is the most potent of the PBGC's enforcement tools. When an unsound plan is "terminated," the sponsoring company must immediately pay into the fund whatever is required to cover its accumulated obligations—even if the sponsor is forced into bankruptcy as a result. And if the sponsor cannot cover the deficit in a terminated plan, the underfunding becomes the PBGC's problem.[5]

But the very power of this tool, paradoxically, limits its usefulness. The drastic nature of an involuntary termination makes the PBGC reluctant to unsheathe its weapon. And even where the harsh step of requiring an employer to immediately pay up on its pension obligations may seem warranted by the condition of a plan, it is not clear that all of the PBGC's constituencies will benefit. For example, if such a termination puts an employer out of business, the interests of the employer's retirees may have been met only at the expense of its currently employed workers.

There are certainly instances that warrant accepting the collateral damage risked by involuntary termination. Even in such cases, however, the inadequacy of the PBGC's resources—both financial and administrative—meant that it had to use involuntary termination sparingly. The PBGC's small staff was responsible for tens of thousands of pension funds. Financial data submitted by plan sponsors was often more than a year old by the time it reached the hands of a PBGC analyst—too late, typically, to use the threat of an involuntary termination as a deterrent to risky corporate behavior.

So, for most of the PBGC's history, the agency had only been involved in the endgame, picking up the pieces when sponsors filed for bankruptcy and left too few resources to fulfill pension promises. After assuming responsibility for these promises, the PBGC would go to court, joining the scramble of creditors seeking to collect what they could from the remaining assets of the failed firm. But in bankruptcy proceedings, the PBGC's claims were almost never given priority, even when, as was often the case, the PBGC was the company's largest creditor.[6] Other creditors, better positioned to spot trouble brewing, had typically locked in contractual protections before bankruptcy, leaving the PBGC among the general unsecured claimants at the end of the priority queue. Throughout the 1980s, the PBGC recovered an average of only eight cents for each dollar of liability shouldered in the wake of a bankruptcy.[7]

In principle, the PBGC has an advantage meant to offset its other handicaps. Unlike most other creditors, it is authorized to hold all members of a corporate "control" group responsible for obligations incurred by other members of the group. Subsidiaries and other entities that are 80 percent or more owned by a controlling company can be sued for the outstanding amount of the pension benefits owed. The catch, though, is that this joint liability holds only for enterprises that are part of the control group at the moment trouble hits. Once separated from a sickly entity by sale or spin-off, the healthy members of the control group are freed from liability. (If the PBGC can prove that the primary goal of a transaction was to "evade or avoid" pension liability, it can make a claim on the assets of former members within five years following the separation from the control group.) Like involuntary termination, this tool was blunter than it appeared to be.

Insured firms had little obligation—and no incentive—to inform the PBGC about control-group rearrangements, and the corporation lacked the capacity to monitor the vast number of potentially consequential transactions in progress in the financial world. So it was often unaware of crucial changes in the control group until after the fact. In 1985 the troubled CF&I Steel was spun off by the much stronger Crane Corporation; within a few years it was bankrupt. This Pueblo, Colorado, steel company, which had dominated the local economy for decades, was unable to pay pension benefits, and the PBGC, no longer able to go after Crane as a member of the "control group," was left holding more than $200 million in pension liabilities.[8]

Sliding toward Crisis?

Given the PBGC's built-in constraints and its enormous potential exposure, it should not be surprising that premiums and investment returns would fail to keep pace with the growth in pension fund liabilities. But the marked increase in corporate restructuring in the late 1980s and the economic recession of the early 1990s left many concerned that the PBGC's financial situation had become untenable.

Much of the PBGC's losses stemmed from underfunding concentrated in a handful of industries, chief among them steel and airlines. Steelmakers had been hit hard by foreign competition, the emergence of domestic "mini-mills," and the fiercely cyclical demand for the product. The wave of corporate restructuring in the second half of the 1980s left already cash-poor airlines highly leveraged and in no position to keep up contributions to their pension funds. When the Persian Gulf crisis sparked increases in fuel prices, several airlines ended up in bankruptcy. The financial collapses of Eastern and Pan Am alone left the PBGC with $1.2 billion of unfunded obligations to retirees.[9]

The reformers who had drafted ERISA in the early 1970s could not have foreseen the subsequent proliferation of corporate restructurings. Thus the law that created the PBGC did not adequately equip it to prevent the resurgence of pension underfunding that accompanied this trend. When recession hit, contributions to pension funds plummeted, leaving shortfalls in the funds at record highs.[10] Much of the ground gained for pension security since the passage of ERISA had been lost, with the worst, many feared, still to come.

A pension plan is defined as underfunded if its pool of investments (assuming realistic returns) would be unable to cover the full amount of pension benefits owed, even if the plan sponsor failed to make additional contributions. The PBGC faces chronic criticism for using such a cautious definition, since most plan sponsors expect to continue to be in business and able to make up any temporary shortfalls over time. But the deteriorating economic conditions of the early 1990s increased the likelihood of insolvency for several large plan sponsors, and underfunding was becoming more than an accountant's quibble. The potential consequences were far-reaching. The rising incidence of underfunding, coupled with higher risk of eventual termination, meant that the PBGC would have to increase its premiums to cover its exposure. Since the PBGC had only a limited ability to discriminate between the sickly or reckless minority of pension plans and the prudent majority, this meant that healthy firms would be burdened with unfair premium increases. Rising premiums could inspire these firms to opt out of the system by shifting from defined-benefit pension plans to defined-contribution retirement plans. If enough employers fled the system, the PBGC would find itself the steward of an increasingly risky defined-benefit system, with fewer and fewer healthy firms to balance the bad bets.[11] Spun out to its logical conclusion, this scenario spelled the unwinding of the insured pension system that ERISA had inaugurated.

There were other, intermediate, anxieties. First, the PBGC insured benefits only up to a basic level. If an employer failed, folded its pension plan, or had its plan involuntarily terminated and taken over by the PBGC, retirees often collected leaner benefits than they had been promised. Even if the PBGC could cope with the rise in underfunding, workers and retirees could still be hurt. Lurking in many minds was the fear that ultimately American taxpayers would be called on to foot the bill, as they had been forced to for the savings and loan industry—to the tune of hundreds of billions of dollars. Could corporate pension plans be the next taxpayer bailout? Looking ahead to the retirement of the baby boom generation, the PBGC projected a deficit of $30 billion, and James Lockhart, director of the PBGC in the Bush administration, warned repeatedly that the pension program was susceptible to the same fate as the savings and loan insurance program.[12] Labor Secretary Lynn Martin agreed: "One would have to be an ostrich with its head buried in the sand to ignore the savings and loan analogy."[13]

This was the setting, in the late days of the Bush administration, in which the seeds of the PBGC's Early Warning System were planted.

The Inaugural Day optimism of many of the newly appointed officials in Bill Clinton's administration was tainted by the mounting troubles of the pension insurance agency, which by now was insuring the pensions of nearly 41 million Americans employed by some 40,000 companies. Between 1987 and 1993, the number of plans the PBGC took over had risen 34 percent, to 1,858; the benefit payments paid out by the PBGC had spiked up 127 percent, to $723 million; the number of retirees dependent on the PBGC for their monthly check had increased 62 percent, to 349,000; the PBGC's deficit was up 87 percent, to nearly $3 billion, and—signaling trouble to come—the amount of underfunding had nearly doubled, from $27 billion to $53 billion.[14]

The administration quickly appointed a task force headed by Martin Slate, a senior bureaucrat at the Internal Revenue Service, to calibrate the severity of the problem. The task force found that the shrillest warnings were unduly alarmist. The system was sound, for the time being. But its long-term integrity was indeed imperiled by the fact that one-fourth of the nation's defined-benefit plans, on which some 8 million retirees relied, were underfunded.[15] There was no imminent danger, certainly nothing on the scale of the S&L disaster, but trends clearly pointed toward serious trouble over the long term.

Shortly after the task force made its report, Martin Slate was named the new director of the PBGC. A short and chronically rumpled man in his late forties, Slate was a lawyer and financial expert with impeccable Ivy League credentials who had chosen a career in the federal civil service. He had a reputation for obsessive commitment to his work, an intense and quirky mind, unalloyed integrity, and a blunt, unpolished style.

Slate rapidly became convinced that the PBGC's cardinal vulnerability was its inability to head off pension-plan problems before they became critical. The PBGC was often blindsided by policy changes or corporate restructurings by plan sponsors, only learning about them once the consequences had exploded as underfunded plans. Even when the corporation spotted problems coming, it lacked the leverage to alter dangerous patterns.

His predecessor at the PBGC, James Lockhart, had launched efforts to create an early warning program.[16] Slate saw the merits of Lockhart's initiative and set out to solidify the program and bolster it with new monitoring and negotiating tools. The focus of the corporation's efforts needed to change from damage control to loss prevention. The first step would be figuring out when and where trouble was afoot.

Recognizing that the PBGC could never monitor all the corporate sponsors whose plans it guaranteed, Slate and his team prioritized: they identified the largest underfunded plans. Though these plans composed only 1 percent of all companies in the insurance pool, they represented 80 percent of the PBGC's potential exposure. From this group they selected the companies with the largest number of participants affected and the highest probability of risk.[17] Targeted companies were assigned to one of two tiers of scrutiny: those with the largest amount of underfunding, problematic credit history, and serious financial conditions were assigned to high-level monitoring. These companies would be the subject of intense research efforts, with the PBGC regularly checking in with senior financial officers; looking for changes in environmental conditions, corporate balance sheets, internal leadership, and funding levels of the pension plans; and watching for any signs that potentially harmful transactions were being contemplated. The remaining companies were assigned to low-level monitoring, involving less frequent checks.

Knowing that his small government agency would have to keep tabs on hundreds of corporate giants in a variety of industries, Slate (again building on Lockhart's earlier efforts[18]) put together a twenty-person staff with private-sector experience. These staff members and others—former investment bankers, industry analysts, insurance experts, and corporate managers—worked to cultivate a network of Wall Street sources and advisors, and they regularly called on these resources to help anticipate company developments and analyze a company's ability to support its pension plan.

The PBGC had begun to watch company moves closely, "as carefully as a cat watches goldfish," in the words of one observer.[19] The Internal Revenue Service, the Securities and Exchange Commission, and the PBGC's own files were mined for information about which companies had recently missed premiums, filed for bankruptcy, or requested approval for a major transaction. The PBGC was newly outfitted with financial wire services and Internet capabilities, allowing analysts to sift through breaking news for events that could pose a danger to retirees. Mergers, downsizings, reorganizations, plant closings, extraordinary dividends, significant stock redemptions, and large loan defaults all had the potential to catapult a company onto the target list.

The PBGC also began to put corporations on notice through an energetic public information campaign. Senior staff members traveled the country, visiting industry conventions and professional organizations. At each stop, corporate managers were reminded that the PBGC had been empowered by ERISA to prevent companies from wriggling out of their pension liabilities. Leaving their pension plans underfunded could have serious consequences—not just for workers, not just for retirees, not just for the federal insurance program—but for them, too. The message spread that the only way to avoid a visit from the PBGC was to keep pension plans in mind during restructuring.

Corporations identified as planning moves that could drain resources away from pension plans were contacted immediately. If they confirmed that they were going ahead with such a move, the PBGC requested a meeting with senior corporate representatives. These sessions offered a setting for PBGC negotiators, armed with research, to review the corporation's legal responsibilities, to spell out the PBGC's concerns about the proposed transaction, and to suggest ways the transaction could be modified to avoid compromising pension security.

Private companies were suddenly being asked to accept the PBGC as a player in the major deals of the day. Some chafed at what they perceived to be unwarranted government intervention, resented the PBGC's readiness to reopen complex transactions, or felt unfairly singled out. Andrea Schneider, a member of Slate's team who had left Merrill Lynch to head the PBGC's corporate finance division, recalls one such reaction: "They literally said, 'Why are you picking on us?' "[20] The PBGC had muscled itself into the collective consciousness of the corporate world as a force to be reckoned with. But no one, including the PBGC, was sure how much bite went along with the bark.

A 1992 court battle with a defense contractor had established the PBGC's right to terminate a pension plan in the context of a corporate transaction if the transaction could reasonably be expected to cause excessive losses to the plan in the long run.[21] But this new weapon remained little tested, its powers and limits poorly understood. Because the PBGC had no history of enforcement or body of precedent behind it, companies might choose to spurn negotiations and take their chances in court. In any case, the PBGC was well aware of the pitfalls of using involuntary termination as a chief bargaining tool.

The Scarlet U: Underfunding

The PBGC has always insisted that making adequate contributions to pension funds is not only the right thing to do, but good business as well. Well-funded plans can mean lower operating and administrative costs, reduced premium payments to the PBGC, better credit ratings, improved cash flow, and higher employee morale. Under Lockhart's administration, the PBGC had added an additional justification for those companies unmoved by these arguments: avoiding bad publicity. The corporation had begun assembling and distributing to the press a list of the fifty companies with the largest amounts of underfunding in their pension plans— the "Iffy Fifty" list. The national business press quickly made an event of the list's annual release. Officials of companies sponsoring underfunded plans could anticipate that their stockholders, competitors, and friends would learn of the shortfalls. As least as significant, in many cases, was the intense local media coverage in cities and states where Iffy Fifty companies had their headquarters or major plants.

Companies were warned months in advance that they had achieved Iffy Fifty status. Some—including Chrysler, Westinghouse Electric, and Bethlehem Steel—scrambled to contribute enough to get off the list. This PBGC stratagem was by no means uncontroversial; many companies that found themselves on the list protested that the PBGC exaggerated underfunding, used gloomy assumptions, failed to distinguish between healthy and struggling companies, and unnecessarily frightened retirees who might mistake warnings of future unsoundness for an imminent halt to their pension checks.

Some companies who made the list were surprised as well as disgruntled. Northwest Airlines executives, for example, were dismayed to learn that by PBGC calculations, their pension plans were $311 million short of what they needed to be. By their own estimates, the plans were fully funded. The discrepancy was in the assumptions about investment returns. The PBGC used a conservative 6.4 percent rate, while Northwest assumed a more optimistic 12–14 percent rate would keep the funds expanding to meet future demands without the need for stepped-up contributions.[22]

The PBGC never claimed that all of the companies on the list were on the brink of abandoning their pension obligations. But most, it maintained, displayed real financial risk, not just temporary and technical departures from full pension funding. A solid company, dismissing pension underfunding as a minor matter of bookkeeping, could suddenly hit hard times and be unable to follow through on its plans to make catch-up contributions to the plan. And the eerily powerful principle of compound interest that lies at the heart of the pension system has its dark side: a small gap in a pension plan today can be an enormous problem down the road. In any case, both defenders and detractors of the Iffy Fifty list might agree on one thing: the stratagem was highly effective in heightening the visibility of the underfunding problem.[23]

The General Motors Experience

The PBGC would gain much-needed new tools in 1994 with the passage of the Retirement Protection Act. But even before these reforms were passed, the early warning program won new credibility after months of arduous negotiations with General Motors produced a landmark agreement.

GM's Hourly Rate Employees Pension Plan was the largest private pension plan in the nation, covering 600,000 current and retired autoworkers. By the end of 1993, it was underfunded by nearly $24 billion dollars.[24] GM had not fully bounced back from the auto industry's troubled transition era of the 1970s and 1980s. With a steadily sinking share of the U.S. market, the company had been hit hard by the economic recession of 1991 and 1992. In 1993, when GM negotiated a new three-year labor contract that actually raised pension benefits after interest rates (which are used to calculate the present value of future pension liabilities) had hit rock bottom, the market did not react well: GM's credit ratings plummeted, unnerving already spooked investors and driving up its cost of borrowing money. GM officials knew they had to come to terms with their pension situation if they hoped to get the company's financial house in order.

When GM approached the PBGC at the end of 1993 with a proposal to strengthen its pension plans, the corporation knew that GM was ready to take substantial steps toward healing its pension woes. The PBGC was equally eager, since it was sobering to contemplate even a remote risk of taking over GM's mammoth liabilities. But the automaker's opening proposal failed to impress the PBGC.

The recent turbulence in the auto industry had left GM strapped for cash and funneling every available dollar into new product development efforts that were vital to maintaining its competitive position. GM's management team was convinced that significant cash contributions to its pension funds, if made at the expense of product development, would be self-defeating in the long run. Management had proposed bolstering the pension fund with a major stock contribution: 185 million shares of GM's class E common stock with an estimated worth of around $6 billion. The value of these shares was only an estimate; the stock represented a claim on the dividends of one of GM's subsidiaries, Electronic Data Systems (EDS), and was therefore linked to that company's performance.

The PBGC had several objections to the proposed stock contribution. While EDS (an information technology company founded by Ross Perot and acquired by GM in 1984) was in good shape and relatively untroubled by debt, the PBGC always looked askance at betting too heavily on any one company within a pension fund's portfolio. GM's executives had expressed their intention to make cash payments to the fund at a later date, but their initial proposal did not bind them to do so. Because the stock contribution exceeded the minimum payment required, GM would actually be creating a credit balance that could legally be used to reduce future contributions to the plan—or to give GM ready access to funds if slow auto sales precipitated cash flow problems for the company.

The PBGC was far from confident that it could negotiate a better deal, however. By this time the Slate team had twenty negotiations behind them, but none had come close to the magnitude of the GM deal. This was the big leagues. GM's legal and negotiating teams would be enormously sophisticated and, with potentially billions of dollars and the company's future on the line, both highly motivated and well financed. The total number of staffers in the PBGC's Corporate Finance and Negotiations Department was nineteen. Could a handful of federal bureaucrats really expect to wrangle concessions from General Motors?

The PBGC knew it had to play its cards adroitly: GM's pension holders had to be protected, as did the PBGC's financial integrity. But adding further financial burdens to the nation's largest carmaker could have disastrous consequences. Both parties knew that the prospect of the PBGC's initiating an involuntary termination was minuscule: GM pension beneficiaries would receive less than they were owed; auto-related industries (many of which had their own pension troubles) would be devastated; an untold number of pension plans holding GM stock would lose big. Terminating GM's pension plan was, as PBGC's chief negotiator Nell Hennessy put it, a "meltdown scenario."[25]

But the PBGC held a trump. When GM had approached the PBGC in November of 1993, it was not only hoping to convince credit agencies and nervous investors that a solution to its pension problem was in the works; it was seeking an explicit assurance from the PBGC that it would not interfere with GM's plans to sell or spin off EDS—an important move in GM's financial game plan.[26] GM had not missed the PBGC's recent propensity to muscle in with a pension-security agenda when a company with large pension underfunding attempted to sell a valuable subsidiary. GM managers were hoping their proposal would appease the PBGC in advance, so future deal-making involving EDS would not get bogged down by PBGC demands.[27]

Both parties entered negotiations with a lot to gain and even more to lose. The process of hammering out an agreement would take months. Compromises did not come easily for either, and at one point tensions were so high that GM walked. But in May 1994, Labor Secretary Reich announced that the two sides had reached a settlement: GM would sweeten its $6 billion stock contribution with an impressive $4 billion in cash; a ten-year schedule controlling access to the credit balance was put in place; the PBGC would help clear the way for GM's actions to receive necessary regulatory approval and give it a green light for peddling EDS.[28]

GM kept its promises. As the company's fortunes picked up, it poured cash into its pension fund. These contributions, coupled with soaring investment returns, ensured that by January of 1997, the fund was fully financed.[29]

The PBGC's high-profile settlement with GM gave a huge boost to the agency's standing in the business arena, removing much of the lingering skepticism about its authority in the context of corporate transactions. And Lockhart and Slate's efforts to assemble a first-rate team had paid off. The GM deal demonstrated that the civil servants could more than hold their own with the most sophisticated private players. Both men had been adamant about getting the best—in resources and personnel—for the PBGC: "You've got to meet these people on their own terms."[30]

The agreement also lent heft to PBGC assertions that it was not in the business of imposing government-issue, one-size-fits-all solutions with no regard to a company's special circumstances. It was willing to tailor agreements, bend rules, and think outside the box to come up with a deal that everyone could live with. "Marty was willing to consider doing things that were creative, innovative, and hadn't been done before," said Gary Ford, a partner at Groom and Nordberg, the Washington law firm that represented GM in the negotiations.[31]

Recognizing that many tough battles lay ahead for the PBGC, Slate was anxious to have the reforms of the early warning program encoded into law. He took a hand in drafting legislation that did just that. The Retirement Protection Act directs corporations whose pension plans are underfunded by $50 million or more to provide the PBGC with detailed financial information and requires privately held corporations to report some classes of transactions to the PBGC at least thirty days in advance.[32] The legislation also obliges employers with a certain level of underfunding to inform their workers and retirees about the gaps in their plan's funding, authorizes the PBGC to file for liens against the assets of companies that fail to make required contributions, raises premium payments for underfunded companies (ensuring that slackers bear the burden of the risk they pose to the system), and closes loopholes that had allowed companies to use unduly rosy assumptions.

Drafting the bill was only the first step; getting it through Congress was a taller order. The trick was finding a legislative vehicle with enough momentum to pull along the complex Retirement Protection Act. Slate zeroed in on the ratification legislation for the latest round of international deals made under the General Agreement on Trade and Tariffs. The GATT bill was must-pass legislation, unlikely to be derailed. Legislative architects allied with the PBGC found ways to knit the proposed pension law securely into the GATT legislation. Administration officials then went to work to shepherd the bill through to passage. Slate quietly but aggressively lobbied key members of Congress. "He had an almost missionary zeal to get the program reformed," said one observer. "There was a bulldog-like tenacity to get it passed."[33] Slate's persistence paid off. The Retirement Protection Act was passed, bundled into more than 2,000 pages of GATT legislation, in December 1994.

Fortified by the new rule-making authority and compliance tools supplied by the Retirement Protection Act, the PBGC's early warning program has continued to negotiate protections for pension holders, often entering the fray at the first sign that a plan faces financial trouble. In case after case, negotiations have yielded financial guarantees from strong companies departing a control group, or additional pension contributions, or assets pledged as security against missed contributions or shortfalls in the event of a plan termination—or sometimes combinations of several such protections in a single deal.

In 1995, the PBGC negotiated fourteen settlements involving pension plans worth a total of more than $740 million; in 1996, eleven settlements with pension plans worth more than $1 billion.[34] Companies reluctant to enter into negotiations found the PBGC was not unwilling to play hardball. "We try to turn every situation into a win-win," Slate observed, " but if companies won't negotiate, we go to court."[35]

The PBGC's successes have had a major impact on the insurance agency's own financial health. Only a few years ago the corporation's director had predicted that the PBGC would face a $10 billion deficit by the end of 1997.[36] Instead its March 1997 annual report showed the agency's first surplus: at the end of 1996, the PBGC had a cushion of assets worth $869 million—after it cut checks totaling $792 million for nearly 200,000 pension beneficiaries.[37] The booming economy of the mid-1990s certainly played a role, but Congress and the PBGC had moved aggressively to exploit the opportunities the good times offered to shore up the pension insurance system.

Black ink for the PBGC, of course, was only one measure—and arguably not the most important—of the improvements in the pension system. The combined reforms of the early warning program and the Retirement Protection Act have resulted in an acceleration in plan funding for those sponsors who had fallen behind and have helped spare the economy the trauma of major plan terminations. And the PBGC has struggled to soften the adversarial tenor of pension regulations and minimize the burden on responsible employers. In order to make employers more comfortable with new reporting requirements, for example, the PBGC has made such filings exempt from Freedom of Information Act requests, ensuring confidentiality. If a company needs to notify the PBGC of a significant financial event, a one-page form is all that is needed. In fact, the PBGC's regulations themselves have been simplified and reduced in volume by 20 percent. When the PBGC issues new rules and regulations, it does so only after consulting with a committee that includes employers, representatives of workers and retirees, and pension specialists.

It is difficult to measure precisely the achievements of the early warning program. One could, of course, add up the number of pension beneficiaries who have had their plans strengthened since the program's inception, or total the dollar value of the protections the PBGC has negotiated, or estimate the amount the agency has saved by avoiding terminations. But these figures would still give an incomplete picture. For instance, we will never know how many companies—persuaded by observing others contending with the PBGC's tough tactics—strengthened their pension plans without further prompting. Indeed, perhaps the program's greatest achievement is that the pensions of American workers are now, by necessity, more than an afterthought in corporate decisionmaking.

In keeping with the spirit of the early warning program, which propelled the PBGC out of its passivity and onto the playing fields, the agency has reconstructed itself as a user-friendly resource that reaches out to its constituencies. Efforts to inform pension beneficiaries about their rights and familiarize them with their own plan's situation have included a home page on the world wide web, an annual newsletter, aggressive radio and newspaper campaigns, and a customer service center and hotline. Hundreds of thousands of pamphlets entitled "Know Your Pension" have been distributed in supermarkets. And the PBGC has launched an Internet search to find people who have not collected benefits owed to them.

The PBGC's internal workings have also undergone a transformation: a new computer system and a modernized premium collection system have made the agency more effective in its basic operations. The PBGC is developing a set of new economic modeling tools that will more accurately forecast its future financial condition; the pension insurance modeling system will be able to project the corporation's health under any of a wide range of economic scenarios.

The new forecasting methodology will be important in limiting uncertainties and helping the PBGC plan for the future. In its early years, the reform effort enjoyed the tailwind of a booming stock market, which boosted investment returns and made it much easier to maintain adequate pension funding. But the ultimate value of the early warning program will be demonstrated in a downturn. The real test, Martin Slate was intensely aware, would come soon enough. "We have to be vigilant. We have been on an up (economic) cycle. Things will not always be like that."[38] In a country where company-sponsored pension plans constitute the largest pool of private savings, the PBGC plans to continue ensuring that those who have earned a comfortable retirement will get one, come boom or bust.

Notes

1. Katherine Pflegler, "Spotting Financial Risks," *Government Executive*, November 1995.

2. Ibid.

3. "Pension Insurance Data Book 1997," Pension Benefit Guaranty Corporation, tables A-7 and A-9.

4. Lauren Dermer, "How the Watchdog Watches Its Money," *Institutional Investor*, February 1997.

5. Companies may initiate such a termination themselves if they meet certain financial distress criteria.

6. The head of the PBGC under the Bush administration, James Lockhart, estimated in early 1992 that the PBGC's claims received priority treatment only 14 percent of the time. Lisa Howard, "Pension Fund Finance Woes on the Rise," *National Underwriter Property and Casualty*, March 23, 1992.

7. Douglas Frantz and Robert Rosenblatt, "Unhealthy Pension Plans Pose Gamble for Workers," *Los Angeles Times*, November 13, 1989.

8. Adam Goodman, "Suit Targets Pension Bailout," *St. Louis Post-Dispatch*, April 19, 1992.

9. "Pension Time Bomb" (editorial), *Washington Post*, March 4, 1993.

10. Companies with cash-flow problems make only minimum contributions to their pension plans or petition the IRS for waivers allowing complete suspension of payments altogether.

11. The Congressional Budget Office warned that raising premiums could eventually lead to employers' pulling out, draining the insurance pool. Jeff Gerth, "U.S. Pension Agency in Deep Trouble, Economists Warn," *New York Times*, December 20, 1992.

12. A taxpayer bailout of the pension program would require new legislation; ERISA did not provide federal liability for the PBGC.

13. Jerry Geisel, "No Guarantees That PBGC Will Survive," *Business Insurance*, September 7, 1992.

14. Christina Del Valle, "Harsh Medicine for Ailing Pension Plans," *Business Week*, September 19, 1994.

15. Martin Slate speech, delivered to the Institutional Investor Institute, March 1, 1996.

16. Lockhart and his team had begun to organize the PBGC to better target and more efficiently monitor underfunding; they were twice unsuccessful at getting legislation passed to bolster their efforts to do so.

17. Risk analysis included assessments of the company's overall financial integrity, the health of the company's industry, and the strength of both the regional and the national economy.

18. The PBGC's Corporate Finance and Negotiations Department was created by Lockhart at the end of 1990.

19. Patricia B. Limbacher, "PBGC Moving Swiftly to Safeguard Pension Promises," *Pensions & Investments*, September 4, 1995.

20. "Protecting Pension Benefits," a Kennedy School of Government case study.

21. Robert S. Metzger, "U.S. Seeks a Piece of Overfunded Pension Plans," *National Law Journal*, February 5, 1996.

22. Del Valle, "Harsh Medicine for Ailing Pension Plans."

23. The "Iffy Fifty" list was discontinued in 1997, once the PBGC judged it had served its purpose.

24. John R. Bell, "Successful Strategies to Reduce Underfunding," *Pension Management*, April 1996.

25. "Protecting Pension Benefits."

26. At this point, Sprint was considering a merger with EDS, which the PBGC learned during the course of negotiations.

27. In fact, without advance approval from the PBGC, these deals would be unlikely to work out in the first place: corporations would be wary of acquiring or merging with EDS as long as the company could potentially be held accountable for GM's pension obligations at some future point. Should GM's pension plan be terminated within five years of EDS's leaving GM's control group, the PBGC could seek a court ruling that the original EDS transaction had been motivated by a desire to "evade or avoid" GM's pension responsibilities, allowing it access to EDS's assets. Whether or not it ultimately prevailed, the PBGC certainly had the ability to tie EDS up in costly and time-consuming litigation.

28. GM's stock contribution was inconsistent with two ERISA limitations regarding the amount and type of stock that a pension plan could hold, thus requiring exemptions from the Pension and Welfare Benefits Administration, the agency whose regulations govern the financial health of pension plans. The PBGC worked with the agency during its negotiations with GM to ensure that the final deal could earn the necessary exemptions.

29. Keith Bradsher, "G.M. Increases Payout and Sets Stock Buyout," *New York Times*, January 28, 1997.

30. "Protecting Pension Benefits."

31. *New York Times*, January 26, 1997.

32. Privately held corporations, unlike those that are publicly held, do not have to file with the Securities and Exchange Commission or notify the public of such transactions in advance. Typically, the PBGC finds out about transactions involving publicly held corporations from analysts who follow the companies or from the companies themselves.

33. Jerry Geisel, "PBGC Executive Director Martin Slate," *Business Insurance*, March 3, 1997.

34. "Pension Insurance Data Book 1997."

35. Peggie Elgin, "PBGC Cuts No Slack for Underfunded Plans," *Pension Management*, May 1996.

36. Howard, "Pension Fund Finance Woes on the Rise."

37. "PBGC Releases 1996 Annual Report," *Pension Fund Litigation Reporter*, April 18, 1997.

38. Jerry Geisel, "Pension Agency Sees Much Brighter Future," *Business Insurance*, May 20, 1996.

INDEX